i

Reading *The Unconventional Chaplain* was almost like what I experienced with Chaplain Andy's remarkable and exciting ministry first-hand. I'm glad I was able to do both. I missed the heat and dust, and the sights and smells; but reexperienced the pulse of the action and the heart of the actor. This is a story of men and ministry that you don't want to miss.

Doug Knighton, SOCCENT
Command Chaplain, 2002–2004.

Prior to 9/11, many senior leaders had opined, one way or the other, whether Army National Guard Special Forces could meaningfully contribute to the USASFC and USSOCOM missions. While that has since been put to rest, in 2002 it was still a yet-to-be-decided issue. As the 5/19th Battalion Chaplain, Maj. Andrew Meverden was an integral part of that unit's first (of many) deployments, and his actions contributed greatly to that deployment's success. Chaplain Andy's contributions did not end when he redeployed to Colorado in 2003; as my Brigade Chaplain, he conceived and implemented the Army's first Yellow Ribbon program. His constant efforts to care for our soldiers, informed by his own experience, better prepared the 2500 members of the Colorado Army National Guard that would follow the 5/19th to OEF and OIF in 2003-2005. His story is the story of all National Guardsmen who deploy to that AOR as an integral part of the finest army the world has ever known.

BG Stuart Pike, USA, Retired

Chaplain Colonel (retired) Andrew Meverden has written a compelling story about the efforts of a deployed National Guard Special Forces unit from Colorado reflecting the winning of hearts and minds of Afghan citizens during the early years of the war in Afghanistan. A personal story, Andy has captured the values that reflect the other side of U. S. military might – compassion, caring, and respect for shared values. A must read for those seeking an understanding of the United States actions in Afghanistan as the war unfolded.

Mike Edwards, Maj Gen, USAF Retired,
Commander Colorado National Guard

Chaplain Andy has lived his life as a conduit for good deeds. My friend touched so many in so many ways, he exuded humility and character. He applied his efforts in a practical, purposeful and devotional manner that cannot be denied. Chaplain Andy stood up with us, and for us. He woke up each day as one of us and looked the world in the eye with a smile. He shared our pain and joys, matched each tear and celebration. Our time together was spent building an army and repairing a culture with the eyes of an anxious country peering down on us. Chaplain Andy faced difficulties and was tasked with challenges that nobody could anticipate, finding and creating unconventional solutions with an unwavering devotion to his fellow man. My friend Chaplain Andy helped make each day a day of hope in a time and place of despair

Dave Martinez, Master Sgt. USA, Retired, Operations Sergeant SFODA 991

Chaplain Andy takes readers along with him on a foreign deployment with a national guard unit from Colorado - the first of which when the majority of deployed Special Forces soldiers in a combat zone are from the National Guard. Readers experience an authentic mission: the challenges, ingenuity, joy, sorrow, humor, and basic humanity encountered among citizen-soldiers, Afghan soldiers, and nearby villagers. The civilian skills of the unit soldiers and Andy's experienced civilian ministry outreach demonstrate the best use of citizen-soldiers in action. Chaplain Andy is a great story-teller. He often starts his oral remarks, describing our relationship downrange - me as Luke, the physician, and he as the apostle Paul, the theologian. It was truly the high-point of my 40+ year military career to serve with this incredible military chaplain - with him saving souls while I was working to save lives.

Robert W. Enzenauer, MD, Brig. Gen. (Retired), Battalion Surgeon, 5/19th SFG(A), 1998-2010

I have been blessed over the years to know and serve with many superb military chaplains. The most effective were not only devout in their own beliefs but also informed and respectful of those of others, capable of serving and ministering to all. They also knew their "congregation" was down in the trenches where the troops were and where life happens. Chaplain Andy is that kind of chaplain. His rich set of life experiences as an enlisted soldier, linguist, missionary, and pastor rendered him a sensitive and culturally aware man of action. When bad things happened, he was capable of positively influencing a very delicate situation with far-reaching consequences. This first-hand saga of his year in Afghanistan is a great read and leaves one confident that, like his unit, he was both special and unconventional. I strongly recommend *Unconventional Chaplain* for all professional soldiers, but especially for aspiring commanders and all who contemplate the unique ministry of military chaplaincy.

Robert J. St. Onge, Jr., Maj. Gen., US Army (Retired)

An excellent look into the challenges and successes of a Special Forces Battalion and their very unconventional Chaplain. Their deployment in response to the 9/11 attack on the Twin Towers and the Pentagon takes you into the hardships and dangers associated with this war. It illustrates the necessity of unconventional warfare and the doctrines in use. It is amazing to see the respect and honor that can be earned when the Chaplain understood that success is obtained by adapting to the customs of the Afghan people. A great read that brings a new perspective to the reader.

Thomas Mills, Brig. Gen., US Army, (Retired)

Many veterans of Afghanistan and Iraq have written novels about their experience, but few of them focus on the Humanitarian Assistance provided to host nations. This book shines a spotlight on the strategic importance of this vital role and the value it plays in not only helping host nations but is also critical in providing safety for coalition forces. Chaplain Andy provides the reader with an excellent blueprint for what successful humanitarian support looks like.

Mark Riccardi, Lt Col, US Army (Retired)

Unconventional Chaplain

Winning Hearts and Minds in Afghanistan

2002-03

By Chaplain (Colonel) Andy Meverden

A15 Publishing
PO Box 66054
Hampton, VA 23665
www.A15publishing.com

ISBN 978-1-970155-10-5

FIRST PRINTING

Contents

Acknowledgements Prologue
In Memorium

Part One: Getting Ready
Chapter 1 – The Ballad of the Green Beret
Chapter 2 – September 10-12, 2001
Chapter 3 – Call to Duty
Chapter 4 – Ordered or Volunteered?
Chapter 5 – Job Interview
Chapter 6 – Baptism by Fire
Chapter 7 - JRTC: Finding my Place in the Unit
Chapter 8 – A Mother's Warning
Chapter 9 – Church Farewell Ceremony
Chapter 10 - Mobilization Station: An unusual request

Part Two: Getting There
Chapter 11 - Hot Air, False Start, and Freedom's Song
Chapter 12 - In-Flight Entertainment
Chapter 13 – Landing at Kabul International Airport (KIA)
Chapter 14 - First Night Fears and Celestial Wonders
Chapter 15 - Digging in and Building up
Chapter 16 – The Fabulous Bombay Lounge
Chapter 17 - Get out there and Do Something
Chapter 18 – Pul-e-Charki School Visit
Chapter 19 – Conversational English Classes
Chapter 20 – Back to the Basics
Chapter 21 - Bomb Threat
Chapter 22 – National Geographic Special
Chapter 23 – Teaming Up to Serve Soldiers and Civilians

Part Three: Getting Settled
Chapter 24 – First Impressions – Oct. 6, 2002
Chapter 25 - Chaplains Drive, Assistants Shoot – Oct. 13, 2002
Chapter 26 - A Prophetic Word Confirmed – Oct. 20, 2002
Chapter 27 – Working through Interpreters – Oct. 27, 2002
Chapter 28 - First Impressions Are Lasting Impressions – Nov. 3, 2002

Chapter 29 - Cool Water for a Thirsty Soul - Nov. 10, 2002

Chapter 30 - Rebuilding an Army on the Golden Rule - Nov. 17, 2002

Chapter 31 - Pointing out the Obvious - Nov. 24, 2002

Chapter 32 – Yankee Ingenuity is Alive and Well - Dec. 8, 2002

Chapter 33 – Worship Off-base - Dec. 15, 2002

Chapter 34 – Christmas in Kabul – Dec. 22, 2002

Chapter 35 – Morning Run – Dec. 27, 2002

Chapter 36 – Bad Soldier, Good Chaplain

Chapter 37 – What's in a Name? – Jan. 12, 2003

Chapter 38 – Spectacular Recovery: Miracle #1 – Jan. 19, 2003

Chapter 39 – A Different Kind of Chapel Bell – Jan. 26, 2003

Chapter 40 – Two Weeks before Christmas – Apr. 13, 2003

Part Four: Getting Busy

Chapter 41 – Meeting the Postmaster

Chapter 42 – First Afghan Battalion Deployment

Chapter 43 – Historic Iftar Meal

Chapter 44 – Eid Celebration and Man-Dancing

Chapter 45 – Rude Wake-up Call

Chapter 46 – Culturally-Appropriate Manly Hugs

Chapter 47 – Whose Soldiers Are These?

Chapter 48 – Hearts, Minds and Hands

Chapter 49 – Wrong Helicopter Right Destination

Part Five: Getting Slammed

Chapter 50 – Human Rights Observer

Chapter 51 - Post-op Visit

Chapter 52 - The Unthinkable Occurs

Chapter 53 – The Saddest Day

Chapter 54 – Padre, Can We Talk?

Chapter 55 – Backdoor Diplomacy

Chapter 56 – When the Church Goes Underground – Feb. 16, 2003

Chapter 57 – Comic Relief: WWF Smackdown at KMTC

Chapter 58 – Operation Christmas Blessing – Dec. 22, 2002

Chapter 59 – Christmas Eve at KMTC

Chapter 60 -- Christmas Eve - Postscript

Chapter 61 – Christmas Day Confession

Chapter 62 – Cat Eye for a Glass Eye – Feb. 9, 2003

Chapter 63 – Splitting Headache...and the Six Days of Christmas

Chapter 64 - New Year's Eve 2002 – Feb. 23, 2003

Chapter 65 – Report to the Embassy

Chapter 66 – The Loose Canon of Kabul Chapter 67 – Civil Affairs 101

Chapter 68 – Emergency Buddy Aid

Chapter 69 - Maharamona: An Ancient Afghan Tradition

Chapter 70 - Making Things Right

Chapter 71 - The Miracle of Pul-e-Charki: A Promise Fulfilled

Chapter 72 – Pul-e-Charki School Renovation – Phase 1

Chapter 73 – Back-to-School Shopping

Chapter 74 – Pul-e-Charki MEDCAP

Chapter 75 – Pul-e-Charki School Renovation – Phase 2

Chapter 76 – Lost and Found: Miracle #2

Part Six: Getting Home

Chapter 77 – If You Go, Taliban and Al Qaeda Will Return

Chapter 78 – Farewell Meal with Female Students

Chapter 79 – Farewell Meal with Faculty

Chapter 80 – Passing the Torch with Tears

Chapter 81 - Graduation Day

Chapter 82 – A Day Off

Chapter 83 – The Curse is Lifted: Miracle #3

Chapter 84 – A Surprising Offer

Chapter 85 -- Final Meeting: "We Are Not Going to Apologize"

Chapter 86 – Lunch at the Golden Lotus

Chapter 87 – Packing Up and Heading Back to KIA

Chapter 88 - Farewell to Arms...and our Afghan Partners

Chapter 89 – Freedom Bird

Epilogue – Part 1 - GTMO Epilogue – Part 2 – Reunification

Glossary/Acronyms:

Acknowledgements

Several individuals helped me birth this manuscript. Without each unique contribution, this story would not have seen the light of day. Lt. Cherisa Clark, Colorado National Guard Public Affairs got the ball rolling by first encouraging my writing and then editing this manuscript and other articles. Brig. Gen. Robert Enzenauer, USA, Retired, comrade, physician and friend, lived this experience with me. He attended my chapel services, invited me into his operating room, mentoring and guiding me through difficult times. If that wasn't enough, he saved my physical life. Col. Randy Hurrt, USA, Retired, played a key role as Civil Affairs officer and friend during a critical period in this deployment. Dr. Jill Montrey, former Army surgeon offered constructive comments on the manuscript with insight and tact.

To the men of the Fifth Battalion, Nineteenth Special Forces Group (Airborne).

Thanks for taking me along, enabling my unconventional ministry and bringing me back, alive.

In Memorium
Abdul Rahman-Abdul Habib

Omran Mohammed-Akram

Aziz Abdul Zahir

Abdul Manan Abdul Manaf

Four boys whose curiosity and initiative got the best of them.

Prologue

While serving as senior pastor of Galilee Baptist Church in Denver, Colorado ('02-'03), I deployed as a chaplain with an Army National Guard Special Forces battalion — The Green Berets. During that absence, I decided to write a weekly update called: "A Word from Chaplain Andy" to replace my weekly church bulletin article entitled, "A Word from Pastor Andy." This new version was subtitled: "On the Other Side of the World." With that update, I would include digital photos related to the event or issue in focus. I took care to avoid operational security breaches by reporting events after the fact. Soon, my email updates were being sent between family, friends, and church members across the country and around the world. Over an eleven-month deployment, I wrote numerous articles describing my experiences.

Upon return to the U.S., several people encouraged me to compile my writings into a book. In 2005, a representative from the U.S. Army Center for History, likewise, urged me to assemble my memoirs, but I couldn't. For some reason, I was stuck. My life had been impacted, disrupted, changed - too many things were going on. With ongoing deployments from my brigade – it was difficult to sit down and do that one thing I hated most as a student: write a "report" of what to me was an amazing chapter of my life.

Fortunately, most of my writing was already done. It was waiting on the hard drive of the laptop I had taken halfway around the world in September of 2002. Before the hard drive crashed, I decided to complete the project I had long intended. It includes my memoirs, musings, meditations, mistakes, a couple miracles, and some mishaps by an Operation Enduring Freedom Army National Guard chaplain who served in the early days of the war in Afghanistan. I trust my writing will educate the general population on our efforts on the other side of the world and serve as another eyewitness perspective on the Global War on Terror (GWOT) for current and future generations. I hope it will illustrate what to do – and not to do – as a chaplain. I will seek to be tastefully honest as I share from my unique perspective as the only noncombatant assigned to a heavily armed Green Beret battalion.

For reasons of security, Special Forces soldiers typically are identified by their rank and first name only. To further ensure the safety and confidentiality of the soldiers and families of the brave soldiers with which I served, I will, where appropriate, change or omit their identities.

"De Oppresso Liber"[1]
Liberate the Oppressed

"Pro Deo et Patria"[2]
For God and Country

Notes:

[1] "De Oppresso Liber" is the Green Beret Latin motto: Liberate the Oppressed!

[2] "Pro Deo et Patria" is the U.S. Army Chaplain Corps Latin motto: For God and Country.

Part One: Getting Ready
Chapter 1

The Ballad of the Green Beret

May 1966

It was a warm mid-60s Friday night in Oconto Falls, Wisconsin, population 2,202. The conflict in Vietnam was escalating as life in small town America continued. For many in northeastern Wisconsin, especially the Roman Catholic population, Friday night was fish fry. Most local bars, restaurants, and supper clubs featured fried perch, walleye, or white fish served with French fries, Cole slaw, rye bread and butter. Eaten with either tartar sauce or ketchup, it was a treat. By age twelve, I had acquired a taste for fried fish, primarily from the Bluegill, Crappie, and Perch I caught in the Oconto River that ran through hydroelectric generators one hundred yards behind our family home. This night however, was special. It was payday. Our truck-driver Dad arrived home early, so the family walked to the Falls Restaurant, just a block and a half down Main Street, for a rare family meal out.

As we sat around a table back by the jukebox eating our fried perch, the owners, Florence and Leonard, came over to greet my father, Glenn, and my mother, Franca. Dad met mom in post-WW2 Pisa, Italy. Glenn was an Army mechanic and driver, proud of having transported General Mark Clark while stationed in Italy. So much so, that he named his third son, Mark, after this man whom he admired. Franca was an Italian teenage gal struggling to survive in post-war Italy, selling chocolate and nylons on the black market. One of two people in our town not U.S.-born, she was simultaneously an oddity and an attraction. At the very least she was unique, because as my kindergarten classmate Suzie said, "she talked funny." She also carried the scars of a bullet wound through her left thigh inflicted during wartime.

After catching up on local happenings, Florence asked my dad if he had heard the new song about Vietnam that had just come out. He hadn't, so she put in a nickel in the jukebox and played the song. The arm of the record player reached over and picked out a 45-rpm black vinyl record and placed it on the turntable. After the needle gently set down, a quiet drum roll began, joined by baritone lyrics:

"Fighting soldiers from the skies. Fearless men who jump and die.

Men who fight by night and day. The brave men of the green beret ..."

The restaurant quieted as all listened to the newly released song, one of the few pro-military recordings of the Vietnam era to become a hit. Several young men from town were heading over there; Butch, Roger, and Teddy, to name a few.

After the song ended, I asked my dad for a quarter for the jukebox. I placed it in the slot and proceeded to play Staff Sgt. Barry Sadler's song five times in a row. By meal's end, I had the lyrics memorized. We finished our fish and left. Later, when the movie, *"The Green Berets"* starring John Wayne, came out, I went to the local Grand Theater two blocks up the street to watch it on the big screen. My older sister, Terri, bought the LP album with all of Barry Sadler's songs. I kept asking her to play it. With the lyrics of those songs memorized, and movie images seared in my pre-teen mind, I often dreamed of what it would be like to serve with the Green Berets.

Thirty-six years later I would have an opportunity to experience that dream and serve with these "unconventional soldiers."

Chapter 2

September 10-12, 2001

Tuesday, September 11, 2001, was to have been a career-enhancing opportunity – during a three-day temporary duty (TDY) trip to Washington, D.C. I had earned the "perk" after serving five years as chaplain for Colorado Army National Guard's light utility helicopter battalion, stationed at Buckley Air Force Base. Colonel Larry Ciancio, former battalion commander, now the State's Army Aviation Officer, made an extra effort to ensure that my name was on the flight manifest for what was to be a routine staff visit to Washington, D.C. The twelve passengers were primarily the Command Team and senior full-time Army National Guard staff members. I was an oddball and felt like it.

I was one of few traditional guard members on board -- the appropriateness of which was questioned beforehand. This was mainly due to the limited number of seats available. In addition to the two pilots, passengers included the Army ground commander – a brigadier general and his aide-de- camp; the state's inspector general; several other department directors; aviation officers: and me – a traditional Guard chaplain, along for some unspoken reason.

Most on the plane had appointments at National Guard Bureau (NGB), the Pentagon, or both. I had an appointment to visit the National Guard Chief of Chaplains, Chaplain (Col.) Father Frank Hill at 9 a.m. on September 11, 2001. I thought the best use of this unexpected trip would be to get an update on the latest chaplain briefings used in support of unit deployments. I had recently helped a Colorado helicopter medical evacuation unit through a six-month deployment to Bosnia and wanted to share with Chaplain Hill what I had developed. I also sought to gather current information on post-deployment briefings. Time permitting, I hoped to make an unscheduled visit to the Office of the U.S. Army Chief of Chaplains, in the Pentagon, across the street from our hotel. In my naiveté, I thought I could just drop by, since I was in the neighborhood.

With the two-hour time difference, most official trips to the east coast from Denver take the better part of one day. With Day Two for scheduled business and Day Three for return travel, I was on a three-day travel order.

The first rays of sunshine burst over Colorado's eastern plains as I arrived at Hangar 909 at Buckley Air Force Base on September 10, with my overnight bag containing my uniform and a book to read. As the group of military travelers assembled, more than one asked me why I was going on the flight. By the third query, I had my reply sounding pretty official: "I'm scheduled to meet with the National Guard Bureau Chief of Chaplains to present deployment briefings I developed in support of recent operations in Bosnia. I also hope to obtain the latest information available to update redeployment briefings for returning soldiers and their families." That seemed to satisfy most of the inquiring minds.

We loaded our bags into the nose and rear cargo compartments of the twin-engine Fairchild turbo prop aircraft. Seats were selected by order of rank, so I settled near the rear of the passenger compartment. Shortly after reaching cruising altitude, the pilot-in-command came back and told me to take his seat next to the co-pilot. I moved to the cockpit, buckled in, and put on the headphones. My former commander and trip sponsor began to give me an in-flight briefing as the plane flew eastward on autopilot. Scanning the cockpit gauges and controls, he would interrupt the familiarization process and conversation with necessary responses to air traffic controllers. Monitoring the almost incessant voice traffic seemed to me a challenging task. My anxiety level remained low, however, and I enjoyed the special in-flight briefing.

Over the previous three years, I had flown countless training flights in well-maintained vintage UH-1 "Huey" helicopters in and around the Rocky Mountain region with this experienced pilot at the controls. He was a former Cobra attack helicopter pilot and most recently, an instructor pilot in the UH-1. He had taken me into and through the Rocky Mountains and up to Camp Guernsey, Wyoming, where we flew many hours NOE (Nap of the Earth), practicing low-level, terrain-hugging rotary-wing tactics, like those showcased in the Disney movie, *Operation Dumbo Drop.*

As I sat in the right seat – the pilot-in-command position – I recalled a previous air assault training exercise in South Dakota to recover the ice cream shop on Mount Rushmore from enemy hands… and give our visiting Slovenian Air Force counterparts a tour of this historic landmark. Helicopters with camera-laden National Guard Soldiers flew around Mount Rushmore in figure-eight patterns to allow personnel on both sides to view and photograph the four granite Presidents. It was a well- conceived and ably executed training exercise for the flight crews, and a great morale boost for the ground crews who supported the aviators, not to mention our Slovene guests.

I was jolted back to reality when the pilot said, "We'll be landing for fuel in thirty minutes, so, I need you to retake your seat." I nodded, thanked him, removed the headphones, and exchanged seats with the pilot-in-command. Several passengers snoozed as I buckled in, but a couple looked at me with an inquisitive look. "Why was he asked to sit in the cockpit?" I imagined them thinking. I knew, but it was none of their business.

After a brief mid-point stop for fuel and lunch at a civilian airport, we took off on our flight to Washington-Dulles airport. I stayed in my seat the rest of the two-hour leg. After landing and taxiing to the general services aviation area, we deplaned, unloaded luggage, and piled into several rental cars. Forty-five minutes later, we checked into the Arlington DoubleTree hotel. I was on the fourth floor with limited view. The senior pilot's room was on the seventh floor with a great view of the Pentagon across the street, and the Washington Monument in the distance. At supper we coordinated our departure times for the next day, as the majority was to have breakfast at National Guard Bureau with members of the Colorado Army Guard assigned there. One or two were heading directly to the Pentagon.

***

It was my first visit to the nation's capital on military duty and I didn't know my way around. I was on time in the hotel lobby as we filled rental cars headed to National Guard headquarters in Arlington, Virginia and the Pentagon. Most of us joined a small group of Colorado Guard members in the cafeteria of National Guard Bureau Headquarters for a short welcome briefing and breakfast. As we were introduced, I met two senior officers who were heading to Jefferson Plaza 1 in Crystal City, where the National Guard Chief of Chaplain's office was located. After the breakfast meeting, I rode with them to Jefferson Plaza 1. This was my first stop, with the Pentagon, my planned second stop, only a thirty- minute walk from there.

Leaving the underground parking structure of Jefferson Plaza 1 with my senior uniformed chauffeurs, we parted company in the main lobby. I pushed the elevator button to the ninth floor according to post-it note written by my wife, who was temporarily filling in for my church secretary. She was able to make a 9:00 a.m. appointment through the senior Chaplain Assistant, Sgt. Maj. Ed Mazekas. I found suite 9500 and met Chaplain (Col.) Father Frank Hill's right-hand man. It was about 8:45 a.m. on September 11.

While Chaplain Hill was finishing another appointment, Sgt. Maj. Mazekas and I chatted. I learned that he was a former Vermont state trooper and, like Father Hill, was nearing retirement. He spoke fondly of his family and his time in the National Guard. As we talked, he received a call from his wife directing him to turn on the television in his office suite. It was about 8:50 a.m. As the station tuned in, we heard a news anchor reporting that an airplane that had just crashed into one of the Twin Towers of the World

Trade Center. Suddenly, Chaplain Hill emerged from his office apparently aware of the incident. He beckoned me into his office with an eye on the television outside his door. It was a brief visit, not more than ten minutes, but it seemed as if we covered a lot. I shared with him paper copies of the mobilization briefing I had developed and asked him for more information on other materials available for preparing returning soldiers and their families. He told me about a new National Guard website that contained sample copies of briefings that I could review and download. He also showed me a copy of recently approved technician position descriptions for full-time support chaplains and chaplain assistants in the National Guard. As he did, I felt like he was sharing with me something of great importance and future worth to the National Guard -- almost like a crowning career achievement. Five years later would I understand its significance when I was hired into that position in Colorado.

At 9:15 a.m., the phone rang again. Father Hill picked up and listened; his face showed alarm. He said he had to leave, so I quickly did what any former altar boy would do in the presence of a senior priest – a monsignor; I asked for his blessing. "Father, may I have your blessing before you go?" Surprised, but pleased, he leaned across his desk, resting his elbows on the blotter, he placed his hands on my head and prayed, "Father, grant this chaplain the courage to sow peace where peace is needed and discord where discord is needed. In the Name of the Father, and of the Son, and of the Holy Spirit. Amen."

Firmly leading me out his office door, on the television we saw smoke billowing from both Towers of the World Trade Center. Sgt.Maj. Mazekas hung up his desk phone. "I just spoke with a police officer friend at the base of the Towers. Something terrible is happening!"

At that moment, the building alarm sounded, and people rushed into the hall to board the elevator and descend the stairs. Unable to board an elevator that opened immediately, I descended by stairs in a stream of exiting blue and green military uniforms. Though no one visibly panicked, faces expressed alarm and confusion over what was transpiring.

As I left the steps of the multi-story building, an explosion echoed to my left. I checked my watch, it was about 9:35 a.m. Several people on cell phones called out about something happening at the Pentagon and yelled commands to take cover. The crowd dispersed as uniformed personnel ducked behind large cement vases that held trees, crouched behind hedges across the street, and generally scattered in all directions. Most of these people worked in the building and knew their way around. This was my first incursion into downtown Crystal City where many Department of Defense offices were located, and I had no idea where I was, or what was happening.

People with cell phones began to exchange reports, "A helicopter crashed at the Pentagon!" one uniformed member called out, "It was a helicopter loaded with explosives!" called another. Suddenly, a cloud of smoke and ash engulfed us. As I looked down, I saw what appeared to be a section of tar paper or roofing material in the shape of huge footprint, which had just drifted to my feet. My first thought was, "I'll bet this is from the Pentagon. Man, I wish I had a big Ziploc baggie to store it." But I didn't have a baggie, and I needed to let my family and church back in Denver know I was okay. They knew I was heading to the Pentagon that morning, and I figured they would be worried.

I opened my Motorola Flip Phone to call, but the local circuits were already overloaded. Reckoning the Pentagon was east of my position, I calculated that the hotel was north. I recalled someone saying that Jefferson Plaza 1 was just a few blocks from our hotel, so I started moving northeast. As I rounded the street corner, I saw streets jammed with cars, delivery trucks, buses and emergency vehicles, struggling to maneuver toward the Pentagon. Passing under an overpass that led toward a Pentagon parking area, I spotted the DoubleTree hotel to the north and jogged in that direction.

Entering my room, I tried my cell phone again to no avail. Using the hotel room phone, I made two calls. No one was home, so I left a voice message that I was okay. I then called the church office and told the volunteer receptionist that I was okay and wished to speak with the office administrator. Again, I assured her that I was alright, and that I was heading back to the Pentagon to see if I could help. I still wasn't sure what had occurred. I only had my dress uniform slacks and short sleeve shirt. Spying my fanny pack, I loaded it with snacks, my cell phone and a pocketknife. Grabbing two bottles of water, I headed back toward the Pentagon to help.

The Arlington Police had already begun setting up a security perimeter. Whereas most of the foot and vehicular traffic was flowing out of the Pentagon, a few people in military uniforms were heading into it. As I crossed toward the Pentagon parking area, I suddenly found myself walking with an Air Force Chaplain who was a Brigadier General. I asked him where he was heading and if I could help. He told me to come along. An Arlington police officer told us that entry was prohibited. When we asked how and where we could help, he pointed to a fire engine parked one block over. As we started toward the engine, a tall three-star Army general, wearing a green beret, crossed into the Pentagon lot. The police officer yelled for the general to come back and that he couldn't go in there. Without breaking his stride, the general looked back and said in a firm voice, "You clearly have the wrong person!" and he strode deliberately back toward the burning complex on "Hell's Bottom."

When the general and I reached the fire engine, we asked how we could help. The engineer said we could stand by with them or retreat to a makeshift medical point being set up in the cafeteria of the Drug Enforcement Agency (DEA) museum across the street. After a few anxious minutes, the Air Force chaplain, probably emboldened by the resolve of the Green Beret general, decided to enter the Pentagon perimeter. I accompanied a group of exiting Pentagon civilian employees across the street, directing them to an emergency medical team that was set up under a tree outside the DEA cafeteria. Once safely across, we asked the half-dozen or so female employees if they were injured or needed anything. One woman had lost a shoe in the stairwell, another left her purse in her office desk, another forgot her cell phone, and another scraped her knee and elbow running across the parking lot. One lady had her car keys, but having crossed the police perimeter, was unable to re-enter to get her car to drive home. Each one had a personal dilemma to upset them. After tying to get a cell signal, and redirecting people indoors to a landline, I introduced myself to the three-member emergency medical team that was rushed down from the Walter Reed Army Medical Center emergency department. We spent the next several hours assisting the exiting Pentagon employees, cleaning scrapes, attempting to make calls and occasionally, praying for a distraught soul.

When the mass exodus was apparently complete, we said 'Good-bye,' disbanded, and headed out; the local medical personnel to their hospital and homes, and I to my hotel up the street. We had done all we could -- pitifully little – as the Pentagon smoldered under torrents of water pumped in by many fire engines.

I got back to the hotel around 4:30 p.m. There were several voice messages from other members of the contingent; one directing me to meet in the lobby at 5:00 p.m. When I arrived, all but a few were present and accounted for. Missing were the general, his aide-de-camp, and the inspector general (IG). Hearing that the IG had business in Pentagon, concern swept the remainder of the group. It was agreed that we would break for supper and reassemble at 7:00 p.m. in Col. Ciancio's hotel room on the 7th floor, a room with the direct view of the west side of the Pentagon that had been hit.

After a light supper, I watched the evening news in disbelief. A total of four civilian airliners had been hijacked and crashed into three separate locations: two into the World Trade Center, in New York City, one into the Pentagon, in Washington D.C.– less than a half-mile from my hotel and one in a field outside Shanksville Pennsylvania.

I got to Col. Ciancio's hotel room shortly after 6:30p.m. Several others had already arrived, including other military personnel in addition to our group. I stepped out onto the balcony to observe the activity. Multiple fire engines poured water into the smoldering wreckage of the Pentagon's west side. Though I had been told that a plane had crashed into the structure, I could see no signs of plane wreckage from the outside. Frankly, it was incredible. I stared transfixed as helicopters landed and took off from inside and outside the mammoth five-sided office complex. Someone offered me a bottle of beer, but I declined and accepted a Coke, instead. Though raised in Wisconsin, I wasn't much of a beer drinker. I couldn't help but stare at the rescue and recovery activity less than a half-mile away.

As we talked and milled around the room and rotated onto the balcony, someone mentioned that the president was going to address the nation. Just a few miles away, Mr. Bush, the Joint Chiefs, and Congress were assembling. Suddenly, the group erupted as our missing inspector general entered the room.

Visibly shaken, but physically whole, Lt. Col. Mark Schoenrock began telling of his intended visit to the very section of the Pentagon that had been hit. At a crucial moment, he turned down a hall leading away from the targeted section. That decision to turn away saved his life. We stood around Mark congratulating him on his safety.

Shortly after, Brig. Gen. Ronald Crowder and his aide, 1st Lt. Rob Bell arrived. Relieved that the last of our group was present and accounted for, we gathered around the wall-mounted television in the colonel's room. The group quieted as the president entered and stepped to the podium. After describing the events of the day, I recall how Mr. Bush asked prayer for those who had been killed and injured, and for their families.

After the president completed his address, the room was quiet. I looked at Brigadier General Crowder and said, "Sir, our commander-in-chief has asked us to pray. With your permission, I will lead us right now." Waiting only a second, I bowed my head and as I did so, all bowed with me. I asked God to comfort the families of those who had lost loved ones, guide the eyes and hands of the rescuers to those still alive and prepare us who served in the military. When I concluded, everyone said "Amen!"

I wandered out onto the balcony one last time. Tractor-trailers loaded with generator light sets were being brought in to illuminate the impacted area for nighttime rescue and recovery operations at the Pentagon. The number of helicopters that had been taking off and landing from the Pentagon courtyard was decreasing. Fires continued to burn, and smoke continued to rise. Watching the events unfold, I wondered what all this would mean

Before going to sleep, I called my brother, Mat, a retired Army first sergeant, who lived near Fort Hood, Texas. I told him where I was and what I had witnessed. We talked briefly and said "Good-night" but not without saying, "I love you."

***

Before returning to our rooms, it was decided that our group would still try to depart for home the next morning, as scheduled. Hearing that all commercial aviation was grounded, our pilots expressed slight optimism that we might be able to take off. We agreed to meet in the lobby at 8:00 a.m.

Arriving together at Dulles Airport, we parked our rental cars and moved into the Signature flight facility waiting room. The pilots were on the phones filing flight plans and checking for clearance. Colonel Ciancio called us all together. He had a plan. Knowing that the Federal Aviation Administration had grounded all commercial flights, he figured that if he filed a flight plan as a military aircraft that included one refueling stop at military airfield, it would have the best chance of getting approved. That, plus the fact that we had a general officer on board, just might get us clearance.

After two hours of calling and waiting, the pilots told us to grab our bags and head to the plane. As we walked through the doorway to the tarmac, several civilian passengers, also waiting to leave, moved to let us by. One of them asked, "Why do they get to leave?" One of the counter agents said quietly, "They are in the military."

As we boarded, the pilots pre-flighted the aircraft. We took our seats and the pilot pulled the door shut. With the clock approaching noon, the engines roared to life and the pilot gave us our safety briefing. At 12:01 p.m., on September 12, 2001, we were the first aircraft to take off from Washington- Dulles airport – and one of the few non-tactical military aircraft that took off in the continental U.S. that day. Our destination: Buckley Air Force Base, Colorado.

Our refueling stop was Scott Air Force Base in southern Illinois. Unlike our flight out, we landed on a U.S. Air Force Base under tight security. Guided to a special aircraft parking area, we had to wait for a bus escorted by security police to take us to the base Burger King for lunch. Though we were U.S. military, the security personnel watched us carefully, scrutinizing the twelve civilian-clad passengers and two uniformed pilots. While we ate, our plane was refueled. Within an hour, we were back in the air.

Radio chatter this time was almost nonexistent. With no commercial aircraft flying, the return flight seemed eerie and surreal. As we approached the Colorado border, the air traffic control tower directed our flight path directly over Denver International Airport — something that would never occur on a regular day. As I looked down, I saw absolutely no aircraft activity at the busiest airport in the Rocky Mountain region.

We landed at Buckley without incident. Upon deplaning, Air National Guard security police in tactical gear with weapons surrounded the aircraft. We unloaded our bags and headed home.

As I glanced at my watch, I noticed that I still had time to make it to church for my Wednesday evening new members' orientation class at 7:00 p.m. I drove straight out of the Mississippi Avenue gate to Parker Road and into the church parking lot which was filling with cars for mid-week activities. Gathering teaching materials in my office, I entered the classroom designated the "Parlor." There waiting, and surprised, was my newest cohort of church members. I booted up my laptop, started my PowerPoint presentation, took a deep breath and tried to pick up where I left off from the previous week. That, I found, would be difficult.

Chapter 3

Call to Duty
February 15, 2002

It was a typical Tuesday morning at the church office. After the busy weekend, I took Mondays off to decompress and rest. As the senior pastor of a multi-ethnic urban church community of 1,000 people, by the time Tuesday came, my inbox was full. My wife was temporarily filling in for my executive secretary who was recovering from surgery. She had just come into my office to hand me something when the phone rang. The receptionist informed me that a chaplain was on the line, and that he said it was important. With my wife standing in front of my desk, I took the call.

"Andy, this is Andrew," he began. After exchanging pleasantries, he got to the point. Chaplain Zeller was the acting state chaplain, in place of our senior chaplain who was mobilized in support of "Operation Noble Eagle". "I spoke with the commander of the Special Forces battalion this past weekend. He informed me that his battalion has been put on alert. He wants a chaplain to deploy with them." As I silently considered the impact of his words, he continued, "Chaplain Bob is deployed, Chaplain Rick is not available, Chaplain…" after he reviewed the reasons why the other two or three chaplains were not available he said, "If you don't go, I'll have to."

Suddenly, I caught myself asking, "So how are your nine children?" "Well, actually," he replied, "Our tenth child was born several weeks ago." I had served and trained in the Army Reserve and Army National Guard for twenty-eight years, and I knew deep inside, it was my turn to go. The Special Forces unit was in my brigade: it was right that I should take the assignment, "After all," I said, "My youngest son is almost sixteen-years-old."

Assuring me that he would go, if necessary, I reaffirmed that, given the circumstances, I was the logical choice. After giving me the battalion commander's contact information, he hung up. I looked at my wife. She had heard the entire conversation – at least my half.

There was little discussion between us the remainder of the morning. I tried to go back to my weekly church routine. I found it difficult to concentrate. The televised words President Bush directed to the armed forces at the State of Union Address replayed in my head, "To the members of the military, I say, be ready!"

How I would get ready was all I could think about. How does a fulltime civilian pastor and part- time National Guard chaplain get ready for combat operations to who-knows-where? I didn't know, but I had a good idea who did. But first I had to inform some key people.

Chapter 4

Ordered or Volunteered? *

March 1, 2002

The next day I called Chaplain Allen Russel. As the endorsing agent for our denomination, CBAmerica, he certified clergy as fit for duty as chaplains, military and civilian. I knew I needed to let him know what was happening and get his advice on how to proceed; how to inform the church leaders, and ultimately how to prepare the congregation for my temporary absence. Al was calm as he listened to my report. He described the protocol of drafting a temporary leave of absence agreement between the church and deploying pastor. He recommended a six-month agreement renewable for an additional six months, should the deployment exceed the initial 180 days. He explained that such an agreement would not only help ensure that I would have my position upon return, but assure that the church would have recourse, should my deployment be extended indefinitely. He agreed to send me a sample document that we could adapt to our situation. Before we hung up, Al prayed for God's direction and protection for the church and my family.

After revising the draft temporary leave of absence document, I contacted the chairman of the church council. As the senior pastor, I was accountable to the deacon board, and worked closely with them, especially the chairman, as he represented the lay leaders and I supervised and led the paid ministry and support staff.

Brother Jake, a Vietnam Veteran, was a committed Christian layman and successful senior executive at a major Denver-based accounting firm. Fluent in Spanish, he became the director of Latin American operations, supervising corporate personnel in Central and South America. We met regularly for breakfast and I learned about the challenges and perks of his job. When problems arose in his company, he would board a plane and take care of business – firing, hiring, and training senior leaders from Mexico to Brazil. Jake was wise and diplomatic, yet firm.

When I told Jake of my call to serve with the Special Forces battalion, he listened with intense concern. When I finished relaying all I could share, he looked me square in the eyes and asked, "Pastor Andy, were you ordered, or did you volunteer for this mission?" Suddenly I realized the deep concern of my Christian brother. He continued, "I could call the commanding general or the Governor and tell him that you are needed here. You don't have to go!"

Rather than becoming offended, I sensed his genuine concern. Still, I struggled with his refusal to let me go. I mulled over my response. "Jake, it's my duty. I've trained many years to be an Army chaplain. You are not qualified to go, but I am." The conversation soon ended. It was hard for both of us. I had walked with Jake through a stroke from which he had recovered amazingly. Still, his emotions were atypically close to the service. We gave each other a teary man-hug, then left.

At the next deacon board meeting, I communicated my call to duty. Members of the twelve- man board asked clarifying questions. With my chaplain endorser's guidance, I presented the proposed temporary leave of absence, along with my plan for substitute staff leadership and pulpit supply. The meeting did not go long. At the end, several men prayed for God's direction and protection for the church, my family, and me. Several, themselves Veterans, hugged me tightly that night, as we adjourned. They knew better than I that it would not be easy.

*One of the challenges that reserve-component members face is the combination of misunderstanding of how soldiers and units are mobilized under current law. Whereas, in fact, entire units are involuntarily mobilized, there is sometimes a flexibility on the part of commanders regarding who they will take. For example, if a unit has excess personnel, the commander may select among the pool of qualified soldiers for a particular specialty or position. In other words, a unit with 100 authorized positions may have 120 personnel assigned, thus creating an apparent option for some personnel to go and others to remain behind in the rear detachment. (Rear Det.).

Chaplains, for example, are assigned to battalion-size units or larger. With the then-current assigned rate of less than 50% in the Army Guard, many units were lacking deployable chaplains. Commanders often would interview an available chaplain and invite him or her to deploy with their unit. In some cases, a chaplain had the option of declining, as in the case of a chaplain who had recently returned from a deployment or had a serious family or professional issue that would render him or her unavailable or ineffective. In such cases, these chaplains may decline a request, and take a later deployment. If a chaplain continued to decline the needs of units in his or her organization, the senior commander may command direct or order the chaplain to deploy, or resign or retire, whatever the case. In some cases, chaplains could serve up to two ranks above the assigned position; meaning that a major or lieutenant colonel could serve in a captain's (O3) position, if no other chaplains were available. In the Army National Guard, only the senior state chaplain (an O-6/colonel) was typically prevented from deploying. Their role is one of recruiting, training, mentoring and supervising subordinate chaplains.

Chapter 5

Job Interview
March 15, 2002

I called the Special Forces battalion commander to set up an initial meeting. Though the options among available chaplains were limited to two, I believed it appropriate to allow the commander to interview me as a potential member of personal staff. We agreed to meet, together with his executive officer (XO) at a restaurant near I-70 and Airport Boulevard.

When I arrived, both men were already there. We shook hands, exchanged pleasantries, and gave the waitress our order. When the food arrived, I offered to say grace before we ate. I recall praying for God to guide the commander as he assembled his team, for a successful train-up, and even gave thanks for the greasy truck stop food we were about to eat.

As we ate, we took turns talking. The commander shared his vision and philosophy of leadership, the XO gave a synopsis of the mission, and I shared my philosophy of ministry and asked a lot of dumb questions. Other than what I saw in the John Wayne movie, *"The Green Berets,"* I knew very little about the inner workings of these unconventional soldiers. After an hour-long meeting, I realized I had much to learn but felt a special kinship to these Special Forces leaders. They both professed a commitment to their Roman Catholic faith but assured me that there was a great diversity among unit personnel – from the devout to atheist.

As we left, I assured them that I would do my best to perform or provide for the religious needs of all their soldiers – including them. We exchanged contact information and went our separate ways. I recognized that I had a lot to learn about unconventional warfare...and I knew just the person to help me learn. It was the same sergeant who taught me how to tie a Swiss Seat* rope harness and rappel from a helicopter hovering at 100 feet in my helicopter unit a couple of years before.

No sooner than I received confirmation of the commander's approval of me joining his staff, I began to hear rumors of concerns about his leadership. Several senior leaders approached me and asked questions that I was unable to answer; questions about unit morale, the confidence of senior noncommissioned officers and my opinion of the commander's general competency. I frankly had no opinion. I was too new. But I sensed something was brewing. Maybe it was just a general concern for the battalion as it was preparing to deploy into harms' way. Perhaps it was

16

something more. I would soon find out in a very tragic way.

*Swiss Seat is a hand tied rope harness that Special Forces personnel use in a field-expedient rappelling operation.

Chapter 6

Baptism by Fire
April 15, 2002

I was in my church office when the receptionist informed me that I had a call from the Colorado National Guard headquarters. That being rare, I quickly picked up the phone. The tense voice on the other end asked me to come immediately to the headquarters conference room in my dress uniform. Little else was said. I hung up and called a couple of staff pastors to let them know that I would probably be out of the office most of the day. I drove home, donned my dress uniform and drove to the Colorado National Guard headquarters.

As I entered the Grove Room, several people were already assembled, including my new battalion commander. When I asked why I was called, he informed me that B Company of our Special Forces battalion that had deployed to Afghanistan had sustained a casualty – a KIA. I could see the sadness in his eyes. Right away I knew it was going to be a difficult day.

As The Adjutant General, entered the room, we all stood to attention. He motioned for us to be seated and asked the Army Deputy Chief of Staff for Personnel (G1) to bring everyone up to date.

I found myself whisked back to a casualty notification class taught by an experienced senior Army chaplain just prior to the Gulf War in 1990. In preparation for the anticipated bloodshed in the Gulf, he distributed several sheets with tips, directions, excerpted Army Regulations and outlines of military memorial, funeral, and burial services.

Back then, as a recently commissioned Army Reserve chaplain, I was attending my first annual chaplain regional sustainment training in Southern California. I recall paying close attention as the buildup in the Gulf occurred following Iraq's invasion of Kuwait. I took copious notes and carefully organized my casualty file.

Vaguely remembering the essence of that class, I was jolted back to the present as the G1 read the name, time, place and manner of the soldier's death. Sgt. 1st Class Daniel Aaron Romero had volunteered to assist a combat engineer Explosive Ordinance Disposal (EOD) team with a cache of recovered munitions outside Kandahar, Afghanistan. He was an 18E, a Special Forces communications sergeant, cross-trained in emergency medical response. Standard procedures required that medical support be provided for such potentially dangerous operations. Dan volunteered so the

EOD team could do its job. Apparently, someone had booby-trapped the site and Dan and four other EOD soldiers were killed in an explosion.

The casualty noncommissioned officer, Staff Sgt. Jim Greenwood, who would later become a close associate in casualty operations, began to review the official procedure for the casualty notification process: "First, we need to contact the wife."

"She lives about an hour north of Denver on a ranch," someone commented.

"And his mother, younger sister, and step-dad live about twenty minutes south," mentioned another.

The plan was to notify the primary next of kin, in this case his wife, followed by the secondary next of kin, his parents, and sister, by the same team.

"We should take two vehicles," someone suggested. "That way, if we find the soldier's wife alone, we can leave someone with her as we go to make the second notification"

"Who should that be?" someone asked. First Sgt. Tami Ferringer somberly raised her hand and said, "I'll do it."

We further discussed how the process would unfold, how we would approach each residence, in what order we would walk, and who would say what.

At that point Mason Whitney, The Adjutant General said, "I will go first, identify myself, verify their identity and give the bad news. Chaplain, I would like you to take it from there. I'll give the bad news and you, please offer pastoral support."

It was then that I realized that our two-star Air Force commanding general was planning to lead the casualty notification process! In a way, I was surprised – not that he had supervised the meeting and planning, but that he intended to make the notification. That part, I had wrongfully assumed, was to be the somber task of the commander or an appointed casualty noncommissioned officer.

"Sir," I said, "You don't need to go. By regulation, all we need is a service member of equal or higher rank – an E-7. Lt. Col. Pat and I, with Staff Sgt. Greenwood's guidance, are authorized to do this." I realized as I heard myself say these words that I might be perceived as contradicting the general's decision – being a chaplain with only the rank of major.

Rather than taking offense, General Whitney looked me in the eyes and said, "Andy, since I have asked our families to entrust their soldiers to me in combat, the least I can do is let them know when one of them dies."

It was a lesson in leadership I would never forget. Rather than delegate what is probably the most painful duty a military commander can perform; this general was leading the way. So impressed was I with his moral courage that day, that I would share that story numerous times, often to his seeming embarrassment … even spontaneously at his change of command and retirement ceremony at the Colorado Military Ball in March of 2007… and, again, here in this book. That day, I saw that effective leaders lead from the front, reserving the hardest tasks for themselves.

Five uniformed people walked out to the parking lot, four in green, one in blue; four males and one female to conduct one of the military's most difficult and somber duties.

An hour later, we found the soldier's wife at home, on a ranch, surrounded by horses and other ranchers nearby. The details of that visit will remain sacred, as will those of the second sad visit to the soldier's parents and sister. The first visit was quick and simple. No one was needed to stay with the Army's newest widow. The second visit was more complicated, as both parents were at work when we first arrived at their home. A neighbor informed us that both worked and usually came home around 4:30 p.m., so we went into town to eat what would be our lunch and dinner.

This experience suggested, and subsequent notifications would confirm, that though it is painful for the notification team to inform a spouse of his or her service member's death, it is often more difficult to tell a parent that their child had been killed in the line of duty.

When we returned to headquarters, it was already dark. Everyone was exhausted, physically and emotionally. I did what pitifully little I could do; compassionate touches on the arm, a comforting hug, a tearful prayer for God's comfort, and a call to the local parish priest, himself a retired Air Guard chaplain. I said goodbye to the members of the casualty notification team, got in my vehicle and drove home. My wife was waiting. She asked me what happened. I told her what I could.

I lay awake, but finally went to sleep.

It took over a week for this soldier's remains to arrive home to Colorado. His casket was escorted by two team members from Afghanistan. I was involved in the dignified transfer, funeral, and burial. Funerals and burials were something I was accustomed to performing as the senior pastor of an old metro church. After the burial ceremony at Fort Logan National Cemetery, a highly decorated soldier wearing a green beret came up to me, shook my hand, and thanked me for taking care of Dan and his family. He said that I had earned the unit's respect, even though I was a "leg," * and that he was glad I would be accompanying them on the upcoming deployment.

*"Leg" is what airborne-qualified soldiers call soldiers who are not airborne qualified. In some ways it's a term of condescension, but not entirely. Without the coveted jump wings that qualify a paratrooper to jump from aircraft, soldiers are limited to ground transportation or movement by their "legs." Author's note: Two weeks following my return from Afghanistan, I was sent to Fort Benning, Georgia, where I successfully completed the Basic Airborne Course – at age 49! From that point on, I was not longer a "leg," but "Airborne! All the Way!"

Chapter 7

JRTC: Finding my Place in the Unit
June 15, 2002

I boarded the C-130 cargo plane with my gear at Buckley Air Force Base for the Joint Readiness Training Center (JRTC) at Fort Polk, Louisiana. There, the battalion would be evaluated on a series of real-world simulations in our fictional host nation "Sand Land." Beyond training in my role as chaplain, I also received training in public affairs and civil affairs.
Near the end of the operation, my skill, along with that of my comrades, would be tested, and videotaped for evaluation.

The public affairs final exam was an interview by a simulated local news agency. The reporter had been sent by the insurgent-sympathetic press with a video crew to impugn the validity of our presence in country. Several personnel had been trained for this prospective role.

In my interview, I focused, as I had trained, on the command messages and talking points. The interviewer (and evaluator) became so frustrated by his inability to get me off topic that he finally ended the interview and said, "This guy is trained, let's get someone else in here." I took that as a sign that I had passed.

The civil affairs training was a bit more complex. I was forced to interact directly with a cast of local role players who had a wide range of problems for almost two weeks. On a daily basis we went from a staged welcome by a religious leader (which was a cover for insurgent surveillance), to locals being dropped at the gate with symptoms of a serious disease, allegations of rape by one of our soldiers, and a demonstration-turned-riot outside our main gate.

The situations increased in intensity and complexity. Though we anticipated a final culminating incident, we failed to adequately prepare for what would occur. Expecting our gates to be eventually crashed, we placed a fire hose for non-lethal use on any civilian trespassers. The rules of the exercise were that we were not to touch the roll players or be touched by them. They were to respond to verbal commands like, "Stop!" "You're restrained!" and "Sit Down!"

The big day came. A crowd gathered at a main gate and claimed a U.S. Soldier had raped one of their daughters. I was called to meet with their local leader. Although I used all the defusing techniques I had been taught, the crowd's emotions quickly escalated, and a riot erupted. They began shouting obscenities, throwing soft objects resembling rocks, and pressing the gate. Before I knew it, someone pushed me aside and several rioters darted through the gate. Looking back, the guards from my unit seemed to get a kick out of watching me get mobbed and shoved around.

When I saw the crowd break through, I ordered the guards to secure the gate and stop the infiltrators. Unfortunately, the fire hose was not connected to the hydrant, so our plan for non-lethal response didn't work.

I didn't know what else to do, so I yelled at one of the young male infiltrators to stop, but he kept running. I took off after him, shouted several more times that he was restrained and to sit down. When it became clear to me that he wasn't going to play by the rules, I grabbed him and slammed him into the side of a military vehicle. Suddenly, he stopped. I grabbed another, then another, until I had restrained four or five rioters. With the cooperation of the other soldiers in play, we managed to capture all who broke into our compound.

Later, when we did our after-action review, a couple of the actors accused me of "unnecessary roughness." It was my word against theirs until other soldiers of my unit corroborated my story.

Looking back, I regret that we didn't have the fire hose attached and ready before the crowd gathered.

At the end of the exercise I thought: "Note to self: have fire hose at main gate ready for non- combatant rioters!" Unfortunately, when we finally arrived in country, there wasn't enough water or pressure to take a shower, much less fill and pressurize a fire hose.

Sgt. 1st Class David Arragon, our unit recruiter, came to me near the end of the exercise. He suggested that we do something to boost morale. We pooled our funds and ordered as many pizzas as we could afford. We had them delivered secretly to one of the back gates. We took the boxes of pepperoni, cheese, and sausage pizza around to the different work centers. At first everyone wondered where they came from. After a few bites, no one seemed to care. The exercise continued, and morale improved. Leave it to a recruiter to smuggle in pizza and leave it to a chaplain to come up with the funds.

The official end of exercise after action review (AAR) noted that the unit was ready for operations. I was not expecting the training in Civil and Public Affairs. Later I would learn the reason why. JRTC was completed, but there was still one thing I needed to do to complete my training: consult with a World War II survivor. My mother.

Chapter 8
A Mother's Warning
July 15, 2002

I had been training with the Special Forces unit for five months. We completed our JRTC exercise with strong affirmation that our unit was ready for deployment.

I also prepped the home front. I remodeled the upstairs bathrooms, bought a new energy- efficient freezer for the garage, had energy-efficient windows installed, purchased an updated four- wheel-drive vehicle for my wife, got the church organized for my absence, and helped our youngest son get his driver's license. But there was one more thing I needed to do before deploying.

Since my 72-year-old mother was a survivor of World War II in Europe, I knew she would certainly want and deserved a visit from her oldest son who was about to deploy into harm's way. She survived the bombing, assault and occupation of Livorno-Pisa in July of 1944. She was a non-combatant caught in the crosshairs of a German soldier whose bullet pierced her right leg, just missing the bone. An advancing U.S. Army infantry squad heard the gunfire. According to my uncle who was present, "a dark-skinned American Soldier (we think an American Indian or a Samoan) with a Browning Automatic Rifle killed the German. An Army medic attended to my mother and evacuated her to an aid station where her wound was cleaned and dressed. Afterwards, she was taken home and given to her parents accompanied by U.S. soldiers, one of whom spoke Italian.

Not only did I feel it was my duty as the eldest son to say goodbye, I wanted to look her in the eye and allow her to give me sound battlefield advice.

It was a quick trip. I flew into Milwaukee on Friday night and drove up to Green Bay where she lived. I spent time with her and my sisters on Saturday, but had to catch a Saturday evening flight home, so I could preach in church on Sunday morning.

As I sat in the living room of my mother's apartment, she became unusually quiet. She looked me in the eyes and said, "You are going to Afghanistan, aren't you? I hear it is a dangerous place."

Then raising her thumb in a familiar European didactic manner, she said, "Rule number one: Always be aware of your surroundings. Look in front, in back and all around you, all the time. See what people have in their hands and if there are bumps under their clothes. Rule number two: I know you American Soldiers, you will get tired of the mess hall food and want to eat in town. If you go into a restaurant to eat, always sit with your back to the wall facing the front door. Look at everyone inside and find the back door. Rule number *"tree"* (she never learned to say "three"): When you pull the pin on a grenade, you get rid of it real fast!"

Though I wanted to smile, I knew that she was dead serious and was speaking from personal experience. She did not smile.

When it was time to leave, I tried to hug her. It was not her custom to give her children hugs, so it was an awkward moment. Maybe it was the privation and stoicism learned in war during her formative adolescent years that steeled her emotions. Or perhaps it was the premature war-time death of her father, combined with the loss of her husband at age thirty-nine. Still, I tried to hug her. Tears came to my eyes. It could be the last time I saw her, as either one of us could die in the next year.

She pushed me away. "No tears. Now go!" she said in a stern voice.

I left, telling her that I loved her while unsuccessfully trying to choke back my tears. I often wondered if she had wept quietly alone in her apartment after I left. That would be something I would never know. As I drove back to the airport, I wiped tears from my eyes.

Chapter 9

Church Farewell Ceremony

This was my first combat deployment and I knew that I needed the advice and help of those more experienced. My chaplain endorser, Al Russell, a retired Army Reserve Chaplain, proved to be a great mentor and friend. Beyond helping me draft a temporary leave of absence from the church, he coached me on a variety of issues, professional and personal.

When it came time to say good-bye to my congregation, he came and participated in a church farewell ceremony. In addition to church leaders and staff members, Chaplain Russell spoke in that special event. But it wasn't an event just for me. Another soldier who had been attending the church, Sgt. 1st Class Dave was also deploying. Though assigned to another unit, he volunteered to deploy with the Special Forces battalion, in part because he himself was a qualified Green Beret, but he also went to ensure my safety and success.

It was not a long ceremony, and I have a faint recollection of all that was said. What I do remember was Chaplain Russell's comment to the church congregation. He said: "God needs Pastor Andy more there than you do here." As I looked around at the ministry team assembled, I saw that he was right. I had a competent, seasoned team of ministers: pastor of worship and music, youth pastor, directors of women's ministry and children's ministries, church administrator and my senior associate, himself a twenty-six-year Army chaplain and Vietnam Veteran. I felt these gifted associates were more- than-qualified to care for the congregation at Galilee. With my retired Army Vietnam Veteran chaplain leading the ministry team and lay pastoral support committee, I felt the church would be left in good hands.

It was still a painful moment. I knew I would miss my family, my creature comforts, my colleagues and my congregation, many of whom had become dear friends. Still, Chaplain Al was right. This battalion of citizen-soldiers needed a chaplain, a shepherd, a pastor to accompany them through the yet unwritten history of this deployment. It was my time, my turn. I must go.

The ceremony culminated in a prayer of commitment for Sgt. 1st Class Dave and me. As the prayer ended, I heard my Green Beret comrade, who knelt beside me, quietly make a sacred vow: "Before God, I promise to bring Pastor Andy back safely!"

After the ceremony, retired pastor, Dr. Charles Cook met me in the church lobby. Well into his 80s, he served as pastor among our significant senior population. Always, positive and insightful, he took my hand in a farewell handshake and said, "Pastor Andy, remember, wherever you go, God is already there!" I looked into his experienced eyes and took great comfort. Not only did his words bring solace, but the anticipation of his continued presence in the congregation during my upcoming absence gave assurance that things would be just fine without me.

Chaplain Russell's declaration, Sergeant Dave's promise and Dr. Cook's reminder were only three of what turned out to be several prophetic statements of the future deployment.

Chapter 10

Mobilization Station: An unusual request
August 22, 2002

A week or so after receiving our mobilization orders, the unit reported to Fort Carson, Colorado, sixty miles south of Denver. Many of us drove our personal vehicles so we'd have transportation in and around and to and from the "Mountain Post." Using the strip map and building number provided, I drove my '94 Jeep Cherokee to a World War II hospital complex typically used for Reserve and Guard barracks and training exercises. I lugged my Tuff Boxes, guitar case and duffel bags into the orderly room and got a key to my temporary lodging. This would be the first of several ancient dwellings I would inhabit during the deployment.

I moved into my long, narrow room furnished with two sets of bunk beds, wall lockers, desks and chairs. I found the electrical outlets and set up my desk area complete with reading lamp and the new laptop and printer I purchased for the deployment from the earnings of my three-week JROTC training.

The next few weeks would be filled with briefings, classes, immunizations, physical training, and teambuilding. I quickly set up shop as chaplain and soon business was booming. Not having an assigned chaplain assistant, I started out as a one-man operation, but soon found several soldiers more than willing to help when needed. Technically, I was assigned to the S1, the administrative section, for accountability and pay, but I served on the battalion commander's personal staff.

One day the First Sergeant came to me and said something unexpected. "Chaplain," 1st Sgt Mike began, "I have a feeling that you will be busy over there. I'm gonna have a company of support soldiers confined on a small base. Whenever you need people to help just let me know. I'm sure they'll be happy to get out a do something different." Unsure what he meant, I thanked him for the promised support and tucked that offer away in the back of my mind.

I spent a lot of time training with the soldiers and traveling to ranges to observe weapons qualification. As one of the first National Guard Special Forces units mobilizing through Fort Carson on this presidential call-up, we had priority in terms of range use and ammunition allocation. After we left, I heard that we had gone through more ammunition as a battalion in two months than the entire Post had at mid-point that year. Though I think that was somewhat of an exaggeration, I did see a lot of rounds go down range through more weapons than I had ever seen in my previous twenty-eight years of military experience.

It was during that training that a team captain, the commanding officer of an Operating Detachment Alpha (ODA, or "A Team") came to me with an unusual request. He began by telling me that he, himself, was a man of faith, a Christian, and that he would never pull my leg over something spiritual. But at the urging of the other members of his team, he felt he needed to enlist my help. He hesitated, and then began to tell me that many of the men on his ODA believed that one of their team members was cursed. He must have noticed my eyes widen, so he raised a hand to prevent my interruption. Here's what I heard.

In 1995, the battalion deployed a company of Green Berets, to Haiti in support of Operation Restore Democracy. One team was called to rescue an American missionary family whose husband- father had been shot by local insurgents. Every ODA has two 18-Deltas, or "super-medics," as I like to call them. These medics are highly trained to the level of a civilian paramedic, EMT-P, to conduct emergency medicine in a tactical environment. So, if another team member gets sick, injured or wounded, at least one other team medic will be available to stabilize and treat until medical evacuation. That was the rub.

Something happened, the team captain told me. Though he didn't know what for certain, ever since that incident, the senior medic who handled that situation seemed to bring himself and his team bad luck. The team wanted me to deal with the situation, exorcise any demon, or whatever necessary to get rid of the curse. I thanked the captain for the intelligence and agreed to pay a visit to the soldier concerned.

A few days later, I made it a point to drop by the team room to see the senior medic, "Doc" Simon. He was sitting on a tuff box cleaning his assault rifle. I asked him if we could talk and he told me to have a seat. It was apparent that he was expecting me. After candidly describing the situation from his perspective – amazingly like the version I heard from his Team Captain -- I asked him what he wanted me to do for him.

"Get rid of this damn curse!" was his reply. "Since Haiti, no team I've ever served on has ever been successfully ex-filtrated! Neither I, nor my teammates, want this to continue."

As he spoke, I could see the seriousness in his face. I recalled an experience as a junior missionary in Portugal in the early '80s when a senior missionary colleague took me along to pray for a woman in a nearby village who reportedly was demon-possessed. Remembering the challenge of that situation, I asked Doc Simon if I could pray for him; that the curse would be removed. After he said, "Sure," I bowed my head.

I could feel him watching me as I prayed, and in a few sentences, I asked God to remove any apparent curse or evil oppression that afflicted him and his team. Confident of the source of all spiritual power, I concluded my prayer, "In Jesus' Name. Amen."

When I opened my eyes, Doc Simon was staring at me — a bit skeptically, it seemed. We shook hands and I left. Only several months later, on the other side of the world, would I come to realize the seriousness of this man's desire to be freed from "the curse."

Part two: Getting There
Chapter 11

Hot Air, False Start, and Freedom's Song
September 2002

I learned several new skills on this deployment. One of them was the proper technique of building military air cargo pallets. When I asked a seasoned soldier how we were going to load our gear onto the aircraft, he said one word: pallets. Eight feet by ten feet aluminum pallets are the standard means for packing, loading, trans-loading and offloading gear and equipment into and out of theater by military cargo aircraft.

A week before we were to be ready to ship out, I went to a warehouse on Fort Carson where these pallets were assembled. The system is relatively simple. It consisted of a flat, almost square reinforced aluminum base upon which to stack the gear with nylon webbing on all four sides and top to hold it onto the pallet, and a measuring stick – eight feet long to make sure the full pallet wasn't packed too high to fit into the transport aircraft.

Teams and sections took turns building their own pallets. At first, I watched, then I helped. Soon I was helping others build their pallets. After building ten to fifteen pallets, I was getting proficient. It was another way I could lend a hand, get to know my soldiers and, hopefully, earn their trust.

When it came time to load my equipment, I brought two Tuff Boxes, a duffle bag, some boxes of Bibles and my trusty old Epiphone guitar in its hard case to the loading facility. Concerned about the guitar's safety, one seasoned pallet builder suggested I place it on top, as that would be the safest place. So, I did, and he was right.

With pallets packed, word came that our cargo plane, a U.S. Air Force C-5 Galaxy would be on the tarmac in a couple days. Life got simpler as ninety-five percent of our gear was now loaded onto pallets awaiting transfer onto the largest cargo plane in the U.S. military's inventory.

Finally, the day came when the mammoth plane arrived at Peterson Air Force Base. Air Force loadmasters driving huge forklifts and transfer equipment expertly loaded our pallets onto the aircraft from the rear. Soon about one hundred soldiers would board the plane.

Family members gathered with those scheduled for this deployment. My wife and four children, ages sixteen to twenty-four were present. My daughter, a student at Colorado Christian University, organized

31

a group of students in her dorm to bake cookies for the departing troops. They included a half-dozen cookies each in a Ziploc baggie with a cardboard heart and an encouraging scripture verse. The cookie bags disappeared in less than three minutes after one soldier sampled the contents and gave his verbal recommendation to the gathering crowd.

My oldest son, an aspiring singer-songwriter, composed a song for the departure. He called it "Liberty." He gave me a recording and a copy of the lyrics as we prepared to board. I hugged and kissed my family goodbye, waiving as I set out across the tarmac. Tears welled up in my eyes, and the eyes of others around me. Quietly and solemnly we made our way in route-step to the rear of the aircraft, up the ramp, and then up a steep flight of stairs to the passenger area in the rear section above the cargo bay.

The passenger area of a C-5 Galaxy is different than most other military cargo planes. In the smaller C-130 and newer C-17 cargo planes, passengers typically sit in jump seats along the sides of the cargo bay. But the C-5 has an area for approximately one hundred passengers in the upper area of the rear fuselage. The seats are more like airline seats, except facing the rear – perhaps because that is a more crash-worthy position? There is a small galley, a restroom and even a uniformed Air Force flight attendant to make sure the passengers stay safe, and don't get too rowdy.

After about one hour on board, word came to deplane. The temperature was too hot to allow for a safe takeoff. We were told to go home and come back early the next day when the air would be colder, denser and safe for takeoff. With glances of frustration, we deplaned and returned to the flight line where most family members had remained to watch the takeoff.

Since my Command Sgt. Maj. lived in Wyoming, I invited him to spend the night at our home about an hour away. After supper and a short night's sleep, we headed back to Petersen Air Force Base for an early departure. We had to take off before the temperature got too warm and takeoff would be aborted a second time. We had to avoid hot air.

With one boarding rehearsal under our belts, and our equipment securely tied down, we boarded a second time without a hitch. Waving our families goodbye, we settled into our rear-facing seats. Prior to takeoff, our lift leader, a Special Forces Major, took the intercom microphone from the passenger attendant and called me up to say a prayer. I took the folded lyrics of the song my son had composed and proceeded to read them to my soldiers. Try though I might, I struggled to contain my emotions as I read the words to the song:

The Price of Freedom[1]

(They Fell in Love with Liberty)

"In a land of the shadows a baby was born,

The most beautiful creature any eyes ever saw.

Some men and women woke from their dark sleep,

To the cries of a child called Liberty.

Soon Liberty grew up in beauty and strength,

And to all who would listen sweet Liberty gave,

A dream that would counter the will of the strong,

But the dream against tyrants would be bloody and long

Chorus:

The price of our freedom is paid for in blood,

Of Soldiers who fight for a dream that they love.

The flag that they wear is the mark of their creed.

They fell in love with Liberty

So, Liberty captured hearts old and hearts young,

And some to their deaths they went singing this song,

For the sake of the oppressed we will gladly risk our lives,

For those we don't know and children we might.

Through peace and through war great Liberty reigns,

Though evil men plot her destruction and shame.

Liberty stands and remains ever strong,

By the blood of the dreamers that still sing her song...

There are some who say that no dream is ever worth the fight,

And they spit on the graves of the ones who died to give
them that right,

Only fools take Liberty for granted as if she was there all along,

But I know better because my Daddy always sang me her song.

Now not every government's actions are pure,

And not every cause reflects Liberty's worth,

But elsewhere the only voice heard is the strong,

And I'll fight for your right to say that I'm wrong...

Chorus:

The price of our freedom is paid for in blood,

Of Soldiers who fight for a dream that they love.

The flag that they wear is the mark of their creed.

They fell in love with Liberty

    The group responded with spontaneous applause to my son's lyrics. I then led in prayer asking God to watch over our families we were leaving behind, and us as we journeyed into the unknown. I handed the microphone back and took my seat. Within minutes we were taxiing and taking off. The journey to the land of the Afghan had finally begun. First stop: Charleston, Air Force Base, South Carolina.

----

[1]Song by Andrew J. Meverden (Copyright 2002 AJM/SOK music)

Chapter 12

In-Flight Entertainment

The first flight was by far the most comfortable. After a fuel stop in Charleston, we hopped over the Atlantic to an air base in Germany in our C-5 Galaxy. There, we could deplane, get a shower, eat and bed down in a huge white high-tech tent, while our pallets and vehicles were trans-loaded onto a C-17 Globemaster. This was the newest U.S. Air Force cargo plane capable of landing in a theater of operation. Though smaller than the C-5, it was still massive and cavernous with a more modern interior.

Passenger seating on the C-17 was along the sides, much like a C130, with the seats facing inward. In between each seat were 110-volt grounded outlets that soldiers quickly used to hook up their portable video players and laptop computers. "How convenient!" I thought, "They put in outlets, so soldiers could entertain themselves on long flights!" Later I learned that these outlets were installed for operational reasons, to include in-flight briefings and preparations for tactical operations. So much for a kinder, gentler Air Force.

The Air Force crew did everything they could to make us comfortable, including showing us how to strap in, use the rest room and get water. As the flight droned on, they even showed us how to stretch out safely on the floor of the cargo bay, on the pallets, or in the vehicles we transported.

About four hours into the flight, the crew chief came up and asked me if I'd like to see the cockpit. They had been rotating soldiers through a few at a time and I was anticipating my turn up top. I climbed the ladder about two stories into the back of the cockpit. Surprisingly, it was quiet enough to talk and hear what was going on.

In the brief introductions, I learned that the pilots were members of the U.S. Air Force Reserve. They had been flying commercial aircraft for American Airlines but had been laid off following the September 11 attacks when the airline industry took a nosedive. They seemed to be in their mid to late thirties, all married with children, and grateful to have their Air Force Reserve jobs to help pay the bills.

Suddenly, the pilots broke off conversation. One pointed out the front windshield into a moonlit sky high above the clouds below. Up ahead, flying a few hundred feet above us was our next fuel stop, a KC-135

Stratotanker. Transfixed by the scene, I watched as the planes approached each other for the delicate task of aerial refueling. It was an amazing sight to see. I had seen it on television and video, but this was my first in-flight refueling experience, and it was grand.

After the operation was complete, conversation resumed. One pilot said, "Chaplain, only in the Air Force will you find a sergeant paid to lie on his belly and pass gas!" We all had a good laugh, but I was sure grateful for the expertise of that fuel boom operator. After thanking them for the experience, I returned to my seat in the cargo bay. As the hours passed, I began to wonder about what might be waiting for us on landing.

Chapter 13

Landing at Kabul International Airport (KIA)

September 23, 2002

After many hours of flight, our lift leader conferred with the loadmaster and one of several Air Force "Ravens" on board. The "Ravens" are a team of Air Force special security forces personnel tasked to secure the landing zone and aircraft on remote or dangerous landing strips. Up until that point they were quiet, mostly keeping to themselves, but when the Raven team leader gave the signal, they snapped into preparation for landing.

They began to kit up, donning body armor and battle gear, a strange sight for Air Force personnel in flight suits. They checked their magazines and weapons and performed radio checks on their intercom units. A few minutes into their preparation, our lift leader instructed our first sergeant to prepare our soldiers for deplaning at our destination. A supply sergeant broke out a box of ammunition for rifles and another for the side arms all Special Forces Soldiers carried.

As the chaplain, I was not authorized nor issued a weapon at home station. Military chaplains and medical personnel are considered noncombatants according to the Geneva Convention. Unlike our NATO chaplain counterparts, U.S. Department of Defense policy prohibited chaplains from carrying weapons for personal defense. A chaplain assistant is typically provided for the chaplain's defense. In my case, an assistant was not yet assigned.

Though I understood the policy and was willing to abide by this regulation, I felt awkward watching my soldiers kit up and not be able to arm myself. As a former enlisted soldier, I was proficient in most Army weapons, including the M16, M1911, M79, M60 machine gun and M2 .50-caliber machine gun. As a chaplain, I knew my weapons were now spiritual, and the Bible I carried was my principal offensive weapon, along with the black-bladed Ka-Bar fighting knife that hung from my load bearing vest.

As we prepared to land, I went around the plane's cargo bay talking with soldiers. I figured that they, too, might be apprehensive. Several soldiers asked me why I didn't have a weapon. I must have explained Army policy at least six times. Most grunted in understanding, but thought it was dumb. A couple of senior Green Berets told me to stay close to them when told to disembark. It sounded like a good idea to me, so I gathered up my rucksack and waited.

Within an hour, our plane descended and eventually hit the runway. When the rear ramp opened, the Air Force Ravens exited first and established a secure perimeter as we prepared to exit. At their signal, our soldiers double-timed toward what looked like a terminal area barricaded with huge wire baskets lined with muslin and filled with dirt. That was my first introduction to HESCO baskets, a modern upgrade to traditional sandbags. As we entered a maze, I saw what appeared to be a Turkish flag flying over the terminal. Inside, we were welcomed to Afghanistan by Turkish International Security Assistance Forces (ISAF) military personnel. The International Security Assistance Force was a NATO-led security mission in Afghanistan, established by the United Nations Security Council in December 2001. Our U.S. forces were a major part of that multi-national mission.

While we waited for ground transportation to our base of operations, one soldier looked at me and said, "Well, chaplain, welcome to KIA!" Suddenly the irony of that greeting struck me. We had landed at Kabul International Airport, coded KIA. With my comrades, I was anxious to get to our base, someplace secure to eat and sleep.

Chapter 14
First Night Fears and Celestial Wonders

It was mid-afternoon by the time we arrived at our destination – the Kabul Military Training Center (KMTC). The small Forward Operating Base (FOB) was located approximately ten kilometers east of Kabul on the Jalalabad road, seventy-five miles from the famous Khyber Pass and Pakistan border. The cluster of one and two-story buildings was made up of old garages, warehouses and sleeping quarters. The base was established by 1st Battalion 3rd Special Forces Group in 2002. It was a base within a preexisting Afghan Army training facility. Our compound was situated on the KMTC grounds. The U.S. base's perimeter was seven-tenths of a mile.

KMTC was constructed in the late seventies with Soviet funds and on September 11, 2001, was reportedly the intelligence center of the Taliban regime. Many of its three-story barracks buildings were damaged by Joint Directed Attack Munitions (JDAM) launched from U.S. B52 bombers in the air campaign against the Taliban in October of 2001. Some buildings had major damage with one or two floors collapsed. These were off-limits, as they were structurally dangerous.

We were conducting a "relief in place," which meant we arrived to take over a mission from troops still present and engaged. One of the downsides of this was there was little room for incoming troops. We were crowded into rooms and stacked onto three-quarter-size metal bunks until Third Group could exit.

After dropping my rucksack onto my bunk, I went to visit the Third Group chaplain. He was a Jesuit priest who had established a chapel area next to the main briefing room. The designated chapel space was in a one and one-half-story slant roof building that looked like it had been a series of garages or storage areas. Most windows were filled with thin plywood for blackout purposes and to help keep out the dust.

When I met the 3rd Group chaplain, Father Tom, he was wearing a ragged T-shirt and running shorts. He was young, probably early to mid-30s and quite congenial and helpful. We talked for about an hour before he had to break for the Commanders Update Briefing (CUB). I sat in with him and was introduced along with a number of other recent arrivals.

After the short meeting, I headed down to the dining facility (DFAC), for the evening meal. After picking up my cardboard tray and plastic wear, I went through the food line for supper. The seating area was small, so there was little time to socialize. It was your basic "wolf and vacate" so others behind could do the same.

It was dark when I left the DFAC. Apart from the few dim lights inside, there was absolutely no artificial lights outdoors. I followed a soldier out to dispose of my tray and paper cup in the trash barrel. The barrels were located about 50-75 feet away from the DFAC. Not anticipating the darkness, I was unprepared, leaving my flashlight with my rucksack. I stumbled twice before running into the trash barrels. After dumping my trash, I froze. All at once I realized that I was standing alone in total darkness. Back home, even if I were out east of Denver in a remote area, if I looked back, I could see the glow of the city off in the distance and the outline of the Front Range foothills. But here, just ten kilometers east of Kabul, there was nary a glint of light. All around me was total darkness.

True confession: as a young boy, I had a fear of darkness. Whether it was from stories of the Boogey Man, one too many episodes of *The Twilight Zone*, or old Vincent Price horror movies, I was scared to death of the dark. Going out at night, I always had a flashlight or lantern in hand. Even then, I was uncomfortable.

Here I was, standing in total darkness, alone. I had no flashlight, nor would I have turned it on without a red filter, for security reasons. Outside the wire were six hundred recruits of the new Afghan National Army (ANA). Some of them could be Taliban sympathizers, if not infiltrators, who would be happy to slit my throat, given the chance.

Yet, even with those wild thoughts cascading through my mind, I felt no fear. I thought a second and a third time; checking my emotions – but strangely I was not afraid. For the first time in my conscious life, standing alone in total darkness, half-way around the world in a theater of operations – a "combat zone" – I felt no fear of the darkness. For some unknown reason, it appeared that God had taken away, at least for now, my childhood fear of the dark. But that wasn't the only amazing thing to occur that first night.

My gaze went upward into the moonless sky. At first, I thought a low cloud or fog was passing overhead. But as I stared upward, I realized that it wasn't a cloud, not of moisture, anyway. Instead, due to the absence of light in my present surroundings, and the 6000-plus feet of altitude, I was looking up at the Milky Way! I stood enthralled for several minutes staring into the Afghan night sky. It was amazingly beautiful; and I was taking it all in with my bespectacled naked eye.

It was then that the thought struck me; God had taken me all this way to show me things I had never seen before. As I stumbled back to my sleeping area, I wondered what other new things I might see!

Chapter 15

Digging in and Building up

Within a couple weeks, the transition between units was complete. That gave us the opportunity to settle in and make this place our home for the next six to twelve months. We transitioned in from August through September. The Afghan summer continued with hot, dry, dusty days and sweltering nights.

Electricity was weak and unreliable. It was supplied by a diesel-powered generator that occasionally overloaded. Water came from two sources; bottled water and a few remote spigots of local water from a cistern perched up on a hill a few kilometers away. That, too, was unreliable and non-potable. Its purpose was to provide water for showers, toilets and front-loading washing machines located in a few tin-clad white shower trailers placed in two separate locations. One trailer was for our Special Forces battalion and the other to support the military police company that was there providing force protection to our forward operating base (FOB).

It wasn't long before our waterline to the showers began to freeze. The decision was made to move the containerized shower unit into a warehouse. With the doorway too narrow and too low and with a lack of available construction equipment, some of our Green Beret engineers offered to cut some concrete posts and steel beams using C4 explosive. I remember the warning for the detonation time of the carefully placed charges. Staying indoors, I listened for the call, "Fire in the hole!" Immediately following a succession of blasts, rock, concrete chunks, and gravel rained down on the tin roof covering the chapel section. After the fallout subsided, I went outside to admire the newly cut opening – along with, smiling, dusty-faced demolition experts examining their work!

The sounds of hammers, saws and drills were everywhere. With limited space, it was a challenge to fit everyone in. It was decided that I would wall off the back 10 feet of the chapel area to build a chaplain's office and two sleeping rooms one for my assistant and one for me. Materials were scarce, but over time we scrounged enough wood to build an adequate parsonage and chapel office. Utilizing a combination of old Soviet weapons boxes used to ship AK-47, RPG, and SPG-9 armament, we were able to build an ingenious system of horizontal cabinets and upright lockers. Interior shelves were made from Meals-Ready-to Eat (MRE) boxes stacked in various configurations.

When all was said and done, we had a functional office area with two computer workstations; one government, and one personal. I had no idea what situations would arise over the next six months, but I wanted to be ready for whatever might come...and eventually, "whatever" showed up in many different forms.

Chapter 16

The Fabulous Bombay Lounge

Forward Operating Base 195 (FOB195) was a dreary place. When it was hot and dry, the dust was two-inches thick. It was so fine; it caused a cloud of dust that exploded with every step. It reminded me of the cloud of dust that surrounded Pigpen in the Charlie Brown cartoons, except we were all Pigpen. It entered our noses, nasal passages and lungs with every breadth and was coughed up the following morning, much like a smoker's cough.

It would be weeks before anyone from higher headquarters would respond to requests for morale, welfare and recreation (MWR) support and send down our first television sets with satellite uplink, and local radio transmitter. With now 400-plus soldiers crammed into our small base, we were going to have to be creative and come up with our own fun.

The ingenuity and creativity of our soldiers manifested itself, again. Capt. Diggs, whose father served as a morale officer in WW2, had a brilliant idea. He decided to begin a *Saturday Night at the Movies* event, only on Thursday evenings. For whatever reason, he dubbed it "The Fabulous Bombay Lounge." Now, you'll have to play this out in the theater of your mind. A sheet was hung from the side of a dilapidated one-story building for our projection screen. A laptop computer with external speakers connected to a borrowed video projector was set up on a small table on top of an aviation pallet – eight feet by ten feet aluminum base. Our premiere movie? *Lawrence of Arabia*, of course!

Initially no more than twenty soldiers showed up for all or part of the movie. I can't be dogmatic, as that night, as in every Thursday night that we held The Fabulous Bombay Lounge, I fell sound asleep at least mid-way into the film.

As we continued the event, more and more soldiers began to attend. We began with one to two pallets for the moviegoers, but over time, more and more pallets were dragged in to accommodate attendance. Many of the soldiers would smoke cigars, a few pipes, and even fewer cigarettes in the outdoor air. I made it a point to bring out the finer delicacies of Care Packages sent to me or the chapel. Soon, popcorn, sausage, beef jerky, candy, whatever people had, was being passed around during the movie. Wise cracks and snide remarks were common sidelines to the dialogue of each film.

To add pizzazz to the event, CPT Diggs took a jigsaw to a scrap piece of plywood and carved out "Bombay Lounge" to greet newcomer and regular alike. Hung from a swing-set like support, this artifact became a regular stop on the soon-to-become- regular KMTC Tour.

Ironically, rumor spread back home that some of our soldiers were frequenting a local Kasbah- style establishment of questionable character. When asked what it was called, The "Bombay Lounge" was named. They could not have been more incorrect. It was "The *Fabulous* Bombay Lounge." It was, indeed, an exotic place of refuge at a critical time, but mostly –a dusty state of mind.

Chapter 17

Get Out There and Do Something

The first two weeks were confusing and hectic. As our unit moved in, the 1st Bn, 3rd SFG(A) we replaced moved out. It was called a relief in place/transfer of authority (RIP/TOA). For a time, we had more soldiers in our FOB than we had places to stay. For this reason, we had to bunk together in cramped quarters.

One day, while tidying up my area, our battalion intelligence officer, another major named Mark, came up to me with an interesting request. "Chaplain, I'd like to recommend that you get out there and start up some humanitarian projects in the surrounding community." Now, at that point, Major Mark didn't know that I served eight years as a missionary pastor in Europe and had experience this area. "What do you mean?" I asked.

"I was thinking that perhaps you could go find a school, orphanage or the like and do something helpful and positive." Frankly, I didn't expect this coming from the intelligence officer. I probably looked dumfounded to him. Then he clarified. "You see, if you do something perceived of value to the local population, and someone plans an attack or ambush, the people whose confidence you have won with your good deeds might warn us of the attack." So that was it. It was all about "force protection."

At first, I didn't know what to think, but I decided to use this recommendation as an opportunity to get out into the community to see what good deeds I could accomplish. I figured I'd start in the local schools, and then see if I could find an orphanage.

A couple days later, as I was leaving the DFAC, the senior cook of our supporting MP unit took me aside. Between the overhang where we ate and the trashcans, were two shipping containers. One had a refrigeration unit, and one did not. The good-natured mess sergeant walked me to the unrefrigerated container and opened the heavy metal door. Inside, were large cans of food; fruit, vegetable, desserts, all kinds of preserves that would make Napoleon proud (Historical note: Napoleon's effort led to major advances in food preservation for his military campaigns).

The mess sergeant said, "We're getting in food faster than we can eat it. It's good now, but in three to four months it will expire. There are so many starving people around us. Do you think you can find some needy people who could use it before it's no good to anyone?" I couldn't believe my ears or eyes. Within forty-eight hours I was challenged to come up with humanitarian projects by the intelligence officer and then, without coordination, I was shown a container full of available food set to spoil if not eaten. I thanked the mess sergeant for his kind heart and promised to look for worthy recipients.

As I walked away, I asked God to show me how to give this food away to Afghans who could really use it. It took three weeks, but God would clearly provide that guidance.

Chapter 18
Pul-e-Charki School Visit

I heard about a school in nearby Pul-e-Charki, so I asked Captain Diggs, a seasoned special forces officer, to go with me to check it out. We found a young interpreter named Tem who guided us to the school. As we entered the grounds, I could see a couple dozen flat-roofed buildings in very bad condition; doors were missing, all window glass was broken, and the grounds were barren and rocky. Some children were playing soccer outside one of the buildings. We pulled into a parking area and got out. The interpreter asked the first person where the headmaster could be found.

We were ushered into the headmaster's office and offered tea, which we humbly accepted. After identifying ourselves with the Kabul Military Training Center (KMTC), we asked if the school had needs that we might be able to meet. Accepting an offer to tour the school, the headmaster led the way.

Our hearts broke as we entered classrooms devoid of just about everything but eager students and teachers. We heard how the Taliban prohibited women from working outside their homes, causing a shutdown of the primary and secondary schools due to fact that eighty percent of the teachers were females. For seven years, this and most other public schools were dormant, causing a backlog in education. Grades one through five contained boys and girls, but in grades six to twelve, the boys and girls were taught separately. The impact was clearly seen in the sixth-grade boys' class. The barren room contained 60 squatting boys ages twelve to eighteen. Surprisingly, the class was orderly, despite our tour's brief interruption. The backlog was not as apparent in the girls' classes, owed in part to the female teachers' audacity in conducting clandestine small group classes for girls in their homes during the Taliban reign of terror.

Capt. Diggs and I exchanged quiet comments and glances as we passed between classrooms. Mid-way through the tour, a younger female teacher of a combined boys and girls elementary glass shocked us. As we asked her through our interpreter, about her biggest teaching challenge, she ignored our question and asked us, "Are you, too, going to promise everything and then do nothing?" When Tem translated her question, I thought, "Where did that come from?" I calmly replied, "We come making no promises. We just want to learn about your needs and see how we might best help." The headmaster quietly led us back to his office.

Mentally concluding that school reconstruction was out of the question, I asked if the school taught English. Gesturing to another teacher in the office, he left to quickly return with another male teacher holding a series of paperback textbooks. The teacher, who had a distinctly Asian look, began haltingly to explain their English curriculum was based on textbooks provided by the United States Agency for International Development (USAID). Capt. Diggs and I quietly discussed the possibility of teaching classes in English conversation, and once agreed I asked, "Would you be open to us teaching conversation classes in American English?" The principal and Afghan English teacher talked between themselves a bit, then replied, "We would like that." "One other thing." I added, "We want to teach both boys and girls." This sparked a lively discussion between the headmaster and other presumably male teachers. Once concluded, he replied, "Okay."

Recognizing that we would need command approval, we told them we would return to coordinate next week. Shaking hands all around, we departed for KMTC. In the vehicle, Capt. Diggs explained that we would need to prepare and present a contingency operation plan (CONOP), before we could begin. Confessing I had no idea how to produce one, Diggs assured me that he would teach me how. I prepared myself to learn something new.

Chapter 19

Conversational English Classes

Without Capt. Diggs' expertise, the English class contingency operation (CONOP) would not have been written. Once complete, we ran the operation through staff channels and received the blessing of the S3 (Operations Chief) before presenting it to the battalion commander, Lt. Col. Nick. After a few questions about security, he signed off and asked us to keep him informed.

Armed with command approval, we returned to Pul-e-Charki school with hopes of beginning classes the following week. The headmaster warmly received us and was pleased to hear of our commander's approval to begin. Then he informed us that though he, the faculty, and high school girls were excited to begin English classes, some of the parents were not too keen on the idea of U.S. male soldiers teaching their daughters. After sixth-grade, men taught teenage boys, and women taught teenager girls separately. Disheartened by the news, Diggs and I replied that if we couldn't teach the girls, then we wouldn't teach the boys. In my mind, I saw the whole opportunity implode. It was then headmaster asked, "Don't you have female soldiers who could teach the girls?" Honestly, I never thought of that, in part because my Special Forces unit was totally male, and because I had a cultural blind spot that I didn't recognize.

Then it dawned on me, "We do have several females in the MP company that provides force protection!" I thanked the headmaster for his honesty and suggestion and told him I would see what I could work out. Back at KMTC I stopped by the MP company commander's office and explained the situation, he was open to allowing his female soldiers to teach Afghan high school girls English. As I left, I knew who I would ask first.

At the evening meal, I looked for Spec. Jessica. She was a college student whose Massachusetts Army National Guard MP unit had been mobilized shortly before ours and sent to KMTC to provide force protection. Specialist Jessica, herself an MP, was a chapel regular. I had gotten to know her as she occasionally dropped by on her free time to hang out with my recently assigned assistant, JJ. She was the same age and year in college as my daughter, Amy.

As we ate our meals, I told her about the conversational English program we were seeking to start at the nearby Pul-e-Charki school. She knew about it as the MP presence patrols occasionally passed through the area. When I explained our need for female teachers, she hesitated. "I'm a criminal justice major, not education." I showed her a sample lesson plan – the first session on the alphabet; with "ABC Song" and simple format, she replied, "I think I can do that."

I explained that I would field test each lesson on Wednesday with the boys and give her an updated copy for the three girls classes the following Tuesday. That would allow her a whole week to prepare. Assuring her of her commander's approval, she said she would think about it and talk with her first sergeant to make sure she wouldn't have duty on Tuesday afternoons. She also said she'd talk with the other females in her unit to see who else might be interested. That would turn out to be a wise move.

The next day, Capt. Diggs and I drove back to the Pul-e-Charki school to confirm that we had secured a female teacher for the high school girls. We coordinated days and times and planned to start the following week.

Chapter 20
Back to the Basics

Armed with a simple lesson-plan, two male soldier teachers, one Afghan interpreter, and one outside guard, we showed up before 9:00 a.m. the first Wednesday of October 2002 to teach five fifty-minute classes of boys ranging from sixth to twelfth grade. My assistant, Specialist JJ, provided exterior security to the rooms where we taught our classes. Capt Diggs, in addition to team-teaching with me, came armed with an M9 pistol strapped to his thigh, and an M4 assault rifle, which he propped up in a front corner of the classroom while he taught the class. I came unarmed but carried a small FM radio with which I could contact JJ, if needed.

At the start of each class, after a brief introduction by the Pul-e-Charki school English teacher, I explained what we hoped to accomplish: improve each student's ability to communicate in English. As we did with many classes, we started with a song. *"A, B, C, D, E, F, G...."* Immediately we discovered we would have to deal with the linguistic nuances between British and American English; like "Ka" and "Zed" for "Kay" and "Zee."

We also had to adjust our lesson plan according to age and number of students. Fortunately, while we had sixty in the sixth grade, there were only six-to ten young men in the upper grades. This, we would find, would allow for some interesting conversation. Taking a cue from my days as a military language instructor at the Defense Language Institute, at the end of every class, I gave a short homework assignment; starting with the memorization of the "ABCs."

In the combined eleventh/twelfth-grade class, one student stood to his feet, after I and Capt. Diggs were introduced. In comprehendible English, he asked with a serious look, "Teacher, you like Afghan people?" I glanced at Diggs, then replied with a smile, "We like the good people of Afghanistan!" Tem, our interpreter, followed up with an interpretation in Dari, to insure all the students understood my reply. The Afghan English teacher, who by the way, attended every class we would teach, smiled from the back of the classroom, giving us a subtle thumb's up.

We left around 3:30 p.m., exhausted.

The next day, I passed off a copy of the first lesson plan to Spec. Jessica. We spoke about our first day with the boys; what went well and what we would change. She listened carefully and made notes. Then she said she had found another female soldier who would help teach. Sgt. Beth, the unit admin clerk, said she would come and observe the first week and decide if she would do it. Before leaving, we coordinated transportation for the following week.

Shortly after noon, the following Tuesday, we arrived at the Pul-e-Charki school; Jess, Beth, Tem, JJ, and me. As we waited in the hall outside the headmaster's office, a man who I didn't recognize walked up, pointed to the two U.S. female soldiers in uniform and asked through my interpreter, "Who are these women? Are they your wives?" Taken aback by the question, I replied, "No, they are not." Insistently, he continued, "Then who are they?"

Suddenly, it dawned on me that this man was asking an honest question from his culture and world view and was trying to make sense out of this unusual situation. I thought about saying they were my sisters, but they were too young, so I replied, "They are my daughters, and they have come to teach the older girls English." After he heard Tem's interpretation, he nodded, grunted, seemed satisfied, and moved on. I justified it, in part, because Jessica had recently started calling me "dad."

The following three girls' classes went extremely well. Due in part to the smaller class sizes (though these would grow rapidly in a few short weeks), and because of the welcoming attitude of the female English teacher, the connection seemed instantaneous. Jessica was a natural with Tem interpreting by her side. It wasn't long before Beth joined in and these two unlikely teachers would model English conversation between females. I took this all in from the back of the classroom, where I stood in each class along with the Afghan female English teacher, who, by the way, entered the class discussion, much to the delight of her students. It wasn't long before other Afghan high school girls and female Pul-e- Charki teachers started to attend the classes led by these two soldiers from the Massachusetts Army National Guard. The word got out and caused quite a stir.

Chapter 21

Bomb Threat

It was mid-October. We were into the third week of conversational English classes at the Pul-e-Charki school. I was running out of songs to teach some of the basics, so I began to ask other soldiers for ideas. One soldier, Sgt. 1st Class Jimmy, who swore me to secrecy, taught me the "Rainbow Song" that he learned from his wife who was an elementary school teacher in Colorado. I wrote down the words and made him repeat the song till I got it right. He did have a good voice, but I couldn't tell any one.

During the daily Commander's Update Briefing (CUB), the intelligence officer (S2) was first up to brief. Prominent in his update was a threat by anticoalition forces (HIG, Al Qaeda, Taliban, etc.) to bomb any Afghan high school that allowed U.S. male soldiers to teach Afghan high school girls English! Suddenly, I felt like all eye were on me.

I stood and explained that we only had female soldiers from the MP unit teaching the girls. The commander thought for a moment, then suggested that we shut down the program out of safety for the school. My heart sank. We were off to a good start; classes were growing and frankly it was fun. But the commander had the final say, rightfully so.

Suddenly, other soldiers - officers and enlisted - began to voice support for the program: "Isn't that why we came?" Said one. "Why should we back down?" Said another. "I commit my team to provide a rotating quick reaction force (QRF) for the chaplain's program." A team captain added. "I have soldiers I can add to the school security detail." Added the support center 1st Sgt.

I think the commander was as surprised as I was, over the unified support for the school program. Conversation briefly continued among the command team and senior staff. After a few minutes the commander said; "All right, I will allow the program to continue, under the condition that the CONOP is modified with an increased security plan; both on site, and with a radio-dispatched QRF."

My eyes caught those of Capt. Diggs. He knew I would need his help updating the CONOP.

Chapter 22

National Geographic Feature Story

Conversational English classes continued with an enhanced security detail. As 1st Sgt. Mike predicted, I would need the assistance of his support company soldiers for my humanitarian projects. Typically, we had four to six exterior guards patrolling the school grounds and perimeter. Soldiers began to bring pockets full of candy for the children. This greatly increased soldier-student interaction and provided weekly variety to many who were otherwise confined to our small FOB within KMTC.

It didn't take long for us to see the benefit of small group interaction in the high school girls' conversational English classes. Jessica and Beth would quickly cover the day's lesson and form into two groups, depending on class size. It seemed like the smaller group format encouraged those who were a bit shy to speak English more. Even the Afghan English teachers would join a group, taking turns talking in English.

Soon, we planned small groups into each lesson plan. The classes grew, in part to more high school girls attending, but also the addition of other female Afghan teachers who had a free period. That led us to invite a third female soldier, Donna, to join the teaching team. Now we had three groups in the larger classes.

The groups would form on the floor mats into what looked like an American football team huddle with heads almost touching. Soon the conversation began, and the decibel level of chatter rose in the room. Still something didn't seem quite right. I was surprised that these young ladies and teachers could be that excited about telling time, learning colors, and simple social greetings. One day, on the drive back to our compound, I asked what was going on in the huddles. From the rear passenger seats came, "Oh, we talk about make-up, hair styles, dating, and stuff like that. They also ask questions about life in America." Rather than be upset, I was pleased that the Afghan female students and teachers were using their new conversational skills to explore topics of mutual interest...and to bond with their American soldier-teachers.

Major Todd Harrell, our public affairs officer, informed us that National Geographic was coming to film a feature story on the Pul-e-Charki girls' English classes. He coordinated, so the film crew would arrive for scheduled girls' English class times. Jessica and Beth were a bit nervous about being televised but did a masterful job. I stood proudly in the back observing and photographing a project that I believe God led us to pursue. In a few short weeks, I would better understand why. The segment aired Thanksgiving Day, 2002 in the U.S. during a National Geographic special.

Chapter 23

Teaming Up to Serve Soldiers and Civilians

I became acquainted with our battalion surgeon at the Joint Readiness Training Center (JRTC) at Fort Polk, Louisiana during pre-deployment training and certification. There I learned that he was smart. So smart that he set a record in accurately diagnosing a virulent "mystery disease" that presented itself at our front gate through our role players. He was also unique in that he out-ranked our battalion commander.

Immediately after arriving in country, Col. Robert Enzenauer started attending the 9:00 a.m. Sunday Protestant chapel service. Initially, he sat in the front row with arms crossed, as if to say, "Bless me, I dare you!" What confused me was that he sang quite well. Over time I would learn a lot of interesting things about "Doc Enz," as many called him, and benefit personally from his life-saving skills.

After the confusion of the "relief in place" (RIP) subsided, our command team published guidelines, "Standard Operating Procedures" (SOP) covering several areas including travel in and around Kabul and to outlying locations where sections, ODAs
and detachments operated.

After each section received its assigned vehicles, a "two-vehicle minimum convoy" rule was established for travel outside a specified radius from FOB195. Upon learning of the new policy, Doc Enz approached me with a proposal. He recommended that we team up and make a weekly trip to Bagram Air Base to allow him to conduct ophthalmology consults and surgery at the combat support hospital (CSH) while I visited our soldiers assigned there as riggers, and to the Combined Joint Special Operations Task Force (CJSOTF), as well as any who might be hospitalized. It sounded like a good plan, so we scheduled our first "convoy" for the following Tuesday.

The CSH commander was a military colleague of Doc Enz from Fitzsimmons Army Medical Center (1989-1994). Colonel Bietler, a 1977 U.S. Military Academy (USMA) graduate, was a renowned cancer surgeon, yet his hospital deployed without an assigned eye surgeon. After President Bush declared "mission accomplished," it was not anticipated that an ophthalmologist would be necessary. How wrong that proved to be.

Our initial convoys were exciting, to say the least. Warlords still manned checkpoints along the way, with Soviet machine guns and rocket propelled grenades at the ready. Per SOP, I drove, and my assistant was ready to shoot, in self-defense. The drive took one hour. Safely navigating the choke point through the narrow gates of "Bagram City," we entered the security control point into Bagram Airfield (BAF). The docs' vehicle peeled off to the 48th Combat Support Hospital, and we continued to the airfield where our riggers lived and worked. There they routinely packed parachutes and prepared airborne bundles specially designed to be dropped by parachute into rugged areas to support isolated troops in remote mountain operations.

After meeting with the riggers and other soldiers assigned to the CJSOTF, we headed to the hospital to link up with Doc Enz and SSG Dean, his eye tech. Finding them preparing for eye surgery on a child with serious eye injury, he asked me an unexpected question: "Chaplain Andy, have you ever been in an operating room or witnessed eye surgery?" "No." I replied. "Would you like to?" He asked. "Sure! Can I take pictures?" I asked. "As long as you don't cross the sterile field. Now let's get you washed and gowned up." He pointed to a chair in the corner. "If you start to feel light-headed, just sit down." In no time they had me looking like a TV doctor – rather more like an amateur operating room cameraman.

I remember being amazed at the skill and smoothness of communication and operation of this two-man surgical team. Only later would I learn that these two had worked together on active duty in the ophthalmology department at Fitzsimmons Army Medical Center in Aurora, Colorado, six miles from my home. A full professor of pediatric ophthalmology at the University of Chattanooga medical school, Doc Enz volunteered to deploy with the Special Forces battalion as their chief surgeon. Like other citizen-soldiers in the unit, he came with a broad skill base and depth of experience rarely seen among active duty medical personnel. As a triple-board certified, pediatrician, ophthalmologist, and public health specialist – a unique and needed combination of skills – the Good Doctor was the only U.S. military ophthalmologist in Afghanistan. That's why we needed to make the weekly convoy along mined roads from our base in Kabul.

As the first surgery began, I leaned in to get a closer look, "Chaplain, remember, not to cross the sterile field!" I pulled back, raised my new HP digital camera and started taking pictures. Rather than get queasy, I got excited as what I was seeing! I started asking questions about the procedures, as I watch two sets of experienced hands treat eye injuries, remove damaged eyes and restore sight to injured and blind; children and adults, military and civilian,
allies and enemies.

Late one day, Doc Enz asked if we could convoy to Bagram hospital early the next morning. He received an urgent request for support (RFS) from the hospital commander, Colonel Bietler. As it turned out, Col. Bietler had been a general surgery resident under Doc Enz in years passed. A serious case was brought in by MEDEVAC helicopter and an ophthalmologist was needed. We arrived early to attend to a twelve-year old Afghan boy injured in an explosion.

Soon, Doc Enz, Staff Sgt. Dean and I were joined by two other Army surgeons, a maxillofacial specialist, a captain, and Col. Bietler, a general surgeon, and an anesthesiologist wearing a shoulder holster with pistol. The young boy lay covered on the operating table, already intubated. I stood back and watched as the three medical specialists conferred. Doc Enz examined the boy's damaged left eye socket. The explosion blew away his upper eyelid, eyebrow and part of the skin on his forehead. "This eye can be saved, but he'll need a new eyelid." The younger maxillofacial surgeon added, "Normally we take skin grafts close to the area, but his head and neck area are burned. We'll have to get it elsewhere." Suddenly, the surgical covering over the boy's midsection began to rise. Colonel Bietler raised the covering and noticed the lad had an erection. "That must be some good gas." Someone quipped. "How old did you say he was?" Colonel Bietler asked. A short discussion about Muslim circumcision ensued, then Col. Bietler, himself Jewish, asked in a Yiddish brogue, "Are you tinking what I'm tinking? And now for da circumcision jokes!" It was quickly decided that Doc Enz and the maxillofacial captain would clean and prepare the damaged eye area for grafts and Col. Bietler would carefully circumcise the youth providing skin grafts according to the size and shape needed to reconstruct the eyelid. In the space of ninety-minutes, the circumcision and skin graft were complete, each step documented with my little digital camera. Three pieces of skin were patch worked into a replacement eyelid and brow. The upper eyelid was attached to a muscle tab that remained and hopefully would open the eye, at least partially. The last step included sewing the upper eyelid to the bottom lid to shape and stretch the graft around the eye. The stitches were to remain for seven days.

The following week, our convoy returned to the combat support hospital. Doc Enz removed the stitches and the young boy's eye opened! This was one of many sight-saving surgeries I photographed during our weekly hospital visits. Unbeknownst to me, I too would personally benefit from the Good Doctor's medical skills.

Part Three: Getting Settled

A Word from Chaplain Andy

As a Citizen-Soldier, a member of the Colorado Army National Guard, I was officially mobilized for duty to last up to two years. Anticipating a shorter deployment, I entered into an agreement with my church congregation to cover my deployment. We established a six-month leave of absence renewable for a second six-month period. After that, the agreement was that the church could terminate my contract and seek a replacement pastor, should my duty extend beyond the two six- month periods.

With a plan in place for my absence, I decided it would be important to keep in touch with my congregation to maintain continuity and communication. To do this I purchased a new laptop and my first digital camera. Armed with these two new tools, I planned to write and submit a weekly article with accompanying digital photos for display to my congregation on Sunday. I titled this communication strategy, "A Word from Chaplain Andy." Each week I planned to send a 250-word article to replace my weekly bulletin insert "A Word from Pastor Andy."

After about six weeks of doing this, I began to get suggestions from church leaders and members that I should plan to write a book about my experiences. The publication of this weekly article became the background and backbone of this book. The following chapters include some of the articles I sent to my home church.

Chapter 24

First Impressions

Word from Chaplain Andy for Oct 6, 2002

I met some interesting people this week; an English-speaking Afghan Army General, a young shop- keeper, an interpreter, and hundreds of school children and their headmaster (school principle). Week one of my "extreme missions' trip" has been a whirlwind of interesting familiarization activity. Though I didn't travel more than five miles from my bunk, I had the opportunity to meet several people from different segments of our host nation's society. Covering a wide spectrum of age and social background, they all had one thing in common – they had suffered at the hands of an oppressive political regime. Two had been imprisoned, one had fled to a neighboring nation, and the rest – the children - had lost up to five years of primary or secondary education due to the closure of their schools by the Taliban. One school I visited has 2500 students – 1200 in first grade – that's right, FIRST grade! I met children ages five to twelve in the same first grade class. Many squatted barefoot on cold concrete floors as their teachers used chalk to write the lesson on the window-less classroom wall. By the way, the classes were amazingly disciplined with up to forty in each class. I was able to communicate with the adult males in English or through an interpreter. Each was interested in establishing a friendship with me – for different reasons, of course, but still unique opportunities to show the Love of God and sow the Seeds of the Gospel. Pray with me this week that you and I will open our eyes to the opportunities God places before us.

Chapter 25

Chaplains Drive, Assistants Shoot

Word from Chaplain Andy for Oct 13, 2002

It is considered by many one of the most dangerous roads in the world. It took about an hour to get from where I was to where I needed to be. Points A and B were safe havens, but the road between was fraught with danger. I was a driver in a convoy. My instructions were to keep engine RPMs up, run one gear down, and watch out for speedbumps, potholes, sticks and landmines. At first, I thought he was joking, but five minutes into the drive I knew my vehicle commander was serious. I passed Afghan militia checkpoints armed with heavy machineguns, AK-47, and rocket propelled grenade (RPG) launchers at the ready. On narrow roads I maneuvered around trucks, buses, bicycles and carts pulled by donkeys. Boundaries between rival warlords were marked with heavily armed checkpoints. Still the most dangerous part of the drive was a road lined by thousands of landmines. Little piles of rocks, some painted white, others red, lined the road for miles like a carefully patterned rock garden. I had to pay attention to the two-lane highway to make certain that we stayed on the asphalt. It was more likely that we would survive a head-on collision than running off the road into a mine field. The good news is that we made it there and back--safely. I did hit a few potholes and speed bumps—and a stick—but I didn't run over any landmines. That was a good thing. As I gratefully reentered our compound, I thought how my trip was like the road of life, fraught with danger once we leave the safety of our mother's womb, until we reach the security of Heaven's Gate. Jesus' words came to mind: "Enter through the narrow gate. For wide is the gate and broad is the road that leads to destruction, and many enter through it. But small is the gate and narrow the road that leads to life, and only a few find it." I wish you a safe journey to your Final Destination, as you travel the most dangerous road in the world...the road of life!

Chapter 26

A Prophetic Word Confirmed

Word from Chaplain Andy for Oct 20, 2002

"Remember, wherever you go, God is already there!" Those were the parting words of wisdom spoken to me by Galilee's Pastor Charles Cook before I left on this extreme missions' trip to the other side of the world. As I was running (okay, jogging) my third lap around our compound at 6:15 a.m., I passed a load of pallets that had just arrived the night before with our final wave of incoming troops. I blinked, and then squinted as I focused in on a U.S. soldier sitting on top of a pallet reading his Bible as the Afghan sun came up. His words came back to me as I ran up to that young Christian warrior and shared with him what Pastor Cook had told me. He smiled, nodded, and I completed my two-mile run. Pastor Cook was right. Wherever we go, God is already there. God is here. I see His fingerprints in the majesty of the mountains that surround our base. God is here. I see His Image in the eyes of impoverished, yet hopeful children giving the "thumbs up" to passing U.S. Army convoys. God is here. I see His Son's image developing in the hearts and minds of believing soldiers, officer and enlisted, who joyfully attend weekend chapel services and midweek Bible Study. In my first couple weeks here, I have seen evidence of God's presence and working in many ways. God is where you are, too! Wherever you go this week, whatever you do, remember Pastor Cook's words: "God is already there." So, you can acknowledge His presence and request his Wisdom, Guidance and Power. Why? Because wherever you go, God is already there!

Chapter 27

Working through Interpreters

Word from Chaplain Andy for Oct. 27, 2002

Every Moses needs an Aaron. Remember the story in Exodus 4:10-16; where Moses told God that he couldn't speak well enough to communicate to Pharaoh what God wanted him to say? God, tired of Moses' litany of excuses, gave him a spokesman, an interpreter, if you will, in his brother, Aaron. Well, God has given me someone to help me communicate in Dari and Pashtu, two of the main languages in Afghanistan. Although I have access to over 50 different host nation interpreters, God has put Tem, an eighteen-year-old student, into my life. Tem has worked with me in all my conversational English classes in a nearby high school and has been my interpreter—my Aaron—in all my training courses at the military training center. Tem is rare, in that his family is still intact, after years of fighting.

He does well in English and learns more every day as he works with me and other U.S. Army personnel training the new Afghan National Army. Tem is with me almost every time I leave the compound. He says he loves Americans for rescuing his country from the Taliban and Al Qaeda. He wants to spend as much time possible with us, helping us train his country's new army and learning English and American ways. After working with Tem for a couple weeks, it dawned that I had a great opportunity to model Christianity before this young man who one day very well might be a leader in his country. Tem has been my mouthpiece as I answer difficult questions raised in my training classes and when inquisitive Afghan soldiers inquire about my role as an Army chaplain or the Christian faith. God has put Tem and me together for this time. Though Army regulations prohibit proselytizing of host nation personnel, it is my hope and prayer that his heart will be opened, and his mind challenged to investigate the claims of Christ while he is still a young man. Who has God put in your life, maybe someone so close to you that you almost don't notice them? Let us commit to being God's mouthpiece on both sides of the world!

Chapter 28

First Impressions Are Lasting Impressions

Word from Chaplain Andy for Nov. 3, 2002

First impressions are lasting impressions. I thought about that as I prepared the flipcharts for my training classes of host nation officers. I was scheduled to be the first instructor in the new training cycle and a U.S. Army General was scheduled for a visit. (No pressure, right?) So bright and early on a Saturday morning, I was standing in front of thirty-plus officers in the world's newest army ready to teach human rights and the law of war. At first the mood of the classroom was heavy with uncertainty as these combat veterans sat listening in molded plastic patio chairs imported from China. As I looked around, I noticed several interesting things: First, all had different uniforms, both in style, cut and camouflage pattern. Second, they all had different footwear. Some wore boots, most wore shoes, some sandals. A few didn't even have socks. Some had big bushy beards with streaks of gray and others sported mustaches. A few were clean shaven. As I began my first class, I looked them straight in the eye and said: "The future of your country is in your hands. Your grasp of these first two classes, and future compliance, will determine your country's acceptance or rejection in the family of nations." Well, I guess you could say I got their attention; so much so that my two morning classes ended taking up the entire first day. During the breaks a group of officers would surround me and my interpreter to ask clarifying questions and share unbelievable stories. Some of these warriors had been fighting for over twenty-five years! Though tired of war, they were still willing to sacrifice towards a lasting peace for their beleaguered country. By mid-day, the mood of the class had changed significantly. I sensed more openness and the building of trust. At day's end every officer waited in line to shake my hand and thank me for leaving my home and family to come halfway around the world to teach them. Their commander left with these words: "These are the most important classes you could ever teach us." Pray that we, your soldiers, will make a good lasting first impression.

Chapter 29

Cool Water for a Thirsty Soul

Word from Chaplain Andy for Nov. 10, 2002

"Like cold water to a weary soul is good news from a distant land." (Proverbs 25:24 NIV). After being here on the other side of the world for over a month, I know this to be true. The first time I tried to take a shower, the water stopped. The soldier in the stall next to me was still covered with soap. As he tried to wipe off the soap he said: "When I get home, I'll never complain about my water bill again!" Water is in short supply here. All our drinking and cooking water is imported. Water for showers is from a local supply and is non-potable. There is almost no water pressure; it's all gravity-fed. Forty-two percent of all deaths in this country are due to water-borne disease. The river running though the capitol city is almost dry. We are in the process of drilling our own well – a slow process! When we travel, people along the roadside call out for "water." So, in typical GI fashion, we bring extra bottles of water and toss them out the window as we drive by. Rather than getting fined for littering, we get shouts of gratitude and "thumbs up" when we recognize their need for water, too! Without water we would all die – most of us in thirty-six to forty-eight hours. Water is precious because it's so essential to life. When we asked a host nation Army officer when it would rain again, he said: "The rain stopped when the Taliban took over." Likewise, good news refreshes our hearts when it is received. Good news, like water, is essential for life. Likewise, the Good News of Jesus' love shown through His sacrifice for us is essential for eternal life. Have you received the Good News? If so, are you sharing it with others? I hope you and I will each share it from our positions...on the opposite sides of the world!

Chapter 30

Rebuilding an Army on the Golden Rule

Word from Chaplain Andy for Nov. 17, 2002

I can see why God has me here. Not only is my ministry to U.S. soldiers active and vital, but I have found an unexpected niche teaching Afghan soldiers classes on human rights and the law of war. I started with officers only my second week here. Then they tasked me to teach all the incoming recruits of the training cycle. Now I am systematically teaching these classes to the entire new Afghan Army; all five current battalions and the future ones we will train. In the process, I have made some new friends – Afghan army officers who appreciate my animated and interactive hybrid training classes – that resemble an infomercial combined with a high school pep rally.

"You are the hope of Afghanistan!" I shout in my opening statement. "Upon your shoulders rest the peace and safety of all Afghan people!" With that declaration, I hook two hundred army recruits, many who are combat veterans, for the next four hours. At the first break they swarm around me and my nineteen-year- old interpreter, Tem. They ask clarifying questions, share insights and blunt opinions regarding their own government. At the end of my first class of soldiers, the battalion commander, a twenty-three-year combat veteran came up, shook my hand, kissed and hugged me; in a culturally appropriate, manly way. He asked to address the soldiers. He passionately pleaded with his soldiers not only to remember but to practice the principles of the class. Then something totally unexpected happened. This senior officer publicly thanked me for speaking of the Golden Rule as taught by Issa (Jesus) in the Ingil (Gospel). He said that they, too, recognized Issa as a great Prophet of God. I could see another reason why God sent me here to the other side of the world.

Chapter 31

Pointing out the Obvious

Word from Chaplain Andy for Nov. 24, 2002

It's not polite to point; so, most Americans teach their children. But here on the other side of the world, that's not the case. Most people, children and adults, are very much in your face both figuratively and literally. If one of our soldiers has a birth mark, it is common for members of our host nation to bluntly ask "What's that on your neck?" -- pointing to the area of interest. Children and adults will come up to us, stare at us and point at our clothes, equipment, weapons, faces, etc. Over time we're getting used to the way most things are here. But there is one cultural practice that our soldiers are here to change – the indiscriminate pointing of weapons. Whether they point at us or someone else, U.S. and Coalition soldiers have orders to fire on anyone showing hostile intent – especially the pointing of weapons at U.S. personnel, vehicles or installations. That has led to some tense moments, to be sure, but firm resolve and great restraint on the part of your soldiers is beginning to make a dent in what has degenerated into a basically lawless society where most everyone has a gun. I was reminded of Jesus' words in Matthew chapter seven, verses three and five; "Why do you look at the speck of sawdust in your brother's eye and pay no attention to the plank in your own eye?...You hypocrite, first take the plank out of your own eye, and then you will see clearly to remove the speck from your brother's eye." So next time you're tempted to point out someone else's fault, remember; It's not polite to point, on either side of the world!

Chapter 32

Yankee Ingenuity is Alive and Well

Word from Chaplain Andy for Dec. 8, 2002

Yankee ingenuity is not dead. In a little over a month; we have turned a carpet-bombed military academy into a secure, functioning base camp. When we began, we had no reliable running water or electricity. There was not enough space for us to eat and sleep, much less work. The first smaller Army unit to occupy this installation basically camped out for a few months in the buildings that serve as our home away from home. That was understandable since our active duty predecessors were primarily trained in unconventional warfare. My unit, however, though possessing the same military skills, also has another set of civilian skills that our active duty counterparts didn't have. These desert camo, uniforms are worn by doctors, nurses, lawyers, a preacher, teachers, surveyors, contractors, carpenters, plumbers, linemen, electricians, computer programmers, network administrators, mechanics, students, police and firemen – and an appliance repair technician – to name just a few. With brick, mortar, two- by-fours, plywood, nails, drywall screws, motivation and creativity, we have been transforming our facilities into a viable base of operations that, hopefully, will endure the upcoming winter as we continue training the world's newest army and fight the war against terrorism. Empty warehouses have been turned into condos and lofts, a fitness center, a motor pool and an electronic repair facility. Metal stakes used to string concertina wire have been reconfigured into clotheslines. Wood has been remanufactured into doors, tables, countertops and stairwells. Why, we even built an enviable chapel office/quarters complex for me and my assistant. It's small but functionally cozy. This has been an excellent example of how the Body of Christ should function. When we all use the gifts God has given us, we can accomplish seemingly impossible tasks...on either side of the world!

Chapter 33

Worship Off-base

Word from Chaplain Andy for Dec. 15, 2002

Last week, I attended one of the most dangerous church services in the world. I don't think it was an exaggeration. My assistant and I attended the Friday service at Community Christian Church of Kabul on November 22. It was the one-year anniversary of the release of the eight Shelter Now aid workers taken by the Taliban for the crime of preaching the Gospel to Afghan Muslims. The man, who invited us to attend, introduced my team (JJ and I) to one of the local church leaders. We were in civilian clothes. He showed special interest when he learned that we were with the U.S. Special Forces. He mentioned that they had recently hired Afghan guards to protect the one-third acre walled compound where the church met. Security was heightened due to the execution of an Al Qaeda assassin the week before. The church had received threats like the expatriate church that was attacked in Pakistan earlier in the month. My assistant offered to guard the outside perimeter, but the church elder suggested that he provide inside security. JJ discretely adjusted his weapon as the worship service began. It was then that I noticed the signs on the walls prohibiting photography. As the service began and announcements were made, I could tell that these believers had learned to worship in secrecy under constant threat of persecution. We were personally briefed on the evacuation plan, in the event of an attack. After an emotional opening where the worship leader recounted the anniversary of the capture and release of eight Afghan aid workers, who attended this church, this multi-national, (no Afghans) multi- denominational group of believers began to worship in English. There was a piano, a guitar and a flute; each skillfully played by people of different ethnic backgrounds. Most of the songs were familiar. There was an offering, sharing, and prayer, singing, poetry, more singing, dismissal to children's church and a challenging message by an Irish preacher on the damage caused by human pride. In the parking area after the service, I encountered an American family, graduates of Denver Seminary and my church's Perspectives course. I met them the day before and brought some care package items that I thought they could use. The mother of three young children smiled broadly as I passed the two bulging plastic shopping bags into her hands. As it turned out, we were standing on the site of the former church building that was destroyed in 1977. Locals believe that the government of Afghanistan was cursed for allowing the church to be destroyed. In January, only fifteen met for worship, but on that third Sunday of November, 150 people packed the ground floor of the historic house lived in by J. Christie Wilson, founder of the Urbana Student Missions Conference and twenty-year tent-making missionary to Afghanistan. After fielding questions by U.S. expatriates on how to contact U.S. forces in the event of attack or capture, we got in our vehicle and left the compound. My assistant had his weapon at ready as we made our way through block after block of buildings severely damaged or destroyed, not by U.S. air strikes, but by years of Afghan civil war. I was reminded again of the preacher's words regarding the damage caused by human pride. I thanked God for the relative safety and security of the U.S. and prayed for family and congregation back home. I also thanked God for the experience of safely attending one of the most dangerous church services in the world.

Chapter 34

Christmas in Kabul

Word from Chaplain Andy for Dec. 22, 2002

This Christmas will be different for us. Over the past eight years, we have celebrated the Advent/Christmas season together in Denver with seasonally appropriate music, Scripture, drama and sermons. This year, in an unforeseeable dramatic twist, I, your senior pastor, find myself apart from family and congregation literally on opposite sides of the world. The temptation to sing the "holiday blues" has been very real. Instead, I decided to do everything in my reach to celebrate Advent with my soldiers here the same way I have celebrated with you in Metro Denver. By the time you read this on Sunday morning, I will have completed two services of the final Sunday of Advent in preparation for Christmas Eve and Day. Last year I remember seeing a short video clip on CNN of U.S. Forces celebrating their first Christmas secretly in Afghanistan by candlelight. Little did I imagine that I would be leading a Christmas Eve Candlelight Service for our troops in the Afghan capital this year. Though separated by distance, our hearts remain united in faith, hope and joy. I miss you all terribly, and look forward to celebrating Christmas with you again, next year, Lord willing. Let us focus on the significance of Messiah's birth. As we do, let us pray that the Muslim people of the world will come to understand that Jesus, indeed, is God's Only Son and Savior of the world, as we celebrate Christmas in Kabul!

Chapter 35

Morning Run

Word from Chaplain Andy for Dec. 27, 2002

Two or three times per week, I get up around 6:00 a.m. to jog. Part of my run takes me outside of our compound and through our Afghan training facility. I wave to our MPs guarding the checkpoint, as I pass to the outer ring of security. Every day except Friday (the Muslim Sabbath), I encounter Afghan soldiers beginning their training day. Now that I have taught most of the soldiers the principles of human rights and law of war, I have become well-known. When the soldiers recognize me, they call out "teacher," "chaplain" or "preacher" in one of two languages as I jog by. Increasingly, soldiers have started to run with me. They have begun doing this, I think, in response to my training class on the law of war. There I seek to teach them to respect and protect non-combatants; innocent civilians, diplomats, aid-workers, medical personnel and religious workers. As a result, some of these young soldiers have taken it upon themselves to ensure the security of my morning run. One day, a young recruit in combat boots ran three laps (approx. 2.1 miles) with me. As we ran, we exchanged greetings, names, and affirming culturally appropriate manly gestures (hand across chest as a sign of humility and thumbs up as a sign of mutual soldierly encouragement). He had to be no older than eighteen or nineteen. He kept pace with me the whole time, making sure I had priority of passage. As we neared the end of my final lap, I veered off toward my re-entry point, the MPs acknowledging my approach. I waved to my unofficial escort, said "Khadofez" ("Good-bye") and "Tashakor" ("Thank you"), as I left this young soldier in the outer ring. I could tell he wanted me to keep running with him, but I had to get on with my day. Though our conversation was limited, (I had no interpreter), I could tell that he was pleased that I allowed him to run with me. As you go through your week, remember to include others on your daily run. If you do it with humility and encouraging gestures, you can make a difference.

Chapter 36

Bad Soldier...Good Chaplain

Word from Chaplain Andy...

I was a bad soldier but a good chaplain...that's how I felt after eating a meal with some of our Afghan day laborers. Any given day we have thirty-five to fifty "korgars" ("workers" in Dari) who are escorted onto our compound to do a variety of tasks. Some are carpenters, electricians and plumbers and others perform unskilled jobs like trash pickup and cleaning the latrines. We also have several permanent "KP" ("Kitchen Police") kitchen workers who wash dishes and keep the dining facility clean. Most of us appreciate their hard work – it frees us up to do our military jobs. Thirty years ago, I completed basic combat training (BCT) at Ft Leonard Wood, Missouri. I had KP duty five times in eight weeks! So, though I am now a field grade Army officer, I still remember the challenges of being a KP – and, hence, really appreciate what they do. At mid-day, the contract workers gather wood, light a fire and cook a pot of stew. One day I passed by and asked what was for lunch, and they graciously invited me to join them. Though against the rules (for preventative health reasons), I remembered all the times I survived mysterious food as a missionary in Portugal and joined in. After a time boiling on the embers, they opened the aluminum pot, poured the juice, vegetables and meat into a metal bowl and proceeded to add small pieces of bread into the sop. It smelled good and tasted even better. There was goat meat, potato, olive oil, tomato and a variety of spices. The workers motioned for me to take the first piece – a gesture of honor and respect. So, in the shade of a KMTC training facility, and in the company of nine Afghan men, I enjoyed my first prohibited Afghan meal. I used my folding knife to cut the meat and share it with the workers. I tried to get them to eat peanut butter from my MRE on their flat bread, but they declined. It was an enjoyable hour of fellowship, food and bridge-building. We sat down as strangers but departed as friends. Whenever they see me now, they invite me to join them for lunch. I confess, I broke the rules – and paid dearly for it for about thirty-six hours -- but I recovered, with the assistance of our medical section. I re-learned my lesson...I was, indeed, a bad soldier...but, hopefully, a good chaplain.

Chapter 37

What's in a Name?

Word from Chaplain Andy for Jan 12, 2003

One unexpected experience I have had here has been the variety of names that I have been called since arriving here on the other side of the world. Back home, I'm typically called "Pastor Andy." In the military, my title is "Chaplain," so most of the time I'm called "Chaplain Andy." Nevertheless, different soldiers call me by different names, sometimes out of jest, other times according to their own religious tradition. For example, some Roman Catholic and Greek Orthodox soldiers call me "Father Andy." Others of Hispanic background call me "Padre," and a few even call me "Rabbi" (Hebrew for "My Teacher"). One soldier from New England calls me "Reverend" --my least preferred title. The French soldiers on our compound call me "Mon Pere." ("My Father") and the Korean doctors, who run the clinic for our Host Nation soldiers, call me "Moxanim." (I learned that title from Korean Pastor Ken Joo at Galilee). But the name I never thought I'd ever be called has come from the host nation soldiers I am helping train. After teaching Afghan soldiers training classes on human rights and the law of war, I started hearing new names being directed my way. At first, I didn't know who they were referring to when I would pass a group of soldiers and they would call out "Mullah!" (Arabic for "Preacher") or "Mawlawee" (Arabic equivalent for "Chaplain" or "Teacher") or even, "Imam!" Initially, I was uncertain as to the meaning of that title or name, but after training several cycles of Afghan soldiers, I have come to recognize those names as terms of respect for religious leaders in their culture and Muslim religion. Because I have taken time to work, teach, run and even play volleyball with my Afghan soldiers, they have had an opportunity, for the first time in their lives – and in the history of their military – to see a Christian chaplain in action. I share all this simply to ask you to pray that what they see in me will somehow create a curiosity and hunger to learn the name of the God that I serve, Isa ("Jesus!"). Why? "...for there is no other name under heaven given to men by which we must be saved." As Paul says in the beginning of that verse, "Salvation is found in no one else!" (Acts 4:12). May we all live this week in such a way that those we meet may want to know the God that we serve!

Chapter 38

Spectacular Recovery – Miracle #1

Word from Chaplain Andy for Jan 19, 2003

"Chaplain Andy come quickly!" I heard the familiar voice and saw our chief medical officer, Doc Enz, in the doorway of my office. Usually, his call meant we were under attack, or a serious injury had occurred. I had come to dread his call, but knew that, during emergencies, my place was in the battalion aid station, when casualties occurred or were anticipated. Yet his time it was different. Instead of a look of distress or professional pain on his face, I saw a look of surprise and almost glee. Just an hour or so prior, I had stopped by the aid station to drop off some medical supplies given to me by a soldier. While there, I noticed one of our men lying on a litter with an intravenous drip, shivering, covered with wool blankets. I recognized the soldier and asked how he was doing. The good doctor then pointed to his ear. It was beet red and swollen to twice its normal size. An obvious infection, initially caused by sunburn, had become infected and he had become seriously ill. As the doc turned away to do something, I looked into this veteran soldier's eyes and asked, "Can I pray for you?" "Sure, I'd like that," he whispered. I was almost through with my prayer asking God for comfort and healing, when the doc came up talking. He didn't notice that I was praying, but when he did, he stopped, apologized for the interruption and let me finish my brief prayer. I patted the sick soldier on the shoulder, told him I'd check back, and went about my day. So, when the good doctor walked all the way over and called me to see what had transpired, I had a fresh point of reference. On the way back to the aid station, the Doc assured me that he believed in prayer, and that had seen it work throughout his substantial medical career as a triple-board-certified pediatric ophthalmologist and public health specialist, veteran Army surgeon and medical school professor; but this was "remarkable." When we entered the aid station, I found the soldier, sleeping like a baby, his ear a normal color at almost regular size. I looked at the Doc with a wide-eyed smile. We were both so pleased and amazed at this warrior's recovery that, at the doctor's suggestion, we stood next to our patient and got a picture to record this apparent miraculous event. For the record, it was the doctor who first uttered the "m-word." He suggested that we practice our professions more closely together for the rest of the deployment! I agreed. Next time, when the Doc calls, Chaplain Andy *will* come quickly!

Chapter 39

A Different Kind of Chapel Bell

Word from Chaplain Andy for Jan 26, 2003

"The valley of the shadow of death." That was a biblical phrase that came to mind as our huge twin-rotor army helicopter descended onto the remote helipad. A dust cloud billowed as the ground crew crouched around the perimeter. Unlike past training exercises, this was the real thing. Throughout the flight, door gunners on the sides and rear ramp scanned the rugged terrain for signs of enemy threat. The soldiers with me locked and loaded their weapons, adjusted their gear and waited to land. As we off-loaded, escorting U.S. Army attack helicopters circled the field like protective mother eagles. On cue, soldiers ran out and formed a line, resembling a bucket brigade passing the many boxes of mail, food and ammunition we transported to waiting vehicles. After a quick hot refuel, the helicopter took off for its next destination. Picking up my rucksack, chaplain's kit and guitar, I entered Camp Harriman, a remote U.S.-Afghan fire base near the eastern border with Pakistan. The camp, named after a U.S. Special Forces Soldier killed in action on March 2, 2002, is located near the Afghan border town of Orgun. Early the next day I put out word that I would conduct chapel at 10 a.m. It was Friday, the Muslim Sabbath, but a regular workday for most U.S. soldiers, so I wasn't sure how many could or would attend. As my assistant and I set up for the outdoor chapel service in an outdoor eating area, I heard an explosion. Stepping out into the open with another soldier, we heard the now familiar whistle of a second incoming rocket, then another explosion. I saw the impact area and called out its location to a sergeant running to a guard tower. All I could think of was "There goes my chapel service!" But, thankfully, no more rockets came. As I turned back toward the parachute-shrouded chapel area, I noticed a group of soldiers forming. It was then that old familiar phrase came to mind, "There are no atheists in foxholes." Over fourteen soldiers showed up that morning. Another fifteen came out that night; Special Forces team sergeants, helicopter pilots and crew members, mortar men of the 82nd Airborne, a Civil Affairs officer and two great army cooks – all gathered to give thanks they had survived another enemy attack in "the valley of the shadow of death!"

Chapter 40

Two Weeks before Christmas

Word from Chaplain Andy for 4-13-03

*There are no atheists in foxholes...*That old saying, coined in previous wars, is as true today as it was when first articulated. I witnessed that on several occasions, but most vividly after two soldiers and an interpreter were seriously wounded in a grenade attack. I walked into the command center; right after the report came in. I stood by to get the details and jumped in the vehicle with my Command Sergeant Major to meet them at a nearby coalition hospital. The scene was tense as the emergency medical personnel worked feverishly on each of the injured soldiers. I sat on a bench outside the operating room module and prayed God would guide the doctors and save those three lives. After what seemed like an eternity, two trauma specialists came out to give us a progress report. It was serious, worse than originally thought, but each was expected to live. One was still in surgery, but I could visit the other soldier, one of my chapel regulars, who was out of initial surgery. I went in and was unprepared for the scene. I could not recognize my brother comrade. His face was so swollen, peppered with shrapnel wounds and covered with bandages; I wasn't sure which one it was. As I took his hand and bent close, he said, "Hey Chaplain Andy, how's my buddy?" Tears filled both our eyes as he squeezed my hand and pulled me close. "Pray for me, sir...and pray for my buddy...he's got a wife and kids back home, don't let him die!" I prayed as requested and he told me that he wanted to recommit his life to Christ. He prayed a prayer of recommitment with me; the Coalition nurses and medics looking on. I then left to let him rest. We came back the next morning and found both men conscious, side my side. They were being prepared for medical evacuation. After squeezing the hand of the one, I said, "God heard our prayers, huh?" He nodded, and I turned to his teammate. I took his free hand and told him that God had spared his life for a purpose. He nodded and told me how he knew that he was dying, as the blood quickly drained from a lower artery nicked by shrapnel. I then asked him about his soul. When he began to tell me of his confusion about what was the right church, I stopped him and said, "Remember the story of Jesus' Crucifixion? There were three crosses on that hill..." I explained how the one thief simply placed his faith in Jesus, was never baptized, never joined a church, never gave a dime, but was granted access to Paradise that day, through a simple, sincere faith in Jesus. When I asked him if he wanted to profess that same simple faith, he said, "Yes, I do!" So right there, with his buddy looking on and the nursing staff standing by, I led him in a prayer of faith commitment to Jesus Christ. Again, tears of joy flowed as we encouraged and comforted our wounded brothers. Much more could be said about this incident, but the simple fact remains...there are no atheists in foxholes!

Part Four: Getting Busy
Chapter 41

Meeting the Postmaster

Shortly after beginning our conversational English classes at Pul-e-Charki School, we noticed the shortage of school supplies. Few students had notebooks and writing instruments. The classrooms were barren and bleak. All students sat on the cold concrete floor. A black rectangle was painted on the front wall of the classroom for use as a chalk board. The school had little chalk. Then I had an idea.

I started to ask around the forward operating base for paper, pencils and chalk. There was little to be found. Even the supply sergeant had a limited stock that was intended for internal use only.

Someone suggested that I write home for help. So, I did.

Several friends, family and church members were contacted. Promises of care packages came in reply. It took a couple weeks before the first boxes started to come. A Soldier came in with a box from some friends he had contacted. The next day, I got a box. Then two, three, four! Within three weeks we had to find room in an adjacent room, then a pallet in our warehouse for the mounting supply of paper, pencils, pens, chalk, rulers; you name it.

As our English classes progressed, we noticed that a lot of unusable items were coming. I quickly drafted a list of approved items that were culturally and technologically appropriate that could be sent out to the growing number of family, friends, groups, and churches that were filling the Army Post Office (APO) pipeline. One item we had to limit was colored chalk. Due to the poor quality of our black wall writing surfaces, only soft white chalk would work. And since there were no concrete sidewalks on which to draw, there was no suitable place for colored chalk. The same occurred with some children's books and other items. Rather than waste our generous donor's money and postage, we tried to channel their efforts – and most were very responsive. Soon my pallet grew to two then three, then a corner of the warehouse. Next, we had to come up with a distribution plan.

One day our unit postal clerk came to my office. He dropped several large packages on the floor and said, "Chaplain, we got us a problem." "What kind of a problem?" I asked. "Well, you're getting so much mail that if I brought all the stuff addressed to you, it would fill up my pickup and no one else would get any mail!" "Really?" I chided. "Really*!*" He replied.

Since I had my own vehicle, a Toyota Land Cruiser, I agreed to follow him to the mail distribution point at Bagram Air Base the next time he made a mail run. My boxy older Toyota Land Cruiser would surely be large enough. Boy was I wrong.

A few days later, I joined the convoy from our base to Bagram Airfield. After passing through the screening checkpoint, we headed for the mail distribution point. The vehicle ahead stopped in a parking area near some large shipping containers. Off to the side was what looked like an entrance to a storm cellar.

I followed the clerk into an old underground Soviet-built subterranean bunker. Down in the cool, dimly lit cavern I waited near the bottom of the stairs. Our mail clerk announced to the sergeant at the desk that he had come to pick up the mail for Meverden. "Meverden," the sergeant shouted. "Who the "F@&k" is Meverden?" On unintended cue, I stepped around the corner. "That would be me." I replied, a bit amused.

When the mail sergeant got a better look at me in the dim light, saw my nametag, rank and chaplain insignia, he replied with an air of relief. "So, you're Meverden – a chaplain – that helps explain it!" "Explain what?" I asked. "Follow me, sir, and you'll see."

Dutifully, I followed the military counterpart of the local postmaster back up the stairs and over to a row of shipping containers; the kind you see travelling highways on tractor-trailers and on ocean- going freighters. He unlocked one from the side and said, "Here you go, chaplain. I hope you brought a big truck!"

Inside, stacked floor to ceiling, were boxes of all shapes, colors and sizes. "Which ones are for me?" I asked. "All of them!" He replied. "So, where's your truck?"

We barely got one fourth of the boxes into my vehicle and my supply sergeant's truck. Several trips later, I had finally cleared out the shipping container.

Feeling a bit sheepish, I stopped down to thank the mail clerk for his patience and help. He said, "You know, chaplain, I was beginning to wonder what was going on. You get more mail than anyone else in country. I understand what you're doing, and that's a good thing. But, do you think you could tone it down a little?"

I promised I would be more careful with my mail order shopping. He grinned. We shook hands and I left. Only later would I see the value of what the good will of the American people sent to Afghanistan.

Chapter 42

First Afghan Battalion Deployment

Camp Harriman was a triangular-shaped firebase or combat outpost in a critical location on the eastern border between Afghanistan and Pakistan. With surrounding mountains, it sits in a saddle or depression that made it more passable in the winter months. As such it was susceptible to attack by anti-coalition forces who wanted to pass through or hit an easy target. It was here that the first battalion (Kandak) of the new Afghan National Army (ANA) was sent on their initial low-level combat operations.

Support soldiers from our unit had been rotating through Harriman for several weeks in preparation for the ANA arrival and mission to impede passage of hostiles from Pakistan. With the ANA Kandak (battalion) newly installed, the Command Sergeant Major took me and my chaplain assistant to visit our soldiers there.

After a false start, the next day we boarded our Chinook helicopter for the forty-five-minute flight to Orgun. Escorted by an Apache Helicopter gunship, we offloaded our people, supplies, equipment and mail for what was to be a two to three-day visit. Here I was introduced to life in "Indian Country," as some of the soldiers called it.

We dropped our gear in our canvas sleep tents and reported to the firebase commander, a Green Beret major who, in civilian life was a California firefighter. Explosive, abrasive, and given to fits of ranting and rage, I listened to camp rules and procedures outlined by the Good Major on what to do when, not if, the camp was attacked. My job was to keep my head down, stay out of the way, and move to the medical aid station – just like I did at FOB195.

The base was Spartan and the tour quick, including a visit to the operations and communications center, the dining facility affectionately dubbed Chuck's Diner (after the Colorado restaurateur who as an Army cook learned to combine U.S. rations with local fare), the shower and latrine facilities (outhouse style toilet seats over fifty-five-gallon drums cut in half that would be removed, contents mixed with diesel and burned for disposal). Then we visited the medical area, brick living areas for the Special Forces Teams, and general-purpose medium-size tents for other attached and visiting US forces.

One of the most interesting stops was the ammo dump where

weapons and munitions recovered and seized in searches was inventoried and stored. Here I got to see all kinds of old, even ancient, Soviet weapons, from small arms (AK-47 automatic rifles), to land mines, artillery shells, grenades, and even functioning anti-aircraft guns. To underscore the amount of ammunition recovered, the caretaker of the ammo dump estimated that they had on hand over one million rounds for the anti-aircraft guns – that's a ton of big bullets. A lot of dangerous material to be sure, but even more interesting was how some of this was recovered. More about that later.

Chapter 43

Historic Iftar Meal

Ramadan was later this year, so our visit overlapped the end of the Muslim month of fasting. The Afghan battalion commander invited the base's senior U.S. Army officers and ODA Team Sergeants to an Iftar dinner to break the month-long daytime fast and do some male bonding.

The fire base commander was the ranking officer, but for some reason, declined the offer to attend—so, by default, I became the ranking U.S. Army officer – an unusual position for me, as chaplain. After sundown, Command Sgt. Maj. Al and I, plus the Special Forces Team that was attached as mentors, advisors and liaison to the ANA Kandak, were invited into the large green canvas tent for the ceremonial Iftar (break-fast) meal. The outside temperature was just above freezing, but the tent was toasty warm from the roaring wood stoves burning at each end of the tent. The Command Sgt. Maj., Special Forces team commander, his team sergeants and I sat cross-legged across from the ANA Commander and his senior staff on woven reed floor mats. The meal reminded me of the Seven-Up commercial where we combined "a little of your country with a little of our country" to come up with the celebratory meal.

Tan cardboard food trays were used to serve, a healthy portion of nuts, cookies and tea. Thinking this was the main meal, I started shoveling in the snack placed in front of me. When the Commander saw how much I liked the Afghan version of camper's mix, he motioned for a refill on my tray. Boy did I goof!

After I ate more, Command Sgt. Maj. Al leaned over and told me that I had just had seconds of the appetizer, and that the main course was about to be served. Really? The Command Sgt. Maj. was right – experienced Command Sgts. Maj. typically are! The Afghan servers replaced our tan cardboard partitioned trays with new trays, filled with Kabuli Rice, nan (Afghan flat bread), and fork-tender cooked meat – a good thing, since the tableware we were given was a set of plastic knife, fork and spoon with napkin like we used in our "dining facility". These were given to us out of courtesy, while our Afghan host ripped off a piece of flat bread and tore into the pile of cooked rice garnished with carrot strings, hydrated raisins and roasted slivered almonds – a very tasty meal.

As usual, I cleaned my plate and was offered seconds, but wisely declined and accepted a second cup of tea. After the meal, I was introduced to something few U.S. soldiers ever experience. What transpired next intrigued me. The experienced SF team captain, Commander Ronco, whispered in my ear that I, as the senior U.S. officer, needed to thank our host Afghan commander. I thanked him for the honor and privilege of celebrating Iftar together on our first combined deployment with the new Afghan Army to the border of Pakistan, the source of much of Afghanistan's problems and woes.

After our interpreter hopefully conveyed my sincere message, the Afghan commander replied with a lengthy soliloquy. The interpreter said, "The commander says, 'We are the ones who are honored and privileged to share this special meal with our American friends, teachers and allies….'" The exchange of compliments, appreciation and praise went on for at least ten-minutes. After I spoke a couple times, the Special Forces team captain, Command Sgt. Maj. and even the other team members chimed in with words of gratitude and praise. Each compliment was countered by escalating adulation, gratitude and praise, by our Afghan hosts.

After my opening remarks, I fell back into listening to the interpretations and observing the expressions of apparent sincerity and gratitude from our Afghan counterparts. It was then that I realized the unique experience I had; an experience that our battalion commander should have had, or even our combined joint special operations task force (CJSOTF) commander, or even Lt. Gen. McNeil, the U.S. Commander headquartered back at Bagram Airfield. I was watching the operational birth of the new Afghan Army – the first Kandak – the first battalion deployed on low-level combat operations on the porous, fragile border of the fledgling new nation of Afghanistan. It seemed surreal and out of order that I, a U.S. Army National Guard chaplain, a lowly major, should have the privilege of being the senior officer at this event. But real it was; as a significant historic moment. But the night was young!

Chapter 44
Eid Celebration and Man-Dancing

The evening didn't end at that. With a wave of his hand, the Afghan commander called a soldier to come to the center of the tent. Kneeling behind the commander with an olive drab plastic water jug before him and two metal rods from an AK-47 rifle cleaning-kit, he began to beat out a rhythm. Caught up in the beat, the Afghan soldier started to sing – in a beautiful voice – what sounded like a ballad, a lament in Dari. I didn't want to ask the interpreter what he was saying, so I kept listening. Suddenly, I picked a word, a name *"Massoud" – "Oh Massoud!"*

Ahmad Shah Massoud – "the Lion of Panjshir," was a legendary Mujahedeen leader who fought the Soviet occupation. He subsequently became the Defense Minister of Afghanistan and commander of the anti-Taliban United Islamic Front. Ahmad Shah Massoud created the United Front (Northern Alliance) against the Taliban. Tragically, Usama Bin Laden had him killed in a staged interview with a bomb concealed in video camera on 9 September 2001 – just two days before the September 11 attacks on the U.S. *"Massoud – our hero, how we miss you, how we love you, how we wish you were here to lead us in vanquishing our enemies!"*

The Afghans, from the Commander on down, sat transfixed and even tearful as the ballad droned on through five or six stanzas. After this, another, more upbeat song was sung; an up-tempo rhythm on the same empty plastic water jug. Then the celebration started.

With the nod of the Commander's head, a soldier jumped to his feet and started dancing. It was like a folk dance synched with the song being sung. Soldiers started clapping and the energy picked up a notch. It was then that I noticed some non-verbal communication between the Special Forces team sergeants. One suddenly got up and left the tent. I wondered where he went. The singing and dancing continued. After a time, the Afghan commander invited us Americans to join in and dance. Looking back and forth at who would take the challenge, a six-foot-six-inch tall team sergeant jumped to his feet and began to do a routine that looked like something out of Michael Jackson's "Thriller." He then switched into the "moon walk" which caused a unified cheer from both Afghan and U.S. soldiers present.

Command Sgt. Maj. Al leaned over and asked, "Chaplain, why don't you go get your guitar and play a song or two?" More of a firm suggestion, rather than a question, I respectfully left, ran to my tent and ran back with my encased guitar.

Upon re-entering the tent, I sat down and took out my guitar, as I did, the group erupted again when the team sergeant who had left earlier returned, dressed in white Afghan garb, complete with formal headwear resembling a turban. He was introduced as "Haji-Ali Echo-Seven." He too, dazzled the assembled throng with some sassy dance moves.

Then it was my turn. Grabbing my guitar, I searched my case for some printed lyrics with chords that would fit the occasion. The first song, "This Land is Your Land," was prefaced by my interpreted wish that the diverse Afghan people would rally in support of their newly elected government and defend it from all enemies foreign and domestic. Then we sang, *"This this land your land, this land is my land, from California, to the New York Island..."* They clapped as I sang and played with minimal U.S. support – primarily because the others didn't know all the lyrics!

My second song was more difficult to choose, so I settled on *"This is the day, this is the day that the Lord has made. We will rejoice, we will rejoice, and be glad in it..."* Totally unaware of the meaning of the song, again, I prefaced it by recognizing the celebration of Eid and our need to thank God for every day of life. Then I lost my guitar to the crowd!

It was after 11:00 p.m. that I made it back to my tent. I slipped into my sleeping bag, zipped it up to my chin and prayed for a good turn-out for chapel. Little did I know how exciting that event would be!

---

[1] **Ahmad Shah Massoud** (احمد شاه مسعود -*Aḥmad Šāh Mas'ūd*; September 2, 1953 – September 9, 2001) was a Kabul University engineering student turned military leader who played a leading role in driving the Soviet army out of Afghanistan, earning him the name **Lion of Panjshir**. His followers call him **Āmir Sāhib-e Shahīd** (*Our Beloved Martyred Commander*). A devout Sunni Muslim reportedly also always carrying a book of Sufi mystic Ghazali with him, he strongly rejected the interpretations of Islam followed by the Taliban, Al Qaeda or the Saudi establishment.[1] His followers not only saw him as a military commander but also as a spiritual leader.[1]

Chapter 45
Rude Wake-up Call

Six hours later, an alarm went off. It wasn't mine, but when I checked my watch, I decided to get up and try to get a shower before breakfast. If it's to be had, it's the early bird who gets the warm water.

I was lucky. Though not hot, it was "warm" (i.e. not freezing), so I counted that a blessing and headed off for breakfast at "Chuck's Diner." Chuck, a Colorado restaurant owner and unit cook, volunteered to run the dining facility at Camp Harriman. He got a local stone mason to build an igloo- shaped bread oven that the Afghans use to bake their flat bread, known as nan.

Nan was a staple food and was made with unleavened bread rolled out in long narrow flattened strips and slapped onto the inside of the wood-fired-dome to bake. When done, it would fall into the center stone area that was kept free of the coals spread around the inside oven edge. Many of us grew to love Afghan nan. Unfortunately, we didn't have a bread oven back at KMTC. We were too close to the flagpole.[1]

Chuck had a knack for taking the issued unitized group rations (UGR), adding a pinch of this and a smattering of that, and coming up with some very palatable dishes. His latest find was a shopkeeper's pile of blood carrots that he prepared in a variety of ways. I ate my warm breakfast on a picnic table under a camouflage net outdoors and went to get ready for the ten o'clock chapel service.

My assistant and I decided the best place to hold the chapel service was in the same place we ate breakfast – outside under the camouflage net. Our setup included, guitar, folding music stand, camo Bibles and chapel programs with lyrics printed on the inside. Once organized, I sent my assistant to visit each sleeping tent and let the inhabitants know that chapel would start at 10:00 a.m. I could tell he was not thrilled with the directive.

He left in a less-than-enthusiastic manner around 9:30 am. I, too, took off to invite personnel in the operations center and team quarters to chapel. After two or three stops and less-than-enthusiastic replies, I heard a whistling sound and then a boom. I saw the dust cloud formed by what sounded like a 107 mm Soviet rocket. I previously had seen and heard them impact around KMTC and knew that they typically came in sets of three to five.

About sixty-seconds later, a second rocket came in. By this time, the entire base was awake and scrambling; some to the helipad, some to gun trucks, some to reinforce the perimeter, and others to the operations center. Chaplains can feel useless during an attack, as they are unarmed non-combatants. My typical battle position was in the battalion aid station to await and assist the medical team with the wounded. With no one apparently injured or wounded, I felt even more useless as the response to the attack unfolded. I decided to check on the guard in the tower closest to the impact. As I climbed the ladder to his reinforced lookout position, I asked if he was okay. He nodded affirmatively and pointed out the two points of impact; one approximately fifty meters outside the perimeter and the other off to the right and a few meters closer. He picked up a radio and called the operations center with impact locations. The personnel there plotted a back azimuth from the impact points and drew two circles at five and seven-kilometer points. These were the probable launch points that would be searched from the air and ground.

As the base response continued, I frustratingly thought; "Well there goes my chapel service." I climbed down the ladder and walked back to the chapel area to gather up our chapel kit, guitar and Bibles with my assistant who had returned from the perimeter to reinforce the defense. Our ministry team response was not well-coordinated, as he should have stayed with me for personal protection. I was not too concerned however as this was an aerial attack. It was good he had an opportunity to respond in perimeter defense. It got his adrenaline flowing – something he seemed to need as the winter season progressed.

Approaching the camo-covered outdoor dining area, I looked up saw a gaggle of soldiers gathered around. At first, I thought they were having a post-attack after action review. When I got closer, I saw they were helping themselves to the Bibles and chapel programs. The rockets did what our personal invitation could not – they roused the sleepy Soldiers from their warm tents and got them out into the cold, sunny fresh air motivated to attend chapel by this itinerant ministry team. After I tuned my guitar, I led the group in a couple repetitions of the same song I had led the night before in the ANA Iftar celebration:

"This is the day, this is the day, that the Lord has made, that the Lord has made. We will rejoice, we will rejoice and be glad in it..."

With the American Thanksgiving Holiday just passed, I asked those assembled for what they were thankful. One soldier spoke out for the entire group and said, "I'm thankful I survived another day in the Valley of the Shadow of Death." Other soldiers voiced joys and concerns. Following that, I led them in a pastoral prayer, concluding with a joint recitation of the Lord 's Prayer; "...and deliver us from evil. For Thine is the Kingdom, and the power and the glory, forever. AMEN!" Once again, it seemed like God's Spirit had guided my choice of chapel theme and topic, as I shared a brief meditation entitled: "How to be Thankful in Tough Times," based on the Apostle Paul's letter to the Philippians, chapter 4 verses 4-8.

Several soldiers came up after the closing prayer to shake my hand and thank me for making the trip. A couple said that they felt abandoned out here on the border. One sassy fellow recommended that I didn't quit my day job and try to make a living by just singing and playing the guitar. I replied by telling him that I would let him lead music on the next visit. He smiled as I poked him gently on the arm on departure. I was grateful for the opportunity to meet with these Soldiers (only one female) in this dangerous location.

One chapel attendee, a UH60 pilot with the 101st Airborne, attached to the FOB, asked me and my assistant if we would like to ride along on a recognizance flight. We looked at each other, and in unrehearsed unison said, "Sure!" We dropped our chapel gear off at the visitors' tent and hiked over to the helipad where the pilot already had his bird pre-flighted and ready to start. As we were belting in, the AOB commander, ran up and asked us in unkind terms what we thought we were doing. When I tried to explain the invite, he just shook his head and motioned to exit. So, we did. The pilot shrugged and continued his pre-flight checklist and, in minutes, was off on an aerial search for the rocketeers.

After the helicopter took off, the AOB commander explained further that the risk we were taking was unacceptable. (Like hanging out on his fire base was a safe place.) Oh well. My thoughts turned to the two gun trucks and UH60 helicopter crew that went out looking for those who launched the attack. I prayed that they would make it back safely. Later that day I would hear their report. But now it was time for a noontime MRE and a foot patrol through the small border town of Orgun.

---

[1] "Too close to the Flagpole" is an old military saying signifying that one's location was too close to the Headquarters and senior leadership's scrutiny. Camp Harriman's remote location had some advantages in this regard, one of them being their daily fresh Afghan bread!

Chapter 46
Culturally-appropriate Manly-hugs

Eid is the Muslim celebration of Abraham's spared sacrifice of his son, Ishmael. After the early afternoon unit formation, select members of the Afghan National Army (ANA) battalion were to make their first presence patrol through the nearby town of Orgun. Before we loaded into vehicles for the short ride to town, the commander wanted to give each Afghan soldier a personal holiday greeting. Again, I had the unique experience of participating in a ceremony that I had never witnessed before, nor ever would again.

As the Afghan battalion formed, the Special Forces Team commander, Capt. Rocco, called me to a huddle along with our visiting Command Sgt. Maj., the Afghan commander and an interpreter. The commander asked if I, as the senior visiting officer and chaplain, would greet the ANA battalion and wish them a blessed Eid, and then personally greet each of the soldiers after the ANA commander. I agreed.

Having become increasingly aware of my cultural ignorance, I took our interpreter aside and asked him how to wish them a "Happy Eid!" At first, the interpreter, a senior Afghan medical student, looked at me inquisitively, then suddenly understood my question. "Oh," he said. "When we greet a family member or friend on Eid we say, "Eid Mubarrak!" Later I would learn that "Mubarrak" means "blessed," so I was wishing them a "Blessed Eid." But for now, I was equipped with a new Afghan phrase I was prepared to employ.

After the ANA commander gave his greeting to the assembled formation, he motioned to me to come forward. In a loud outside voice, I shouted, "EID MUBARRAK!" Their response was spontaneous, "EID MUBARRAK!" they shouted in reply. I said a few more words which were interpreted by our trusted medical student interpreter and followed the ANA commander to the left end of the formation.

To my surprise, the commander grabbed the first ANA soldier by the shoulders and pulled him into an embrace kissing him by touching cheeks on both sides. As he stepped to the next soldier on his right, I mimicked the Afghan commander's actions, put out my hand, which was firmly grasped, and we pulled each other into a manly embrace, my clean-shaven cheeks rubbing against mostly bearded Afghan faces. As we passed through the formation, I used the "Eid Mubarak" greeting along with alternating Dari and Pashtu greetings and blessings that I had learned. The ANA commander smiled back as he heard me rotate among the four or five greetings that I knew.

Then the Afghan commander gathered about twenty soldiers into a circle and they began to dance – the Afghan national dance. It reminded me of an Israeli folk dance – the Miser Lou, with the men turning in circle in a grapevine, counterclockwise fashion. Most were in good step...even I got the step down and joined in the dance. The surrounding Afghan soldiers sang, laughed and clapped as the inner circle danced.

After about 250 Afghan man hugs, I was ready for the patrol. The Afghan commander put his arm around me and walked me to the awaiting vehicles. About seventy ANA soldiers piled into the back of five-ton Russian-made trucks for the short ride to the border town.

When I got into the Russian-made Waz jeep with my Command Sgt. Maj., I expected razzing or criticism. Instead, the seasoned Special Forces soldier looked at me and commented that it was a culturally appropriate thing for me to do...but if I ever tried that with him, he'd knock the s@#t out of me. I smiled back and told him not to worry because I had come to prefer unshaven males!

Chapter 47

Whose Soldiers Are these?

Eid was also being celebrated in the nearby Afghan border town of Orgun. The ANA unit was to conduct a presence patrol through the main street business area. This would be the very first such patrol by the fledgling army in an area of strong anti-coalition/anti-government activity. Risk was moderate. Given the previous day's rocket attack, it was clear there were people nearby who wished us and our Afghan partners harm.

As our vehicles pulled up, the ANA soldiers dismounted. The Command Sgt. Maj. and I were given the option of riding in a jeep behind the Afghan patrol, but I chose to dismount and walk with this group of men I had helped train. I wanted to see if the principles of human rights and the law of land warfare made any difference in the way they conducted themselves in real-world operations. I would soon see.

The patrol led by the Afghan battalion commander and senior noncommissioned officer began at one end of the main street. As it was a major religious holiday, most men were congregating in the center of the town. The platoon spread out equally on both sides of the street with the battalion commander in the lead. The Special Forces mentoring, and liaison team disbursed among the platoon and kept a low profile.

I positioned myself with my assistant to the middle left of the formation and began to walk a leisurely pace – more like a shopping stroll. As we approached the first cross street, a crowd of men was gawking at a group of soldiers they had never seen before. What they saw were Afghan soldiers dressed in U.S. woodland camouflaged uniforms, with Swiss helmets, Soviet weapons and other load- bearing equipment from countries like Spain, Greece and Italy. Though neatly and uniformly dressed, they knew they weren't U.S. or NATO personnel, but were not sure exactly who they were in the company of the U.S. Special Forces team.

Suddenly, the Afghan commander stepped off to the side, engaged some of the men with "Eid Mubarrak!" ("Blessed Eid"). The men of Orgun responded enthusiastically, and a lively interchange ensued. In a flash, the Afghan commander joined in a circle of men who clapped and sang what sounded like the words to the Afghan National Dance I had learned earlier. I joined in. Around the small circle I danced to the cheers (and jeers?) of the crowd of men and children.

After a few minutes – short minutes – I felt a strong hand pull me from the crowd and back into the patrol. Something told me that my participation in the dance may have been a bit too risky. To regain situational awareness – like my mother warned – I began to scan my environment for threats.

Within ten steps the Afghan soldiers on my flank closed in around me; one at my front, one at each side and one in the back with my U.S. Army assistant. At first, I thought this was just happenstance, but as we moved forward, I realized it was intentional. Finally, it dawned on me what they were doing. They had formed a tight walking perimeter around me – like a mini Roman phalanx – to ensure my safety. I called to the interpreter and he walked closer. "What are these soldiers doing?" I asked. After a quick exchange with the ANA soldier next to him, he said, "They remember how you taught them to treat protected persons, places and things. Since you are an unarmed religious worker, they must protect you in this dangerous place." I smiled to him and to the Soldiers around me. "Tashakor." ("Thank you.") I said. "Tell them they are good students!" My mini personal security detail smiled when the interpreter relayed my message. We continued our patrol.

Another significant occurrence caught my attention. At a small shop selling fruit and sundries, an Afghan soldier stopped and pointed to a small box of laundry soap. When he asked how much, the shopkeeper motioned for him to take it. The soldier could have taken it. Instead, he reached into his pocket and pulled out new Afghan currency and paid the asking price. The old shopkeeper looked shocked as he made the sale to a soldier carrying an automatic weapon. I was encouraged, as that was another principle I taught in my human rights/law of war training classes – integrity and the rule of law.

Near the end of the main thoroughfare, was a mosque under construction – more likely, reconstruction. Out front were several men, one who appeared to be the imam. As the ANA patrol approached, one of the men called out to the Afghan commander, "Who are these soldiers?" The ANA commander stepped over and with a smile said, "These are Afghan Soldiers." The man replied, "They sure don't look like Afghan soldiers, and they sure don't act like Afghan soldiers – they are too disciplined!" The interpreter softly said to me. The commander called a couple of his soldiers over and let them talk to the men in front of the mosque. Standing back a few yards, my interpreter relayed the conversation to me. Inside, I felt like we had done a good job of taking these Afghan volunteers and turning them into disciplined soldiers of the world's newest army. I couldn't wait to report to our U.S. special forces battalion leaders what I had observed in Orgun.

Chapter 48

Hearts, Minds and Hands

While at Advanced Operations Base (AOB) Orgun, I visited the medical section. Major Bronson White, DO, better known as "Doc White," shared a couple amazing stories. One of the missions of The Green Berets is foreign internal defense (FID). That involves training indigenous people to defend their homeland; the very thing we're doing at KMTC and "field testing" at this outpost. A critical element in this effort is earning the trust of the people being defended and trained, in other words, "winning the hearts and minds" of the local population.

Back in Kabul we attempted to do this through wide range of humanitarian projects. This included English classes and distribution of school supplies at the Pul-e-Charki school and food, clothing, school supplies and toy distribution and extensive medical support of the Allahuddin orphanage. It also included a significant number of community-based medical civic assistance programs (MEDCAP). In fact, six of ten planned MEDCAPs in Afghanistan during our presence were carried out by our battalion under the direction of Doc Enz and his medical section. These efforts help develop good will and trust with the Afghan people, and often lead to valuable information on insurgents and bad actors.

An amazing example of that occurred at Orgun. One medical civic assistance program (MEDCAP) conducted by the Special Forces team at Harriman provided medical and veterinarian services in a neighboring village. The day after, local citizens came back with detailed information on the locations of weapons and caches of rockets, mortars and ammunition. This led to capture and destruction of war materials that most likely would have been used by the enemy in future attacks, bombings and rocketing.

One story from this border MEDCAP must be told. Doc Bronson showed me photos of a young boy who scalded his hand in a boiling pot of tea. Somehow, he burned his arm halfway up to his elbow.
In Afghanistan, when poor people lack medical care or any type of first aid training and materials (bacitracin, Neosporin ointment, band- aids or sterile gauze, etc.), they improvise. Children with burns of all kinds were often treated with the blue or black ink from ballpoint pens.

When his dad, saw the injury and immediate blistering, he told his son that he would take him to the American soldiers for help. The young boy cried and said, "No daddy!" When he asked why he didn't want to go to the Americans he said: "Because they will kill you, daddy!" The boy's father believed differently and took his son to the Camp Harriman.

Doc Bronson treated the boy, keeping him in his small medical facility for a few days. There he carefully debrided the burn, removed the dead tissue, and provided physical therapy to prevent the scaring from reducing his hand and finger movement. I saw photos of the boy's hands after two weeks of daily treatment. Though some scaring was visible, new pink skin was growing and the young boy lost almost no flexibility in his hand. After about ten days, that young boy became fast friends with his American Special Forces doctor.

Doc Bronson beamed as he showed me before and after photos of the boy's hand and arm. The expert medical skills of this Special Forces physician effectively won the hearts and minds of not only that little boy, but his entire family and village!

Chapter 49

Wrong Helicopter—Right Destination
Word from Chaplain Andy for Feb. 2, 2003

It was Sunday morning, my traveling companion and good buddy, the Command Sgt. Maj. (CSM), was trying to get us a flight to Kandahar to visit our Soldiers stationed there. Flight operations told us that this would not be possible, so we prepared to return home through Bagram Airfield.

I had originally scheduled chapel for 0930. After a quick cold shower and hot cup of coffee, I received word that a "bird" was inbound at 0945. My Command Sgt. Maj told me to plan a short chapel service, so we could make our flight back. Instead, I moved the meeting to 0900 to ensure enough time for my Advent Chapel service. I changed the sign on the mess tent and began, along with my assistant, to notify the various sections of the time change. In a combat zone, every day is Sunday, so chaplains provide services every day, if necessary. On this visit, Saturday chapel was Thanksgiving and Sunday chapel was Christmas.

Once again, I wondered how many, if any soldiers would make it to chapel. Set up outside under a camouflaged parachute canopy, the Afghan sun began to warm the early morning mountain air. I got out my guitar, tuned it and began to practice the chapel songs. Over fifteen soldiers showed up to sing, pray, hear a message and observe the Lord's Supper. As the final prayer was said, I heard a helicopter off in the distance.

I said good-bye to the soldiers and quickly packed up my guitar and chaplain's kit. My rucksack, body armor and helmet were already stacked and ready to don. Suddenly Apache pilots ran from the chapel area. An incoming helicopter had taken gunfire and the attack crews scrambled to meet the threat. My assistant and I followed the CSM to the helipad. (He always makes sure I am close by – he thinks I'm too careless about my personal security.) I lugged my gear into the helicopter right behind my CSM and sat down. After a couple minutes, the crew chief gestured for us to get off the aircraft – engine problems.

The helicopter had to be "jumped" to a secondary site for inspection and repair as several other mammoth cargo helicopters suddenly lumbered over the ridge. It was controlled chaos as the rotor wings of the Apaches beat the air at take-off. The dust cloud and engine roar made communication, visual and verbal, extremely difficult.

After about twenty minutes, the crew chief of the helicopter we originally boarded motioned for us to return. We ran into our helicopter, buckled up and took off, attack helicopter in trail. The rear cargo ramp was down, manned with a gunner, tethered with a safety strap. I watched as Camp Harriman faded in the distance.

I intermittently dozed and looked out the lateral porthole as we flew low and fast toward our destination. After observing terrain that I hadn't noticed before, we landed – over two-hours later. The jolt woke me up and I looked for the familiar sights of Bagram – but we weren't in Bagram!

As our helicopter taxied, we passed by a sand-colored, clam-shaped terminal – one I had seen on CNN many times – Kandahar? We had landed in Kandahar! I looked at the CSM who shrugged in the deafening din of the cargo hold. After checking on possible flights home, we stopped in to visit our ODAs temporarily stationed there. We found some very demoralized soldiers. As we listened to their concerns, it became clear that some serious misunderstanding had occurred. One ODA had just succeeded in capturing a key Taliban leader, Shaw Wali, who was now on his way to Guantanamo Bay, Cuba. A previous report of their ineffectiveness and inactivity was clearly inaccurate.

Had we not accidentally dropped in, no one back at our FOB would have ever known the ground truth of their activity. As I stood with the CSM, I said to the ODA Captain, "If we hadn't taken the wrong helicopter, we would have never known the truth. Clearly, God had us get on the wrong helicopter to get to the right destination!"

Smoldering Pentagon from hotel balcony on 9/11

Colorado 14 who flew to DC Sept 10-12

Church dedication of Pastor Andy & SFC Dave

Building pallets...and relationships.

Boarding C5 Galaxy

Mess Sgt who suggested food donation

The *Fabulous* Bombay Lounge

Capt Diggs teaching boy's English class – armed!

Chaplain Andy teaching 7th grade boys ages 12-18

Jess & Beth teaching girls during Nat Geo filming

Eating forbidden food and learning why

First class Human Rights & Law of War

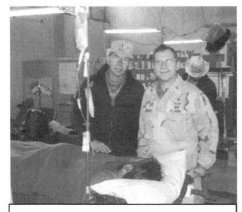

"It's a miracle!" Doc Enz' diagnosis.

Collaborating with French Army priest

Cpt Diggs, interpreter Temour &
Chaplain Andy at Allahudin Orphanage

Off to Orgun with CSM Al, mentor & protector

Taliban captive, Silke, sharing at KMTC Christmas Eve service

Andy with Afghan officials at first orphanage food delivery

Andy & USO WWE wrestler, John Bradshaw, after making up!

FOB195 Multi-national Christmas Eve choir

Maj John offloads Maharamona sheep for presentation

1600 villagers served in Polycharky MEDCAP!

Local workers build the school perimeter wall

Newly constructed male latrine facility

Chaplain with fathers of 4 boys killed in training accident after meal with salt.

Faculty farewell lunch for chaplain & GEN Eikenberry of OMC

Student farewell lunch for female soldier teachers!

Examining "the list."

Conciliation: Team Sgt & bereaved Father embrace with tears.

"Go in peace. You have done your job well. We forgive you!" (Afghan Fathers)

Part Five: Getting Slammed
Chapter 50
The Ten Principles of Human Rights
Word from Chaplain Andy...3-30-03

I've written before about my opportunities to teach classes on human rights and the law of war to our host nation soldiers. It was a subject that I had taught to U.S. several times to troops back home, but never did I think I would have to practice what I taught.

A few days before Christmas, we had two soldiers and an Afghan interpreter seriously injured in a grenade attack in Kabul. The report was on CNN. Heroic action and public cooperation not only saved the lives of our three KMTC personnel, but also resulted in the apprehension of the suspect.

After visiting our injured soldiers in a nearby coalition hospital, I returned to base. I confess that when I saw the injuries sustained by my soldiers, I became angry and wished I could return the favor to whoever it was who attacked them.

As I was about to collapse on my bunk, someone knocked on my plywood door. It was MAJ Ken the battalion operations officer. He informed me that the suspect was on his way to our compound and that he would be interrogated in the conference room adjacent to the chapel office and my quarters. He then asked me something I never expected: "Chaplain, will you be the human rights observer of this interrogation? You have taught the classes many times and are the best person for this task. If at any time you feel his human rights are being violated, you may step in on the suspect's behalf." What? Me ensure that this assassin's human rights weren't violated?

I looked my comrade in the eyes. He could sense my apprehension. As a veteran Denver police officer, he calmly said: "Andy, you can do this. I have had to arrest and safeguard people who had just killed fellow officers. Under the circumstances, we feel you are the best person to ensure his safety." I nodded and got dressed.

In a few minutes, the assassin was outside the chapel. I can say assassin because he had confessed to the dastardly deed in the previous interrogation – and was proud of it!

After the interrogation team arrived, I led the assassin and the security detail guarding him to our medical facility. We woke up a doctor to give him a medical check before the interrogation – to verify his condition upon arrival. As he stood there naked for the exam, I noticed that he was just a young man; seventeen or eighteen-year- old. I also noticed something else; he had no beard and no body hair below. I was puzzled at first, but later realized why.

This young man had not only intended to kill U.S. soldiers, but he had purified himself by shaving all the hair off his body in preparation to kill himself in the process – only he had failed.

The interrogation proceeded through the night. He was even allowed to sleep for a time. Not once did I hear U.S. voices raised or see any mistreatment. The next morning, I examined the young assassin. He was leaving in the same physical condition he had come. Only by now he was not so proud of what he had done. As he was again blindfolded and led away, I thought to myself: "I only hope our enemies treat their prisoners as well as we treat ours!"

I recalled the words of Jesus: "Love your enemies, do good to those who hate you." (Luke 6:27) As an instructor of human rights and the law of war, I witnessed first-hand the fact that our soldiers practiced what Jesus, and I, taught. I kept the blindfold and sandbag used to cover his head as a reminder of this unique encounter between the chaplain and the assassin. I didn't how significant that would be.

Chapter 51

Post-op Visit

After I inspected the person under custody (PUC), I traveled with Command Sgt. Maj. Al to visit our two wounded Soldiers. I promised Sgt. 1st Class Chris that I would come back the following day to check on him and his buddy, Mike. In my twenty-five years as a pastor and missionary, I had made many hospital visits. These would be my first serious combat casualties. I prayed for the right words to say.

As we entered the equivalent of the intensive care unit, we had to work our way through a crowd of medical personnel; doctors, nurses, all members of various NATO units working together at Camp Warehouse in the International Security Assistance Forces (ISAF) complex. I couldn't help but notice several female medical professionals – you know, the ones with stethoscopes hanging around their necks. I quickly realized why our sick and injured Soldiers were quick to ask for treatment in this facility; the blonde Swedish nurses were quite attractive.

Sgt. 1st Class Chris smiled and gave us the thumbs-up sign and said: "Chaplain, Mike wants to talk with you." I turned to Mike, ignoring the forum of medical personnel quietly watching and said: "How are you doing, buddy? You almost bought the farm yesterday. Would you have been ready to meet your Maker?" Sgt. 1st Class Mike just nodded and through streaming tears replied: "Chaplain, I don't know what is the right church…" It was like breaking into a conversation between two people, and not really knowing what was said before, but I quickly caught the drift. These two soldiers must have been discussing Eternity before I got there.

Leaning closer to Mike, I began to share with him the story of the three crosses on Golgotha -- the ISAF medical team politely and quietly observing and listening -- how, as Jesus hung between two thieves, one challenged Jesus to come down off the cross and bring him and the other condemned man down with him. I explained further how the humble thief told the other guy to "shut up" and that whereas they deserved their punishment, Jesus was innocent; and then asked Jesus to remember him when he entered His kingdom. I then told him how Jesus responded; "Surely I say to you, you shall be with me today in Paradise." I explained that at the end of the day at least two of them went to Heaven - Jesus and the repentant thief, for sure. Then I asked, "How did he get there?" He didn't have time to get baptized, join a church, give an offering or perform any act of service.

"How could he make it into heaven, Mike?" I asked. "Because he believed in Jesus," came Mike's reply. "Would you like to make that same faith commitment before we head out to the medical evacuation helicopter?" "Yes," he said. Mike responded with a prayer of faith commitment to Jesus Christ. As we ended our prayer, I suddenly realized all eyes were on us. For a few sacred moments, we were touching Heaven. Now it was time to return to earth.

Both Soldiers asked me to accompany them to the medical evacuation helicopter. I went on ahead to meet them at the helicopter landing zone (HLZ) back at KMTC. There, I helped load them onto the Oregon Army National Guard MEDEVAC helicopter to Bagram Airfield with a final prayer for health and safety.

Chapter 52

The Unthinkable Occurs

I had recently returned from my trip to Orgun via Kandahar and Uzbekistan with Command Sgt. Maj. Al and Spec. "JJ." The Christmas Holiday was approaching, and I was busy preparing. During the last two lessons of our conversational English classes at Pul-e-Charki School, we sensed an ever-increasing bond with students and faculty. We were sad that the winter break was approaching.

On December 14, the school year in Afghanistan was over. The cold weather, windowless school and unheated classrooms, made formal teaching impossible. We heard discussion among the female high school students of a desire to continue the English classes, but we didn't know how this would be possible. The heavy sheets of plastic stapled to the exterior window frames by Master Sgt. John's ODA were already shredding in the wind. It would take a climatological miracle to meet through the winter.

Turning my attention to holiday planning, I dropped by the operations center to discuss options for proposed Christmas activities. Peanut butter and jelly sandwich in hand, I entered a room with several soldiers huddled around a radio receiver. Glancing at my watch, I saw that it was about 1:45p.m. When I asked what was up, the operations officer motioned for me to be quiet. As he feverishly wrote I heard him say in proper radio protocol; "One dead, several wounded...now two dead...over. We are sending all available medical personnel and an ambulance, over!"

The assistant operations officer took me aside and began to paint a picture of what had just transpired. Our ODAs were conducting a live-fire exercise on nearby Gharib Ghar Mountain firing range. A battalion of Afghan soldiers were organized into rifle companies with indirect fire mortar support. It was a simple shoot, move and communicate exercise; testing the Afghan battalion's ability to assault an objective located mid-point on the mountain. The intent was to fire volleys of suppressive mortar fire on the mock objective to allow the Afghan infantry the opportunity to move into assault positions to defeat the notional emplaced enemy.

Prior to the commencement of the training exercise, the range management team had cleared the area of all people and animals within the range fan[1]. In the process of scanning and clearing the terrain, a group of school-age boys were chased off the range twice. We had a challenge keeping Afghan children away; partly due to natural curiosity, and partly due to their desire to pick up expended brass casings fired from weapons, as well as aluminum from mortar and rocket rounds fired into the mountainside. Years later, I also learned that the Afghan mountains contained substantial veins of lapis lazuli, a blue semi-precious stone used in jewelry making. The explosive impact of mortar and rocket fire occasionally dislodged deposits of lapis that the boys could sell to local jewelry makers. After chasing away the group of boys and a few goats, the range was declared hot, and ready for operation.

But, regardless of geography or culture, boys will be boys. These ten boys, age twelve to sixteen, were not going to be deterred. They proceeded around the backside of the mountain, climbing up and over through a draw that led them down to the very spot on the slope where the first three mortar rounds hit.

With the final casualty report in, four Afghan boys were dead, one seriously wounded and a couple more slightly injured. The medics were bringing the dead boys back to KMTC to be examined and prepared for return to their families. I figured that I should be there when family members of the dead boys arrived. Not sure how soon they would get the news and arrive, I decided to make a stop to see our senior interpreter for some language and culture instruction.

Through my conversational English classes, at the Pul-e-Charki school, human rights and law of war training classes with Afghan soldiers, and other humanitarian projects, I got to know several of our Afghan interpreters. Colonel Sammy, a former Afghan military officer, was our chief interpreter. I went to his office desk and sat down. If anyone could help me, surely, he could.

"Colonel Sammy, how do you say, 'I am very sorry?'" He looked at me with sad eyes and asked if I intended to speak with the families that would soon be arriving. "Yes." I said, "And I want to be able to express condolences in a culturally appropriate way." "I see." He said. He rubbed his chin for a few seconds and replied, "Mung-der-ram-gen-you!" I wrote it on the back of his business card, repeated to check pronunciation and thanked him.

I then asked him another question: "When you have an accident, or if someone is injured or killed, like in today's training accident, do you have a way to bring reconciliation or make a formal apology?" Again, he listened to my question, thought for an even longer time, then spoke with another interpreter standing nearby, and then said, "Yes. We have an ancient custom called 'Maharamona.' We do it when someone accidentally kills a goat or a child by running over them with a car or truck." He said. "Can you tell me more about it?" I asked. "First you go and give the boys back to their families. Then come back I will explain it to you." "Okay," I replied and went off to do one of the saddest pastoral duties of my deployment…and life.

The day was overcast. That, in part, contributed to our range personnel's inability to see the boys climb back over the mountain on the backside. The clouds were low and covered the top portion of the range. It was under this cover the boys slipped in, undetected. After, being told by the surviving few boys of the horror on the mountain, a father in Pul-e-Charki drove at breakneck speed to the range and broke through the checkpoint. When the range guards saw the car enter the range area, they immediately called a cease-fire. The car stopped, and the man began to shout that there were injured boys up the slope. Immediately, the range personnel called all available medics to follow up to the site indicated by the frantic man.

The scene was gruesome….

Chapter 53
The Saddest Day

I waited on the KMTC parade field for the bodies of the young boys to arrive. An ambulance entered the compound and drove to a medium-sized tent for examination, documentation, photography and clean up. Who would do this mortuary procedure, I wondered. Later I would learn that SSG Dean was more than qualified for the task. He was an experienced technician who routinely harvested organs and tissue from donors through the Rocky Mountain Lions Eye Bank. An experienced eye tech and preventive medicine NCO, he was uniquely skilled for this solemn, specialized task. Under the guidance of the battalion surgeon, each boy was carefully examined, cleaned up and photographed to document the nature and severity of their wounds. As our medical team completed the examination, communication with higher headquarters transpired on how to proceed with the processing and return of the boys.

It didn't take long for news of the tragedy to spread through the nearby town. One by one, family members came to the main gate to ask about their sons, brothers or nephews. Interestingly, no women came. As family members arrived, the interpreters would indicate who they had come for and their relationship. A fine drizzle began to fall and soon everyone gradually got wet and started to shiver. One U.S. soldier came up and asked if he should try to find something to serve as protection from the rain. I said it was a good idea. In a short time, he returned with sleeping bags. We offered them to the Afghans and some wrapped themselves to keep warm.

One by one I squatted next to a family member and said, "Mung-der-ram-gen-you." ("I am very sorry."). Several looked at me and seemed to understand what I was trying to say. I moved next to a middle-aged man. He was wearing the round rolled up woolen hat that the Afghan freedom fighter Masood typically wore in his photographs. I repeated my condolence phrase to him a couple of times. At first, he didn't acknowledge me, but after my third statement, he turned his head and simply glared at me. I could see the anger, confusion and pain in his eyes. Neither my presence nor my words could bring any comfort.

After what seemed like hours, someone came up to tell me that the boys' bodies were almost ready to be returned. Finally, I heard a HUMVEE ambulance start up in the distance by the medical clinic. A few minutes later, it slowly made its way to the assembly area where the family members waited.

Sgt. Maj. Dan, our operations sergeant, took control of the identification and transfer of remains. After coordinating the ensuing chaos at the front gate, with men in taxis demanding entrance, the sergeant major established a discrete security plan. In a polite, professional and compassionate manner, he worked through an interpreter to identify the next-of-kin of the four boys in the ambulance.

Through the interpreter he called the first family member into the ambulance. Faced with the dilemma of not knowing who was in each bag, he opened one. The man looked relieved, as it was not his son. Upon opening a second bag containing his son, he burst into tears. Sgt. Maj. Dan gave a nod for the body to be lifted out of the ambulance and into an awaiting taxi. One by one, the boys were identified and returned to their families. Wailing broke out as each one was identified, and the bag was zipped shut.

Three passenger vehicles, mostly Afghan Toyota taxis with their distinct yellow paint, were allowed onto the receiving area just inside the gate. Two carried the bodies of one son, but a third taxi carried two boys. Later I would learn that this makeshift hearse carried the son and the nephew of the man who glared at me in mute rage. One by one, the tragic identification and return of the four boys took place. After the last vehicle departed, I knew I needed to go back to see Col. Sammy.

Without my realizing it, Colonel Sammy had observed and helped supervise the U.S. soldiers and interpreters throughout the entire process of retuning the four boys. He saw the genuine, sorrowful, dignified care with which my men handled the bodies of the boys. I realized that he had been out there after entering his office and noticed that he was even wetter than I was. I sat in a chair by his desk. Two men, both fathers in their late forties looked at each other with pain-filled hearts, and tear-filled eyes.

"Tell me about 'Maharamona." I asked. Colonel Sammy picked up where he had left off. "First, you must visit the families of the dead boys, explain that it was an accident, drink tea, and eat what they serve you. You must not delay, for they must bury their dead within twenty-four hours." He explained. "Similar to Jewish practice." I thought to myself.

My Afghan mentor went on to describe the process whereby the offending party desiring conciliation would approach the local elders for their assistance in communicating with the offended family. The village elders would go to the family and facilitate the Maharamona. If the injured family were willing to undergo the conciliation process, they would host a meal and cook the food with salt. The party who inflicted the injury or damage would bring a sheep to compensate for the family's loss. If the meal had salt and the sheep was accepted, "Maharamona" would be

116

accomplished, and the families would be reconciled.

I then asked Colonel Sammy two questions: "How old and how big of a sheep was required?" and, "What if the food isn't salty?" He answered that the size and age of the sheep had to do the with the amount of damage; big damage, big sheep. As for the question on the lack of salt, he basically said, "You'd better run, fast!" After that cultural lesson, I left to see the commander.

I found the battalion commander in the operations center speaking with the intelligence officer. When they finished, I asked if I could make a recommendation. Given the tragedy unintentionally inflicted by our forces, and the Muslim practice of burying the dead within twenty-four hours, I recommended that the commander accompany me to visit the bereaved Afghan families. He listened and then asked the intelligence officer what he thought.

The Intelligence officer thought a moment and replied. I heard him acknowledge the Muslim burial practice, but express hesitation about the command visit. He felt there was a risk of retaliation or ambush. I further explained that I recommended that we go into the homes with boots, body armor, and weapons left at the door. The dead boys would be most likely laid out on the floor of their main room and entering with battle gear would be offensive. The intelligence officer expressed even greater hesitation at my second recommendation. The commander thought for a few moments and decided not to go. Frustrated and fearful of the consequences of not going, I nodded, and returned to my chapel office. My job was to recommend, not decide.

On my way past the dining facility, the chief cook waved me over. He said that he heard what had happened and was very sad over the accident. He then said something I didn't think of nor expect. "Chaplain, I've got some ice cream in the freezer that I've been saving for Christmas. What do you think about us putting some of that out for dessert tonight? It might help pick up morale?"

I looked up into the sad face of our MP company cook, who back home in Massachusetts was a chef at a restaurant on Cape Cod and smiled. "Good idea!" I replied. "You know, food has a big impact on morale." He said. "You know that better than anyone!" I replied and slapped him fraternally on the arm and continued. Everyone on our FOB was impacted, even the cooks...and everyone wanted to help.

Before I could make it to my office, another soldier stopped me. "Chaplain, here." He shoved a wad of U.S. currency into my hand. "Use this to help the families of the boys who died today." Before I could reply, he looked away with tears in his eyes and slipped off. I put the cash in my pocket and walked on, only to be stopped two more times with similar offers. Before I could get to my chapel office, I had a pocket full of bills. I counted three hundred and fifty dollars. I had to put that in a safe place, so I went to the operations center to see Sgt. Maj., Dan, whom I had come to love and respect. "Sergeant Major, can you secure this for me?" "What's this?" He asked. When I explained, he nodded, and said he would count it and put in a sealed envelope in the safe. It was time for the daily commander's update brief (CUB), so I entered and sat in the back of the room.

Rather than conduct the briefing as usual, the focus was the day's tragic accident. As in all serious incidents in the U.S. military, an investigating officer was appointed, and an internal inquiry was ordered. The process was reviewed. It was a sad, somber time. Just before the meeting was to adjourn, Major Bruce, another member of our platoon of majors, himself an experienced Green Beret officer, spoke up and said, "I think the chaplain should offer a prayer for the tragedy that occurred today."

Feeling a bit sheepish that I didn't think of that myself, I stood, took a deep breath, and said, "Let us pray…" In my extemporaneous prayer, I recall asking God to comfort the families of the boys who were killed and thanking him for the heroic efforts of all who responded especially the medics and docs. I specifically remember ending my prayer that "…somehow, God may you bring triumph out of this tragedy…fire out of these ashes. Amen." The sounds of "Amen" echoed throughout the room. The meeting ended shortly thereafter. I felt sad, emotionally drained, and apprehensive. Somehow, I knew I had to do more.

Chapter 54
"Padre, Can We Talk?"

After patting a few backs and saying good night to several others on the way out, I walked the seven steps from the door of the conference room, through the chapel into my office and sleeping area. I was ready to turn in when someone knocked on my door. "Come in." I said, and the door opened to the saddest American face I had seen all day. "Padre, can we talk?" He asked. I beckoned him to sit, and he dropped into a white molded plastic chair.

He began by telling me of his previous experience in Somalia; how he had to shoot a young teenage boy who refused to put down an AK47 the lad had pointed at him. "I promised that I would never allow myself to be put in that kind of a situation again, but today, I'm responsible for the death of four young boys. I came here to kill terrorists, not young boys!" As he put his head into hands and sobbed, I leaned forward and hugged him. I could feel the pain in his soul reverberate throughout his entire body. I cried with him.

After a time, he regained composure. Looking me straight in the eyes, he said, "Padre, you've got to get me out of here. I've got to go home. My wife has wanted a child for so long, but I've always been gone. You've got to help me go home!" Sobs again punctuated his plea. He then handed me his weapons. "Here, take these. I don't want them anymore. I've got to leave this place." Sensing the depth of his emotional pain, I took his weapons, placed them in my metal wall locker, turned back and looked him in the eye.

"Go get some rest. If there's water in the morning, get a shower, eat a hot breakfast, and come back and see me. We'll figure something out." He left; one of America's best, blindsided by a second tragedy he never could have imagined, much less avoid. I surreptitiously watched him enter the door of his team room just down the covered walkway from the chapel. Figuring him safe with his Team, I flopped exhausted onto my bunk. Tears came unbidden; I crammed my face into my pillow and cried myself to sleep. I needed rest from the day's tragedies, so I could get to work the next day...on what I wasn't sure. I prayed and asked God to show me what I could do. I slept, no dreams, just hard sleep.

Chapter 55

Backdoor Diplomacy

After morning hygiene, devotions, extra prayer, and breakfast, my new assistant, Specialist Russell, and I went to pick up an interpreter. A senior medical student that I had worked with before, got up and greeted me. I asked him if he knew about Maharamona. He said that he did. As we left, I explained what I had learned the day before from his boss, Col. Sammy, and my desire to somehow see if we Americans could work that process with the offended Afghan families. We got in my vehicle and headed for the school at Pul-e-Charki, about seven kilometers away.

Leaving a guard with the vehicle, we went to the headmaster's office. School was out of session, but I didn't know where else to go. Fortunately, the "mudir" (headmaster) was in his office. We went in, sat down and began a long conversation. "You heard what happened." I said quietly. "From all I can see, it was an accident." The headmaster replied. "I know. I've been telling the parents of this village to watch their children...you know I have...but some just wouldn't listen. I know it was an accident." He hung his head and sighed. Cultural and linguistic distance aside, I sensed he somehow felt a share of the blame.

I then explained how our entire base was saddened and upset by the incident. How the soldiers had chased them off only to have them run around the backside of the mountain and climb up and over into the impact area. He just shook his head. Looking him in the eye, I got to the point of my visit.

Through my interpreter, I asked if Afghans ever dedicated buildings or rooms to the memories, or in honor of past students. "Yes, sometimes we do that." He affirmed. "So, what if my soldiers wanted to renovate a couple classrooms in memory of the four boys, would that be viewed as a positive expression of sorrow and remembrance?" I asked. "I think it would. What are you thinking?" After two and a half months teaching conversational English in his school, we seemed to have developed a good relationship. "I'm thinking about renovating the double classroom with help from our soldiers and friends back home. Would you help me find local people to do the work?" I asked. "Yes, I know people who can do the work." I told him it would take a couple weeks to get the money together, so we agreed to meet again in two weeks to start the project in memory of the four boys.

Before I left, I asked him if he thought the families would be willing to do "Maharamona" with the soldiers of my military unit at KMTC. He was surprised that I knew of the custom. I told him that Col. Sammy had told me about it. "Give me a week and I will speak with the families." He said. We shook hands and said good-bye.

Later that day, I paid a visit to the commander of Charlie company. Maj. John received me with his Sergeant Major. We discussed the recent tragedy, its impact on his soldiers, as well as the pain and loss experienced by the families. He asked what we could do to help rectify the situation. In addition to Maharamona, I explained to him how local Afghan burial custom included visitation of the bereaved families by neighbors, friends and family. These people would come to grieve with the families, some from a distance. It was the responsibility of the bereaved family to provide food and beverage for all who visited and lodging for those who came from a far. This would put families of lesser means in debt, as they would end up borrowing food from neighbors when their own stores had been exhausted feeding everyone. Hence, a funeral could put a family in a financial hole.

The concept of providing the families with a sheep for Maharamona, plus some money to help with the cost of the burial was outlined. When I asked how we might fund this, the Sergeant Major said his unit would take care of that. When I told Maj. John about the spontaneous donation of money for the families, we came up with the idea of receiving an offering on Christmas Eve that would go toward restoring a classroom in memory of the four boys. The desire of these two leaders to help make these families whole with the funeral expense, and work conciliation through their cultural traditions made me proud to be a part of this unit.

As I left, Maj. John asked me to keep them in the loop, as we probably would try to do the ceremony after the start of the New Year. I thanked them for their compassion. Sgt. Maj. Dean told me to "get the hell out of here and figure this out!" I smiled and said, "Yes, Sergeant Major!" It was the first time I had smiled in a couple of days.

On my way out, I ran in to the battalion commander. I told him of my conversation and developing plan with Charlie company. He listened intently. Then I told him about the spontaneous donation of money from the soldiers and asked if he would approve of a special voluntary offering that would be received at our upcoming Christmas Eve services. He thought a few moments and agreed that would be acceptable, and the money could go toward restoring a classroom in memory of the four boys. I thanked him, affirmed his decision and left. Christmas was just around the corner, and I had another project in the works...one the MP Mess Sergeant had asked me to do.

Chapter 56

When the Church Goes Underground

Word from Chaplain Andy for 2-16-03

When the church goes underground, it's a scary thing for believers in other lands, especially countries without religious freedom.

Several weeks ago, I wrote about the most dangerous church service in the world. I had hoped that things would improve, but they didn't. When a fellow Christian soldier and I contacted the church in the city, we found that, due to heightened security concerns, the growing congregation had decided to split up and meet in several secret locations. Since there are few street signs, we arranged a known rendezvous point and linked up for our zigzag journey through town to their secret location.

After our guide confirmed the location of the service, he led us several blocks away to the gated compound of another non-governmental organization (NGO), where we could safely park our vehicle inside with a guard. We transferred some special cargo into the back of a tiny car and squeezed our bulky armored bodies into their eighteen-year-old coupe.

When our guide assured the gatekeeper that we were safe, another metal gate opened, and we entered. At the entry, we took off our shoes and were greeted by believers from the United Kingdom, Africa, Europe and the United States – there were even several women from Colorado Springs working out of the home we visited.

After we removed our body armor and my comrade carefully placed his machine gun in a safe place (but not far out of reach), we entered the rectangular living room where the service would be held. There was little furniture. Cushions like I have on my bunk, lined the walls with pillows every couple feet. Within a few minutes, the place was packed with over sixty-five expatriate men, women and children who had come to worship.

And worship we did! Many new songs from the UK were played and sung. Scripture was read, prayer was offered, songs were sung, and a British woman gave a sermon on hope.

It was an inspiring time for my comrade and me. I could see tears in his eyes through mine as we heard the testimony of one of the eight Afghan aid workers who was captured and imprisoned by the Taliban for fourteen weeks in 2001. She and her team were eventually rescued by U.S. Special Forces. When she learned who we were, she came up and vigorously shook our hands and thanked us!

At the close of the service, someone asked if there were going to be any Christmas Eve services in town. No one said anything, so I looked at my comrade (one of my company commanders) and he nodded to me. I spoke up and said, "We at KMTC have two services planned, 6 p.m. and 11 p.m. You are all welcome. The password at the gate is 'Chaplain Andy – Christmas Eve Service.'"

Several asked for directions, including teachers of the local international school where most of the children in this congregation attended. They agreed to come and do a special children's program for our soldiers on Christmas Eve. Unfortunately, things would change.

Chapter 57

WWF Smackdown at KMTC

Word from Chaplain Andy...2-23-03

Yes, it's true. I really did it. I must confess. But, first some important background information. It was Sunday, December 22. We were staging our convoy to the orphanage for "Operation Christmas Blessing," when the convoy radio operator called me over. The command element had asked that we delay our departure time by fifteen to thirty minutes.

The reason? A USO Bird (helicopter carrying USO celebrities) was inbound. Most of us weren't all that excited as we had heard that it was just the Jaguars' NFL football team cheerleaders on board. When I asked the identities of known passengers, the radio operator replied, "One cheerleader, two female movie stars, a country and western singer and his guitar player, and a WWF wrester!"

Now that was exciting; a country and western singer and a WWF wrestler! I was sure my sons, would recognize who it was, so I waited to get his autograph and a photo.

As the group stepped off the helicopter landing zone (HLZ), I saw the motley looking crew walking our way. A small group of soldiers gathered at entry control point one (ECP1) to wait for the USO VIPs. Suddenly, there he was. Big, about six-foot, four-inches tall, long black wavy hair – I didn't know who in the world he was. I was wearing my body armor and Santa hat, so my rank (Major) and branch insignia (chaplain's cross) were not visible.

As the big guy stepped through the gate I walked up and said: "Hi, who are you?" He looked down at me and spoke in that fake WWF voice, "I'm Bradshaw, who the f%$k are you!?" I don't know what came over me, but I reared back and slugged the foul-mouthed wrestler in the right shoulder and said: "I'm the battalion chaplain, that's who, and you'll kindly watch your language on my compound!"

He was as surprised as I was. He began to stammer and say, "Oh, sorry sir, I didn't know who you were. I would have never cussed at you. Please forgive me!" I smiled and said, "Just kidding. My sons watch WWF and I was wondering if I could get a picture with you?" He put his hand on my shoulder continuing to mutter apologies as a fellow soldier took a photo. He then thanked me and my soldiers for the sacrifices we made for the

American people.

As we shook hands, so he could meet the next waiting soldier, that same uncontrollable urge came over me (I guess three months in a combat zone will do that to a person), and I reared back and hit him even harder on the same shoulder a second time and said, "But just remember to watch your mouth!" He smiled and said, "Yes, sir!" My convoy team mounted up and went on our important mission.

Wrestler John Bradshaw then spent the next two-hours meeting the other members of our base. He told the Commander; "You sure have some tough soldiers, sir." When the commander asked why he said that, Bradshaw said, "Why your chaplain just decked me twice for cussing!"

So, the word is out. I share this story, in the remote possibility Bradshaw asks for a rematch. My executive officer, Major John, was a former judo competitor. He has agreed to tag team-wrestling match with me against Bradshaw and a wrestler of his choice, in exchange for $500,000 for Afghan orphans – and my medical expenses! The moral? Watch your mouth around us Special Forces Chaplains.

PS The events in the above story are true. The names have been left the same to embarrass the guilty!

Chapter 58

Operation Christmas Blessing

After Action Report

On Sunday, December 22, Command Sgt. Maj. Al and I led a convoy of vehicles guarding a five-ton cargo truck loaded with precious cargo to the Allahuddin Orphanage in Kabul, Afghanistan.

The genesis of this mission came one day when I was speaking with our mess sergeants (head cooks).

They told me that they had inherited from the previous unit, an excess stock of canned goods, powdered milk, juice concentrate and literally a ton of other foodstuffs. This food was good now, but would eventually go bad, if not consumed before its expiration date. They felt it was morally wrong to allow good food to spoil with so many people around us starving. Several times during the fall they would put boxes of food by my chapel door to take to the local school where we taught weekly classes of English conversation. Taking several boxes each week didn't even make a dent, as excess stock continued to grow, and the huge storage containers began to fill.

Then I received a letter from the parents of one of our soldiers whose work took him out and about to various undisclosed locations. His mom and dad had read about two Orphanages in Kabul full of needy children. The article described the estimated one million Afghan children who had been orphaned over the past years of fighting and how the initial aid received immediately after the fall of the Taliban had dwindled dangerously as winter approached. They asked me to verify the need since their son could not. They wanted to help and asked for confirmation of the need.

After reading the article, I thought how good it would be if we could donate our excess food to these orphanages as a base-wide project. After several failed attempts at locating these orphanages, we finally made contact through Mary MacMakin, the American director of an Afghan aid organization, Physiotherapy and Rehabilitation Society of Afghanistan (PARSA), who knew exactly where the orphanages were. When Mary took us to visit the orphanage, the director and staff were more than eager to receive our food donation. Regulations required that the U.S. Army give the
donation through a recognized national NGO who would assume liability for the food, specifically. Mary agreed to accept the donation and liability, but needed

help delivering the food items. We told her we would handle that.

The commander gave the approval, the cooks became excited, the Plans and Operations section got working, and volunteers were solicited. In a few short days, "Operation Christmas Blessing" (the CONOP name) underwent staff review (just like any military operation), a route recon was completed (we used a GPS to get exact grid coordinates in case we needed reinforcement, rescue or close air support) and volunteers were solicited for this important mission. Following our Sunday morning chapel services, the convoy assembled. As the truck was loaded – thank God for forklifts – I prayed that our convoy would make it through the congested downtown area through which we had to pass. Several recent terrorist attacks against U.S. and coalition forces, made this more than a routine food delivery. Over twenty heavily armed soldiers boarded their vehicles for the estimated forty-five-minute trip to the orphanage. Excitement was high, but the sense of potential danger was real, as the team was briefed.

Though delayed twenty-minutes by an unexpected USO visit by several U.S. celebrities, we arrived on time as the orphanage gates opened wide for our truck loaded with precious cargo. The orphanage staff greeted us, director, doctor and other administrative assistants. When asked where to off-load, the director asked if we would wait until an Afghan national TV crew arrived. We agreed, completed our greeting with the staff, and turned our attention to the children. They were the reason we were there. Our psychological operations (PSYOPS) team began distributing backpacks with school supplies and other soldiers distributed candy as they talked and played with the children. A group of young girls came out dressed in traditional costumes to sing folk songs. They sounded good and were cute as could be.

A taxi suddenly dove up and several important-looking gentlemen got out. They were introduced by the orphanage director as the national ministers of education and social services. After exchanging greetings, I explained (through my interpreter) what we had brought and why; that we had come to celebrate our Christmas, by giving what we could to the orphans of Afghanistan. They, too, asked that we wait for the TV crew before unloading our Christmas gift. Once again, we waited. By now the orphanage courtyard was filled with approximately seven-hundred-fifty of its nine-hundred residents. Only the infants were kept indoors, but we could see them in the arms of veiled female attendants looking out the widows of the two-story dormitories that surrounded the courtyard. From our collective fatherly experience, we estimated that the children present ranged in ages from two to eight-years-old.

The national Director of Orphanages told us that there were 2000 children in two Kabul orphanages, nine hundred in the facility we were visiting and eleven hundred at another facility. The current number of registered orphans was 50,000 with a nation-wide estimate of one million. Sadly, current laws forbade the adoption of Afghan children to foreigners (read "Non-

Muslims"). Children placed in these government-run orphanages would stay until they were old enough to leave and find a job. That disappointed some soldiers who had come, hoping to adopt a needy child.

Finally, Command Sgt. Maj. Al came to me and told me that we would have to unload by 3:00 p.m. Daylight was running out and we needed to be back before nightfall." At 3:00 p.m., I looked out at the group of fifteen soldiers playing with the children and couldn't bring myself to pull them away. For most, it was the first time in three months that they had played with a child, and they had come expressly to do just that.

Many, like me, were fathers missing their children this holiday season, and this visit was assuaging the pain we felt in our hearts as Christmas away from home loomed.

So, I did something very un-officer and un-gentlemanly-like. I jumped into the back of the five-ton truck and began unloading large cans of fruit, vegetables and pudding (vanilla, butterscotch and chocolate!). I could tell it surprised the Afghan ministers, as they figured that I was the senior officer in charge and diplomatic liaison – and they were right. But just then my soldiers needed a few more minutes playing time with the children, so I did what I believe Jesus would have done, and I got my hands dirty. As I passed the huge cans off the back of the truck, suddenly, the minister of education stepped forward, took a can and placed it on the growing pile. It took about forty-five-minutes to unload the estimated 5,800 pounds of canned food, plus two-dozen cases of other food stuffs.

In addition, we unloaded forty boxes of clothing, toys and school supplies donated by family, friends, co-workers, church and civic groups across America that had accumulated in section of the KMTC warehouse. That's over three tons of humanitarian aid. It was good food that would have gone to waste, if it wasn't for the wise stewardship of the cooks of the Massachusetts Army National Guard!

By 4:00 p.m., we had to call it quits and say good-bye to the staff and children of Allahuddin orphanage. We got back into convoy formation, soldiers locked and loaded their weapons, and we headed back to KMTC. The trip back seemed to go much quicker, probably because we were traveling a lot lighter – over three-tons lighter in terms of food, clothing, toys and school supplies – but even lighter and happier in spirit because we had taken the time to share a few moments with the orphans of Afghanistan and those who care for them -- all in the spirit of Christmas. When we got back, everyone who accompanied the convoy came up and shook my hand, thanking me for the opportunity to visit the orphanage. Some had tears in their eyes and could only nod their head confirming that it was a worthwhile trip.

Do pray for the orphans of Afghanistan...and pray for another convoy that is being planned, this one laden with de-worming medicine, disposable diapers, vitamins, toothbrushes and toothpaste, doctors, a dentist and medics for a medical mission to that same orphanage.

Looking back, we all agreed that "Operation Christmas Blessing" was a huge success. Why? Because we did it in honor of Jesus' birthday…and for the orphaned children of Afghanistan!

*CONOP stands for "contingency operation." To conduct any operation or "mission," a plan must be drafted and approved by the commander to be staffed, supplied and executed. Over the course of my tour, I submitted 8-10 CONOPS for various missions completed "outside the wire" of KMTC.

Chapter 59

Christmas Eve at KMTC

Word from Chaplain Andy...3 March 03

Christmas Eve at KMTC was a very special event. To make this an inspiring time for our soldiers, we tried to bring in a children's choir from the local private expatriate Christian school. We also organized the KMTC multinational choir, made up of U.S. and French soldiers. We practiced our songs by caroling on the compound two nights before Christmas.

At the last minute, due to increased security concerns, the children's choir backed out. I felt bad for our soldiers who were so looking forward to hearing the children sing, besides, we were the safest place to be in Kabul on Christmas Eve. But God had other plans.

He wanted one of the eight Afghan expatriate aid workers from Shelter Now, International (SNI) taken hostage by the Taliban last year, to come instead and share her story of survival. Silke and seven coworkers were captured and held for fourteen weeks by the Taliban. They were finally rescued by U.S. Special Forces soldiers in November 2001.

Silke wanted to come and say thank-you, to the U.S. Special Forces for their rescue. At 5:50 p.m., few people had shown up at our conference room filled with eighty-seven chairs. The room was beautifully adorned with Christmas decorations sent by my family. By 5:55 p.m., the conference room was packed, and we scrambled for more chairs. There were French, German, Spanish, and Dutch soldiers; State Department and OGA (other governmental agencies – including CIA) personnel, heating contractors, and the Afghan commanding general of KMTC, General Assifi.

When I had the Afghan General stand, he told us that it was his third Christmas celebration. His first two were as a young exchange artillery officer at Fort Sill, Oklahoma thirty-years ago. He said he wanted to see how much our Christmas celebration had changed. Plus, he "wanted to hear Chaplain Andy preach."

The KMTC choir processed in with candles singing, Adeste Fidelis (O Come All Ye Faithful, in Latin). We lit the Christ Candle of the Advent Wreath, read the Gospel accounts of Christ's birth in Matthew and Luke and sang traditional Christmas carols. After the reading of "The True Meaning of Christmas," by Doc Enz, there wasn't a dry eye in the place. We received a special offering for the renovation of a local school, heard the story of the Afghan aid workers' rescue, and I brought a message entitled, "I'll Be Home for Christmas."

We closed the service singing "Silent Night" with candles, the same way we did in my home church (and with my home church candles!), but we sang it in English, French and Spanish!

The results were beyond expectations: In all over 110 people attended the 6 o'clock service. Another twenty gathered at 11:00 p.m. The offering came to over $1100 and my Special Forces Team guys held the visiting Afghan aid worker hostage for
ninety-minutes, asking her questions about her captivity and rescue.

When I asked the Afghan general about the service he said: "I liked it very much." Do pray for this man who has heard the Gospel as a young officer and now as a mature General, and for all who came on Christmas Eve. Pray for eternal results to spring from Christmas Eve at KMTC!

Chapter 60

Christmas Eve at KMTC - Postscript

-----Original Message-----
From: "Kim Doyle"
To: Chaplain Andy
Subject: Wanting to come to your Christmas Eve service in Kabul - please contact
Date: Mon, 23 Dec 2002 15:57:32 +0430

Dear Andy,

We met you at the church service in Kulle Fattulah last Friday. Three of us are very interested in coming to your Christmas Eve service. Our office is having a Christmas party for our staff on Christmas Eve afternoon, so we wouldn't be free until 5:00 or so. Could you please call us with directions????? We will not be able to check our email again before Christmas. We have a car and so can drive there ourselves. We understand that folks from IAM do not have permission to go, but we still do. If you want, we can teach your guys one of the songs that the 8 prisoners wrote when in prison last year. It's not very 'Christmassy' per say, but we are sure they will like it. Sorry, none of us plays the keyboard.

Silke and Kim 070-280-XXX Shelter Now

-----Original Message-----
From: Andy Meverden
Sent: Monday, December 23, 2002 4:32 PM
To: kimdoyle
Subject: Re: Wanting to come to your Christmas Eve service in Kabul - please contact

I'll try to call. Go East on Jalalabad Road past Camp Warehouse (on Right), KMTC is next Military Entrance/Gate on Left. There are two howitzers (cannons on wheels) at entry. Afghan soldiers and U.S. MPs at Gate. Tell them you are here for the 1800 Christmas Eve Service as a guest of "Chaplain Andy". Hope you make it. If you come early, you can eat with us.

Chaplain Andy KMTC ☺

-----Original Message-----
From: "Kim Doyle"
To: Chaplain Andy
Subject: Thank You & Happy New Year! Dear Chaplain Andy,

Hello, Hello, Hello. And happy new years to you and your troops there. Silke and I are just popping in to say thanks sooooooooooooooooooooooooooooooooo much for the wonderful evening on Christmas Eve. It was truly an evening to remember for all 4 of us who came. We are glad that we pursued coming. Silke, especially wants to say thanks for opportunity to share!! And all of us appreciated the warm welcome. And oh, the gifts. We were so blessed. The next day we divided all the boxes up and took them to some of our teammates and others. We had fun eating and giving out what you gave us. On the way back into town that night we got stopped a lot at alllllllll of the checkpoints. We gave the Afghans at the checkpoints cookies (that you'd given us) and gave out many, many Christmas blessings, saying "this is our Eid" etc., etc. It was sooooooo fun. I think next year we will also get a whole load of cookies and drive around and do it again. HA.

It was refreshing to see someone with a real heart for the Lord and a message of Evangelism at such an occasion. May the Lord give you a fruitful season here in Afghanistan.

Kim & Silke Shelter Now

Chapter 61

Christmas Day Confession

My assistant, Spec. JJ, requested, and was granted a four-day leave for Germany. I thought I could get by without him for a few days, hoping it would help him out of his growing winter funk. We drove to Bagram Air Base and got him to the military air terminal. He signed in and was told he would-be put-on stand-by for the next flight to Ramstein. I helped him lug his stuff to the tent where he could camp out until he was called.

Deciding to drop by the Base Exchange (BX) on my way out to look for Lectric Shave, I parked near the combined joint special operations task force (CJSOTF). I started to walk across the gravel parking lot, when I heard my name called by a familiar voice. Looking in the direction of the voice, I was shocked to see the Task Force 180 senior chaplain Rogers with the U.S. Army Chief of Chaplains, G.T. Gunhus and another chaplain. We approached and shook hands all around. I noticed that the chaplain general's aide was caring a shoulder bag. "Chaplain Andy, tell Chaplain Gunhus one significant thing that you've done recently."

Well that was easy. "Well, sir, we recently had four Afghan boys tragically killed in a live-fire training accident. My soldiers were so distraught that we decided to receive an offering at our Christmas Eve service last night. Over $1,100 came in and we're planning to restore a classroom in their memory in the school where I've been teaching ESL." Chaplain Gunhus glanced over at Chaplain Rick and back to me. Without a word, the chaplain assisting him handed him a token in the shape of the Pentagon, which he passed to me. "Keep up the good work, Chaplain Andy. May God bless and sustain you as you care for our Soldiers." It was less than a five-minutes exchange, but little did I realize that I had just confessed to two breeches of operational policy. I wouldn't learn about it for two weeks.

Encouraged by the "divine appointment," I stopped by the small base exchange only to be disappointed again at not being able to find any Lectric Shave for my electric razor. I got back into my mini convoy and headed home to KMTC. I was beat from the late-night activities and early rising on Christmas Day, but I still had Santa duties to complete.

My wife and children wanted to do something special for my soldiers, so they sent a large box containing individual bags of Doritos, shiny pencils and cellophane Christmas stockings. In transit, the bags of Doritos broke, and their contents smashed. Still tasty, I poured the crumbs into several large plastic bags and set them aside. With the remaining items, I filled the stockings with pencils and other goodies that I had accumulated and set out to deliver them to the members of our base.

Wearing a Santa hat, most of the Soldiers accepted the stocking gifts with a smile. Some just waved me off and others suggested that I give them to local children, instead. I tried to explain that Christmas held no meaning here in Afghanistan, and, as a result, some caved in and took a stocking. After about two hours of deliveries, I returned to my chapel area, exhausted. The events of the past couple weeks were taking a physical and emotional toll. As I thought about New Year's Eve, I prayed that it would be an uneventful, boring night. Again, I would be proven wrong.

I went out to check the plastic fuel can that fed the diesel potbelly stove we had scrounged out of the junk yard at Bagram Air Base. Diesel was in short supply, so I tightened the drip valve to slow fuel consumption. Anticipating a cold night, I stuffed my sleeping bag with an extra poncho liner and changed into a sweat suit with hood. Part way thru my nighttime prayers, I fell asleep.

Chapter 62

Cat Eye for a Glass Eye

Word from Chaplain Andy for Feb. 9, 2003

On Christmas day, 2002, several Afghan children were playing with some deadly UXO – that's the Army acronym for "unexploded ordinance." In addition to the estimated ten-million landmines emplaced over the previous twenty-five years, primarily by the Soviets, there is an unimaginable amount of unexploded tank and artillery shells, rockets, aerial bombs and other types of military and home- made explosives stockpiled and laying around. Some munitions are duds; but many are still live and deadly.

These children were playing with some UXO that suddenly exploded. It is believed that a rock became a secondary missile and hit a four-year-old boy in the eye. Pediatric ophthalmologists are in short supply in Afghanistan, but we happen to have a world-class pediatric ophthalmologist and medical school professor from Tennessee as our head surgeon. We also have as one of our medics, the chief operating officer, and surgical eye tech of one of the world's largest eye banks, located in Denver. They were called in to do eye surgery on the injured four-year-old.

It became obvious in the first few minutes of examination that the child's eye could not be saved. But, to prevent the child's eye socket from shrinking and his face collapsing on that side – like the infamous Mullah Omar some of our ODAs have been hunting – the Doctor needed a prosthetic device, a "glass eye," to fill the void and maintain symmetry of the child's face.

Glass eyes also are in short supply, especially one the proper size for a four-year-old. Doc ENZ said to his eye tech, "Does anyone have a marble?" A marble? U.S. soldiers bring many things for recreation, blow guns, Game Boys, playing cards, Scrabble, but not marbles! Another soldier nearby heard the request and said, "Wait, my mother sent me some marbles for Afghan school children. I put them in the chapel distribution box. Let me see if I can find them."

After searching through the many boxes and bags of donations pilled in the back of the chapel area, he found the bag of marbles from his mom. He brought them to the doctor who measured one and found it to be just the right size. They sterilized it and carefully placed one chosen marble into the eye sack and closed the wound.

Because of this surgery, this child will have the opportunity of one day having an appropriate prosthetic eye—not to mention, not having to look like the infamous Taliban leader, Mullah Omar.

God knew that that child would need this surgery, so he sent with us one of the best pediatric ophthalmologist teams available. I believe that he did it for this child and many other people who have sustained eye injuries since we have come. A soldier's mother sent the marbles, hoping that they would bring joy to some poverty-stricken Afghan child. Little did she know that God directed her to send Christmas marbles for your world-class pediatric ophthalmologic surgery team.

Chapter 63

Splitting Headache...and the Six Days of Christmas

"On the second day of Christmas..." I woke up with a splitting headache. Having to pee like crazy, I made a stop at the nearby porta-potty, before checking to see if there was any water at the shower point. Now that winter was in full swing, frozen pipes were common. Though some of our water lines were buried, not all the line was protected underground. Fortunately, I was able to get a less than freezing shower before breakfast. The longer I stayed in the outside air, the less my head hurt. By the time breakfast was over, I was feeling pretty good. I thought about dropping by the medical clinic to see the Docs, but I was too busy. I felt better and, had larger concerns. I needed to see about the families of the dead boys and needed to meet with a local contractor to help get the classroom renovation started.

"On the third day of Christmas..." My thoughts went something like this. *"Man, my head sure aches again! And the skin on my face is so flush. Once I get into the fresh air, I get to feeling better quick."*

"On the fourth day of Christmas..." The issue continued. *"Something's not right. I must be coming down with something, like a flu bug or a virus. I'll feel better once I get moving."*

"On the fifth day of Christmas..." The problem worsened. *"It must be the cold weather. I froze last night and could hardly get out of my sleeping bag to pee in the Gatorade bottle. Man, I wish that headache would go away. Must be the cumulative effects of all that dust we inhale. I better stop by the clinic to get some Advil or Tylenol."*

"On the sixth day of Christmas..." I didn't wake up in my bunk as usual. "Gee, Doc, how did I get here? I don't remember walking over...man, my head hurts like crazy. It's been hurting since Christmas Day." Doc Enz looked over to SSG Dean and told him to go check out my diesel heater. "We're taking you to the ISAF hospital for an x-ray," he said. They wrapped me in a blanket and put me in a vehicle for the short trip to Camp Warehouse. There the ISAF emergency department personnel checked me out, confirmed probable carbon monoxide poisoning and sent me back to KMTC for rest.

Doc Enz was still concerned as my pulse oxygen saturation remained unusually low. Back in the battalion aid station, they tried to put me on oxygen, but the small tank and mask system didn't seem to work well. I was very groggy and just wanted to sleep but could hear their conversation about getting me to the combat support hospital in Bagram. A call was made for aerial medical evacuation (MEDEVAC), but the weather was too bad for a non-emergency flight. The decision was made to keep me under observation until the next morning when the logistics convoy was scheduled. I asked if I could go lay down, but the good doctor wanted to keep an eye on me. A medic arranged a bunk for me in the rear of the aid station and I laid down. Within seconds, I was fast asleep.

About noon, a medic dropped by to see how I was doing. He told me to get some lunch and drink plenty of liquids. I ate a peanut butter and jelly sandwich and returned to the aid station to sleep. I woke up around supper time and decided I'd stay in my own bunk. When I got there, the diesel stove had been torn out and diesel fuel had spilled over a large portion of the chapel carpet. With the overpowering fumes and lack of heat, I headed back to the medical clinic. When I told the Doc what I tried to do and what I found, he told me that I'd be spending the night in the clinic. When I asked where, one of the medics dragged a metal bunk between the Doc and Dentist's bunks and was told, "There!"

That night I slept between two of the finest, most compassionate medical professionals I'd ever meet. Only later did I learn that they took shifts through the night watching me to make sure I didn't stop breathing. I slept hard…didn't even get up to pee, and the next morning, they wrapped me in a sleeping bag and put me in the back of a military police HUMVEE along with a medic for a convoy to Bagram Airfield. There I was checked into the combat support hospital, examined, given some inhalation therapy and eventually put into a bed in the intermediate care ward (ICW) along with three U.S. personnel, six Afghan males and a four-year-old boy I had watched our ophthalmologist operate on just a few days before. When I checked my watch, I realized it was December 31 – I would be spending my Afghan New Year's Eve 2002 in a combat support hospital.

Chapter 64

New Year's Eve 2002

Word from Chaplain Andy - Feb. 23, 2003

New Year's Eve 2002 wasn't what I expected. I hoped for a slow evening, maybe watching a few celebratory illumination rounds fired by our mortar crew along with a glass of sparkling cider. Instead, I was in the Intermediate Care Ward (ICW) of the 48th Combat Support Hospital (CSH) at another base undergoing treatment for carbon monoxide poisoning.

The diesel pot-belly stove in my building malfunctioned and I almost died of asphyxiation a couple days prior. In the middle of the night, on his way to the chemical toilets, the battalion surgeon, noticed smoke coming out of the chapel area. He called nearby soldiers and they found me on my bunk unresponsive and pulled me into the fresh air. The medics subsequently took me to the nearby German hospital for oxygen and chest x-rays. Afterwards, I was returned to my base for bed rest, but my medical team wasn't satisfied. They kept me in their quarters overnight, sleeping in a bunk between the senior surgeon and the dentist.

The next day they bundled me up and drove me to the 48th CSH at Bagram Airfield. After x-rays and respiratory treatment, I was taken to the ICW. There were three U.S. soldiers, including me, six Afghan men and a four-year-old Afghan boy. What I saw was simultaneously heart-warming and heart-rending.

One man just had his foot amputated after stepping on a landmine. He was depressed and spoke little at first. Next to him was a younger man with his right arm in suspension. He had lost several fingers and his friend next to him had lost his nose when the vehicle they were traveling in hit an antitank mine, killing two other occupants with them. Another, more talkative man had his right foot in traction after taking two bullets fired by an Al Qaeda terrorist. He had a section of bone removed from his hip and grafted into his shattered ankle. The young man next to me had been injured by a rocket-propelled grenade and had lost motion and feeling in his left arm and hand. Across, to my right were two beds pushed together. Another older man with his foot in traction was sleeping next to the four-year-old boy. This was the child that our Surgeon had previously attended, removing his damaged eye and fitting it with the sterilized marble that a soldier's mother had sent. The little boy had earlier looked at the man, who spoke his dialect and asked, "Are you my uncle?" The compassionate man smiled at the maimed young child and said, "Yes, I am." Through the combined care of the professional medical staff and the love of his surrogate "Afghan uncle," little Sahib, was recovering quickly. He came over to my bed and shook my hand, giving me a big, one-eyed smile. All spoke only Pashtu, the first dialect I started to learn prior to coming to Afghanistan. I was able to greet them and, after the ward interpreter left, help the nursing staff with the patients.

Before lights out, I walked over to each one, took their hand and prayed for them—they didn't know what I was saying, because I was praying in English, but they knew that I was an Army chaplain -- because I told them in Pashtu. I sensed they appreciated my blessing and concern.

At midnight, eighty-one illumination rounds were fired from mortars positioned around the base perimeter; one for each of the U.S. servicemen killed so far in Afghanistan. No, it wasn't what I expected, but it was a gratifying and memorable way for your pastor to celebrate New Year's Eve 2002!

Chapter 65

Report to the Embassy

A runner from the Operations Center told me to report to the new Operations Officer, Major Bill. When I asked Bill what was up, he said that there was a message for me to report to Major General Karl Eikenberry in the Office of Military Cooperation at the U.S. Embassy. When I asked the reason for the appearance (I had yet to make it to Bagram to see the TF-180 senior chaplain and was a bit skittish), no specific reason was given, except that it had something to do with the death of the four boys from Pul-e-Charki. Time and date of my appointment, noted, I went to see my buddy, Operations Sergeant Major, Dan. He, too, had no idea why I was being called in but told me not to worry. I still did.

I drove with my assistant to the now familiar U.S. Embassy. After identifying myself to the Marine Guard, I was told to wait for my escort. I looked around at the lobby, noting the damage caused during the recent Taliban regime's occupation. The thick security glass protecting the Marine reception cage was damaged from gunfire. Some bullets almost penetrated, causing spider web-style fractures emanating from the point of impact at several places. I tried to imagine whether this resulted from an actual firefight, or just vandals ransacking our abandoned embassy. Given the size and intimidating presence of the US Marines there now, I suspected it was probably the latter.

"Chaplain, your escort is here. Please enter through the door on your right." I nodded thankfully to the Marine, as the security door buzzed opened. A man in civilian clothes motioned me to enter, shook my hand and asked me to follow him up a white stone stairway. The entire facility was made of cut stone, metal and tempered glass. As we climbed, I wondered if there was any wood used anywhere besides furniture. Entering a second security door, we passed through a hall with high windows to a large office.

Inside were three men in Army uniform, MG Karl Eikenberry, his deputy, LTC Allen, and an Army major I had never met. A glance to his collar, and I saw that he was a staff judge advocate – a JAG – an Army lawyer. "What trouble am I in now?" I wondered. After we shook hands, the general said, "Chaplain, take a seat. I was back in the United States over the holidays, and I read the news reports about the training accident that took the lives of the four Afghan boys. They paint us in a very negative light. What can you tell me about what happened, and what has been done to help rectify the situation? When I asked who our man on the ground was, your name came up. I understand you've been teaching conversational English at the local school where the boys attended. Brief me."

So that was it. Somebody higher up, the U.S. Ambassador to Afghanistan, or perhaps people further up the chain of command, were concerned about the families of the boys injured and killed. Immediately, I was encouraged. Senior leaders were concerned about what happened and what had been done. Taking a deep breath, I started in. Quickly I described my limited second-hand knowledge of what occurred from those on the scene, but went into detail with my research into Afghan customs and traditions in dealing with accidental deaths, etc. When asked if anyone from the battalion had spoken directly with the families, I explained how my recommendation to make a command visit prior to burial was not accepted, but how I started working behind the scenes through the headmaster of the Pul-e- Charki school to remodel a room in memory of the four boys with funds from a special Christmas Eve offering, and other donated U.S. church funds.

Next, I explained the Afghan conciliation ritual called "Maharamona," and how I thought we should give a mature sheep to the families, for each boy killed and seriously injured. I then got sidetracked on the importance of entering a culture as a learner, and not try to impose Western values in matters of the heart...I kind of lost my train of thought... "Focus chaplain, focus!" Maj. Gen. Eikenberry exhorted when I took an anthropological rabbit trail. "What is your recommendation on how to resolve this situation?" End state. That's what he wanted. How could we effect some sort of culturally appropriate conciliation with the victims of this unfortunate, unintended tragedy?

I started down a list of what I thought could and should be done. "I recommend that we meet with each family that lost a son and give them a sheep along with $500 to them and a smaller sheep to the family whose son was seriously injured. The sheep is a culturally acceptable way of compensating them for their son's loss, as they have no 'social security' for their old age. Sons typically care for their parents; no son, so security." When I mentioned the sheep, the general looked over to the JAG. The JAG leaned forward and spoke quietly into the general's ear. Straightening up, Maj. Gen. Eikenberry said, "The U.S. Army doesn't do sheep."

I glanced over to his deputy, the Lieutenant Colonel, himself a Special Forces officer. With low, gentle hand motions, he mouthed "It's okay." Advising me not to push the issue with the JAG present. I sure hoped the Deputy knew what he was signaling. I believed that we needed to follow Afghan custom, but I also knew I only had the ability to recommend – the decision had to be made by the chain-of-command.

The general then queried, "What's the $500 for – indemnity?" "No. Courtesy." I replied. "Afghan custom dictated that each bereaved family receives mourning members of their families and friends. Social custom requires that these visiting mourners be given hospitality; food, drink, lodging, depending on how far they come. Initially, they will use the food they have. When that runs out, they borrow from neighbors, and friends, or local shopkeepers, who they must pay back. This can easily put a family into a financial hole. On top of that were the burial expenses; plot, grave. It's mostly funeral expenses," I said.

"What else?" General Eikenberry asked. "Well, I think there should be some sort of compensation made to the families for the accidental death." Was my reply. "Kind of like a death gratuity?" He asked. "Whatever the legal term, it would be like an accidental death insurance policy payment." I suggested. The JAG remained silent. I felt uneasy in his presence.

"What else?" He continued. "Well, given the impact on the local area, the village and school, I recommend the restoration of the Pul-e-Charki school we've been teaching at, the sinking of a well, building of a wall with a gate, and a Medical Civil Action Program (MEDCAP) mobile clinic, to bring health care to the village. I believe that this incident is so significant, and has garnered such negative press, that the way we handle this will have strategic impact on the future of U.S.-Afghan military relations..."

The general raised his hand to cut me off. "Chaplain, my dad taught me long ago that once you have made the sale, shut up." I was dumbfounded, if not confused. "What do you mean?" I asked. "Lt. Gen. Daniel McNeil, commanding general of Task Force 180, has given us a blank check to make this right. You will work with the Civil Affairs people at the combined joint civil-military operations task force (CJCMOTF), and your battalion, to carry out all these things you have outlined. I ask that you keep me updated on the various aspects of the project, especially when you have these conciliation meetings with the Afghan families affected, so I can participate, as able."

You could have knocked me over with a feather! "One more thing, sir." I added. "What's that, chaplain." He replied. "Well, sir, I jumped the gun on the school restoration project, and, using privately donated funds, already started the renovation of a double classroom in memory of the four boys. We also received an offering on Christmas Eve of $1,100 for this purpose, and I didn't know that I needed Lt. Gen. McNeil's authorization. I thought battalion commander approval sufficed – I was wrong. If you could put in a good word for me with Chaplain Rodgers at TF180, I'd really appreciate it." The general nodded and said he would have a talk with the chaplain.

We shook hands all around and I departed. I left somewhat incredulous at what had just transpired – "a blank check!" Now that female schoolteacher at Pul-e-Charki might get her wish, after all. Still, I wondered how my visit with the TF180 chaplain would go in a couple days. I sure hoped Maj. Gen. Eikenberry would see him before then. My new assistant, "Piper13," was anxious to get back to the compound, as it was getting dark. I got behind the wheel, he locked and loaded, and we exited the Marine checkpoint. Our conversation back was interesting, to say the least.

Chapter 66

The Loose Canon of Kabul

A couple weeks after the excitement of the events prior to Christmas, and my near miss with carbon monoxide, I received a short email from the Task Force180 command chaplain. He said he needed to see me in his office as soon as possible. Checking with the combined joint special operations task force (CJSOTF) chaplain, I gathered that Chaplain Rogers was upset with me over my actions surrounding the death of the four Afghan boys. With that understanding, I sent him an email asking if he needed more info on my activities. His reply was curt: "No more info needed. Get here as soon as you can." I wrote back to ask if I could see him the next logistics convoy the following week. His reply was even more curt: "Yes." Unsure as to his source of heartburn, I prayed that God would get me through whatever I had done to cause the problem.

Feeling better, but still under my 9:00 p.m. daily curfew, I let the convoy commanders know that I needed to get back and asked him not to leave without me. I gave him my personal FM radio frequency and headed off to the TF180 chaplain's office. He was at a meeting when I arrived, so I sat outside his office, like a schoolboy awaiting the principal, fidgeting for about forty-five minutes.

When he arrived, Chaplain Rick motioned for me to follow him into his office. Closing the door, he directed me to sit. I quietly sat in a white molded plastic chair and waited for him to speak. Without formalities or small talk, he got right to the point.

"Have you read the Field Standard Operating Procedures (FSOP) on field offerings in Afghanistan?" He asked. "No sir, I never saw a copy, but I secured authorization from my battalion commander, prior to receiving it on Christmas Eve," I replied. He picked up a thick stack of stapled papers and said, "It says that all chapel offerings need to be approved by the three-star commander." "I didn't know that," was my reply. "And did you know that you also broke army regulations by conducting illegal contracting, in your renovations of the school?" "No sir," I replied. "I figured since it was privately donated funds, with most of it coming from donors in the U.S., that would not be a concern." I was sunk.

Suddenly I realized that I had confessed both breaches of FSOP in front of him to the Army Chief of Chaplains, two weeks prior on Christmas Day! What an idiot I was. Not only did I not follow FSOP, but I even reported it first-hand. Then came the final blow.

"Further, when I checked your check-in and checkout times from the hospital, you were in just shy of twenty-four hours. Your complaint at not seeing the hospital chaplain during your stay with us was exaggerated. Next time, you might think twice before you drop a dime on a ministry colleague." Strike three – I didn't see *that* coming. Having visited the combat support hospital (CSH) almost weekly the previous three months, I had never run into its assigned chaplain. In fact, I had heard repeatedly from hospital staff that they saw me more than their assigned chaplain. I guess I thought I was simply providing important feedback to senor chaplain. It was clearly not taken that way.

I was wrong. Guilty as charged, mostly due to ignorance, partly due to wrong assumptions at the appropriate availability of another ministry colleague, and the way I approached giving my feedback. I nodded my head and apologized for my ignorance and presumption.

Chaplain Rogers sat down. "Sounds like you properly safeguarded and accounted for the chapel offering. Your heart was in the right place. I recommend you get some training in Civil Affairs before you decide to start any more remodeling projects." "Yes sir," was my reply.

Then he seemed to soften. He sighed and said, "You know the difference between you and me—our ministries?" By now I was too afraid to venture a guess. He continued, "Everything I say, do, or write is scrutinized by lawyers, but you are out in the field doing ministry." With a wry smile he said, "Next time you do something creative or on the edge, don't get caught!" I heaved a sigh of relief. For a while I thought I might be sent home – in shame. From the turn of the counseling session, it looked like I might be given another chance.

"Come with me," he said as he rose his chair. We walked to an adjacent room, just a bit larger than a closet. It was waist-high full of boxes of…care packages! "Take what you can carry, but don't take the last item." He smiled, like old St Nick, telling a young boy to choose his own Christmas presents.

I gathered some electronic gear, batteries and other high-end stuff to take back. He had another meeting to attend, so we shook hands and said good-bye. I left, realizing that I had just had my wrists duly slapped, and subsequently received a pat on my back for effort and creatively. As he walked out, he asked, "Do you know a Lt. Col. Randy Hurtt with Civil Affairs?" Caught by surprise, I had to stop and think. "Colonel Randy…I don't think so." "Well, he said he knew you back when you were enlisted." With that he left. Could it be my old friend Randy Hurtt? Last time I saw him, he was a Captain and I was a Specialist Five…but that was over twenty-five years ago.

Chapter 67

Civil Affairs 101

I was relieved by what had just transpired. Not only had I been admonished, corrected, affirmed, and supplied in the same session, I was informed that an old Army buddy might be in country. When I got back to my office at KMTC, I sent out a personal email to my old friend, Randy. Within a couple hours, I received a startling reply.

As it turned out, Captain Randy was, indeed, now "Lt. Col. Randy," and a senior reserve officer with the U.S. Army Civil Affairs (CA). He had recently arrived at Bagram. As the senior civil affairs officer, he sat on the general staff of the Task Force 180 command, next to the Task Force 180 chaplain. Himself, a solid Christian, he immediately involved himself in the chapel program at Bagram.

As it turned out, when Chaplain Rogers mentioned an issue with a Guard chaplain down range named Andy, this senior Civil Affairs officer queried, "Chaplain Andy Meverden?" Chaplain Jim replied, "Why yes, do you know him?" "I've known Andy since he was a language instructor at the Defense Language Institute in Monterey, and later supported him as a missionary in Portugal. Andy's a good guy!"

I had no idea that God had already placed an advocate on my behalf on the Task Force 180 command staff. He contacted me by email to let me know he was in country. We agreed to get together as soon as circumstances would allow. Not only was Randy instrumental in helping me through my encounter with the Task Force 180 chaplain, he would soon be training our unit...and me in the fine art and fundamentals of U.S. Army Civil Affairs – something that would come in handy.

Armed with Lt. Col. Randy's email, we set up our first meeting during my next trip to Bagram. After a big hug and time catching up on personal and family issues, I briefed him on our tragedy, and what we were planning to do. Given the seriousness of the incident, and the wide range of humanitarian projects our unit was involved in, he recommended a "teach and train" visit to get us on the right path in Civil Affairs.

Coordinating with our battalion operations and lone civil affairs officer, Maj. Rob (another member of the platoon of majors), we scheduled a visit to KMTC for the following week. With key command team present, we got smart with a Civil Affairs 101 briefing that clarified a lot of confusing issues. As it turned out, rather than limit our operations, this training facilitated and enhanced our future medical and humanitarian projects. With everyone on the same page, we had a clearer idea of what we could do and how to do it – according to regulations!

Chapter 68

Emergency Buddy Aid

Word from Chaplain Andy...4-06-03

"Chaplain, I need to see you. I've got to get some things squared away before we move out. I'll drop by this evening." We had spoken previously about an Emergency Buddy Aid card I had produced that explained how to minister to a dying soldier in the absence of a chaplain. It was good for all combat soldiers to carry, but especially field medics.

Several teams were moving out, taking with them some of our newly trained Afghan soldiers. Their destination was a secret mountainous area known to be inhabited by a fierce, well-supplied anti- coalition faction more radical than their predecessors.

This man was the Green Beret Delta, team medic, responsible for the healthcare of his special operations team and the host nation soldiers deploying with them. His concern? How he would care for the spiritual needs of any soldiers seriously wounded in their upcoming area of operation in the in the absence of a chaplain.

Back at our Colorado mobilization station I had met this peacetime Denver Metro area certified emergency medicine physician's assistant (PA-C) - turned-warrior. He had come to me over a previous spiritual concern and we had developed a close relation over ensuing months. We were neighbors and spoke often. I sensed his genuine concern, not only for the physical, but also for the spiritual well-being of his men. He didn't want any soldier in his care to die without spiritual consolation.

So, I took out the Emergency Buddy Aid card and reviewed the proper care of wounded and dying Protestant, Catholic and Jewish soldiers in their end-of-life spiritual need. I even showed him how to conduct an emergency field baptism. I could tell he was serious, as he paid close attention. Finally, he asked, "Chaplain, how can I make sure that God will be with me in my duties."

I picked up the Buddy Aid card we had just reviewed and turned to the section on Emergency Christian Baptism. I looked him square in the eyes and asked him: "Are you now truly sorry for all your sins?" "Yes." He said. "Do you now truly believe that Jesus Christ died for your sins, and on the third day rose from the grave?" "Yes." He said. "Do you now confess Jesus Christ as your God, and as your only savior?" "Yes!" He said. We then bowed, and I led him in a prayer of confession and faith in Jesus Christ.

There were tears of joy in both our eyes as this expert medical professional citizen-soldier, left my room for even more hazardous duty with a newfound faith in Jesus Christ Who, alone can provide the ultimate emergency Buddy Aid!

Chapter 69

Maharamona: An Ancient Afghan Tradition

With the indispensable help of the Pul-e-Charki school principal, Matiula Safi, we were able to schedule a meeting with the fathers of the four boys who were killed, and the one seriously injured, in the training accident. A Charlie Company ODA provided the five sheep, and funeral funds, as well as security for the meeting. Several Afghan officers of the KMTC cadre, in local dress, wisely attended the meeting, along with the school principal. Major John, the Executive Officer, Maj. Todd, public affairs officer, my assistant, Specialist Russell, and Doc Simon, the 18-Delta/PA-C who helped saved the life of one of the boys, also attended. I asked a mature interpreter, and medical school graduate, to sit with me and interpret for me. Looking back, I could see that the right mix of people had been assembled.

We met at the home of one of the village elders. I led the way into the home, taking off my body armor, and boots, and leaving them inside the front door. Most of the soldiers with me followed suit. Russell, my assistant, kept on his body armor and placed his rifle behind him as we sat on the carpeted floor. Part of me didn't want him armed, but the Special Forces Team in charge of security, directed him to do so, as the internal guard.

Stocking-footed, I sat cross-legged on the floor between my interpreter and one of the KMTC Afghan officers in the rectangular ten by twenty-foot room. The Afghan fathers, one wearing an Afghan Army officer uniform, sat close together in a group near the entrance. Thanking them for receiving us, one of the fathers nodded and then called for a boy with a metal water jug, basin and towel. He started around the room pouring warm water onto the hands of all assembled. I listened carefully to the coaching of my interpreter, as the boy came to me. After all hands were washed, hot tea was poured, and we awkwardly picked at the nuts and snacks served. After seeking to make repeated eye contact with the fathers, amidst small talk, plates of food were brought in. By now I recognized the traditional Kabuli rice with carrot strings and hydrated raisins in a mound covering the cooked meat in the center, garnished with a tomato-base sauce, onions, tomatoes and radishes, and topped with a U.S. GI boot- size-thirteen piece of fresh, hot Afghan Nan flatbread.

After someone uttered what I think was "bon appetite" in Dari, I broke off a piece of bread, dipped into the sauce, and twisted a small piece of meat. It was delicious…and clearly cooked with salt! Remembering the lesson given by Colonel Sammy, I looked up, smiled as big as I could and said,

"This tastes good!" Grunts of affirmation came from all my fellow Americans and it almost seemed like the social atmosphere warmed one or two degrees. Reminding me of the fantastic cooking of my Italian Aunt, I sopped up every drop of sauce. Convinced of the salt content of the victuals served, I thanked God for their culturally displayed openness to conciliation and prayed for God to guide the words I would soon speak. After a cookie and a chaser of green tea, the floor was cleared, the vinyl tablecloth was folded up, and removed. Catching the eyes of my comrades and Afghan officers, I asked my Afghan interpreter, if it was time to begin. He nodded a quiet, "Yes."

Through my interpreter, I initiated the dialogue: "We thank you for allowing us the honor and privilege of eating together in one of your homes. The food was delicious and your hospitality gracious." The faces of the fathers showed little emotion, as I continued. "We wanted to come sooner, but for several reasons were unable." I breathed deeply and got personal. "I am sorry it has taken us so long to arrange this meeting. Several things had to be done in preparation, and it took longer than it should have." I decided to be truthful. "Sometimes our military is slow to respond in situations like this." I prayed for God to give me the right words. "We come to extend our personal condolences and seek 'Maharamona' with you. According to your custom, we have sheep outside for each of you."

The father in uniform, who glared mutely at me the day of the tragedy as I tried to speak words of condolence while squatting in the rain, looked at the other three fathers and began. "I will speak for all the fathers." I wondered what he would say. "You did not need to bring us anything. The fact that you have come here to meet with us shows that you consider us to be more than mere animals." I was simultaneously encouraged and intrigued by his response and wondered if he was making a comparison between us and the Russians who had previously invaded Afghanistan in 1979. As our eyes met, his next words took me by surprise. "I remember you from the day our sons were killed, how you tried to speak to me. I was so angry over my son, and my brother's son's death that I could not understand what you were trying to say. I was rude to you. Please forgive me." Me forgive him? I replied, "Sir, I have been a chaplain for many years, and have sat with many who have mourned over the tragic loss of their loved ones. Long ago I learned to not take offense over the words and actions of those in the throes of grief. You are very kind." The father nodded after the interpretation.

So far, the conversation seemed to be going well. I went on to discuss how many of us were fathers and could hardly imagine the grief they must be experiencing. How we wanted previously to come and express our sorrow and assure them that this was a terrible accident that we would regret for the rest of our lives, but the military system delayed our visit us until now. Soon came the expected reply. "Allah willed it. It was their destiny to be martyred."

After several exchanges of sympathy from other members of the group, along with words from our fellow Afghan officers, the spokesman for the bereaved fathers said something that we would never forget. "Our country has been at war for most of our lifetimes. During the past twenty to thirty years, hundreds of thousands of innocent children, women and elderly have been killed. But since the coming of you Americans, for the first time in our lives we have a feeling of hope and peace for our future. The death of our four boys was worth the peace you have brought."

I was flabbergasted at what I just heard! Could he really have meant what I heard through our interpreter? I looked at the fathers and back at the interpreter in disbelief. I then looked to my American team members as if to make sure I was hearing correctly. Their response was a combination of surprise and humiliation at the word of a man who lost not only his son, but his nephew on that tragic, fateful day.

Major John, the Executive Officer, nodded, as if to tell me to continue. I regained mental focus and then asked the question that I had practiced the day before; "Will you accept this sheep as Maharamona for the accidental death of your son?" I directed my words to the spokesman of the fathers. The Afghan colonel looked me straight in the eyes and said: "Nay - No, I cannot receive anything for the death of my son." I insisted: "Lutvan – please." He looked down and said, "As you wish." I then asked him a second time, "Will you accept this sheep as Maharamona for the accidental death of your brother's son?" Again, he replied, "Nay – no, I cannot receive anything for the death of my brother's son." "Lutvan – please." He looked down and said, "As you wish." I went through the same verbal exchange with each of the fathers. Each replied the same way. After I insisted, they acquiesced. The ceremony was coming to its culmination.

After the offering of sheep, I then explained that we understood the added, unplanned expense of mourning and burying a son, so wanted to help them with that. I told them that the "little army" – my battalion of Soldiers wanted to help in this regard and that we had an envelope for each who lost a son. I went on to explain, that immediately following the accident, my soldiers gave money of their own to help their Families, and that money was given from them and friends in America to renovate the large classroom at the Pul-e-Charki School in their memory. Work had recently begun, and we asked them to come see the work when it was done. They looked quizzically at each other and nodded ascent.

154

Suddenly, it seemed like the atmosphere had lightened. The fathers started smiling a bit more. There were two things yet to do, so I continued. "This is a very special day – a day we have come to remember and honor your sons who were taken from life too soon. With your permission, we would like to go outside and take a group photo by which to remember this important occasion." "Will you also take a photo of our sons' graves" One father asked. "We sure will!" Major Todd, the public affairs officer almost shouted in reply. I stood up and motioned for the fathers to lead us outside. At the door, I put on my boots, and picked up my body armor, but didn't put it on.

The public affairs officer gathered us for a group photo. The lightened spirit seemed to turn almost joyful. The fathers grabbed the arms of the nearest American Soldier as photos were snapped. The street outside the home began to fill with neighbors, especially children. They were peeking into the Humvee pickup with square canvas cover to see the noisy cargo it contained. After the last photo, Major John and I walked to the back of the vehicle. We opened the upper flap and inside were five pairs of sheepish eyes staring back at us. The bed of the truck was high and though we beckoned the sheep to jump out, they stood frozen, almost fighting to stay in the back of the pickup. I think the Afghans were enjoying our dilemma, when Major John reached in and put his arms around the front and rear legs of the closest scraggly sheep and lifted it up and set it on the ground. Grabbing the rope tied to its head, I looked back to see the other four sheep jump out as if they suddenly decided it was okay to exit their foreign import ride.

Grabbing all the sheep securely, I took a large one by the rope and walked up to the who was the group spokesman and through my interpreter again said, "Will you accept this sheep as "Maharamona" for the death of your son?" "Nay – No." "Lutvan - please!" "As you wish." Grabbing another for his nephew, I repeated my plea. I went to each father and we went through the same exchange; each hesitating, but finally accepting with my insistence. Afghan children were everywhere. It was then I remembered I had a large bag of candy in my vehicle. Sergeant Russell retrieved it and I handed it to the Afghan father spokesmen and gestured for him to distribute the candy to the children. He was suddenly swamped, much like we were in similar situations. At least I had learned that lesson! After watching the bag of candy disappear - in about ninety-seconds - it was time to leave. We shook hands, all around. When I went to say good-bye to the father who had lost two family members, he put his hands on my shoulders and drew me close. We both had tears in our eyes – from the dust in the air, I'm sure. Few words were exchanged, just knowing glances between soldier-fathers about the same age.

Though grateful for our visit, signs of pain remained. We entered our vehicles and returned to our FOB. Little did I realize that was not the conclusion, but rather the beginning of the reconciliation process.

Chapter 70

Making Things Right

At the nightly command briefing, I reported on the Maharamona ceremony. Some were amused and made snide comments about the future of the sheep. Most were intrigued and later asked serious questions regarding the cultural meanings of the meal with salt and offering of sheep. After I outlined in detail the process we were entering, to include renovation of the Pul-e-Charki School, upcoming medical civic assistance program (MEDCAP), drilling of well, and other projects, the group sat quiet. The extent to which the U.S. Army wanted to make things right, seemed to sink in.

On the way out, several offered to be a part of the process, helping any way they could. One ODA team captain offered to provide security any time I needed it. I had to turn away after a quick handshake as tears came to my eyes. What I heard him say was that he didn't want me to get hurt, that he would risk his life to safeguard mine. There are not too many situations in life when you feel that kind of cohesion (that's the military code word for "brotherly love"). I stepped into the darkness of the night, still unafraid.

Within a couple days, I received another message to report, this time it wasn't to the U.S. Embassy but to the combined joint civil-military operations task force (CJCMOTF) staff judge advocate (SJA or JAG). Just when I thought I had learned all the Army's acronyms; I'd run across a new one!

Finding my way to an office in a small Army compound in Kabul, I introduced myself to two JAG officers who appeared to me to be in their mid-thirties to early forties. They explained to me that they were tasked to calculate and deliver a sum of money, akin to an accidental life insurance payout to help compensate the families for their loss. It was an interesting discussion, as both men were fathers of children close to the age of the younger boys accidentally killed. We spent more time discussing what this proposed payment was not, than what it was. I sensed that we were breaking new ground, or at least forging into an area with unclear definition.

Near the end of our meeting, they asked me to arrange a meeting with the parents. Sensing that they might be looking for the signatures of both parents, I explained that we would be more likely to secure the signatures of the fathers. I told them I would do my best to arrange the meeting and left.

I admit that I was a bit apprehensive, why I wasn't entirely sure.

Perhaps it was all those bad lawyer jokes or slimy corporate movie roles I had seen, or my limited contact with attorneys. I wasn't sure. Hesitant to upset the conciliation process, I dropped by the Pul-e-Charki school, already under partial renovation, to see my friend, the school principal, Matiula Safi, who helped arrange the original Maharamona meeting.

Greeting me with a hug, I explained the need for another informal meeting with the fathers – no meal, just some tea and discussion with representatives of Big Army. After discussing the issue with the interpreter in my presence, he looked at me with his amblyopic eyes, smiled, and said in English, "Yes, I will do!" He took pleasure in using the little English he had picked up in our conversational American- English classes.

A few days later, I linked up with the CJCMOTF JAG officers, and took them to the Pul-e-Charki School where we picked up the principal. Directing us to the home where we were to meet, we stopped; this time, a much smaller delegation. Leaving an exterior guard with the vehicles, we entered the home, all parties taking off their boots inside the door.

Directed to sit on the floor, we were again served tea, nuts, and cookies, after the traditional washing of hands with warm water. Expressing gratitude for their hospitality and the opportunity to sit with them again, I introduced my companions to the fathers. Explaining that they were representatives of the "Big Army," I ceded the floor to the JAG officers...and prayed silently. What followed astounded me. As these two fathers, U.S. Army Reserve JAG officers on deployment with a Civil Affairs unit in Afghanistan began to speak, I listened closely.

Through our interpreter, first one, then the other began by offering their personal condolences over the loss of the four
boys – their sons. Each one explained, through tears, that they, too, were fathers of two and three children each, and could not begin to imagine the pain of the loss that they and their wives, children and larger families must feel. Glancing over at the three fathers, again, huddled close to each other around their spokesman, I saw tears well up and run down their faces in a mirror response to these two U.S. Army Reserve attorneys who demonstrated genuine sorrow over the loss of their sons.

Suddenly, I felt the sting of conviction. As I observed the words and actions of these two fathers, who happened to be military attorneys, my preconceived notion of what a JAG was, and how uncompassionate they might be, dissipated. After what seemed an appropriate amount of time and dialogue, the lead JAG explained the reason for their visit – to offer a sum of money in recognition of the tragic and unintended loss of their sons in a training accident. Both men expertly and diplomatically answered the fathers' questions through the interpreter. When they were satisfied there was a correct understanding of the settlement, the Afghan fathers signed the documents acknowledging the receipt of money and were given a copy of the translated document, along with an envelope containing the specified amount in U.S. dollars.

After a second cup of tea, we thanked the Afghan fathers for this second opportunity to acknowledge the loss of their sons, and for their gracious hospitality. Standing, the JAGs each one shook the hands and hugged the Afghan fathers on the way out.

Entering our vehicles, we conducted an after-action review of what we intended to accomplish, what happened and what, if anything we might have done better. When they asked my opinion, I fessed up. I admitted my apprehension, and negative preconceptions of their profession. I apologized, they laughed, and thanked me for my honesty and help in this most difficult task. Upon departing, I commended them for their sensitivity, empathy and humility in following my suggestions on how to proceed – instructions they didn't need after all! After firm handshakes and manly hugs all around, we said good-bye. I was glad that this second emotional meeting was over; hoping it would be the last meeting...but it wasn't!

Chapter 71

The Miracle at Pul-e-Charki: Promise fulfilled...almost.

Shortly after meeting with the JAG officers, I visited with the senior engineer of the CJCMOTF. He was assigned the task of supervising the contracting and renovation of the Pul-e-Charki School. We set up a visit to the school and met with the headmaster, Matiula Safi.

Always trying to improve my conversational Dari, I walked into his office and said, "Mudir Saheeb ast?" ("Is the headmaster here?") He looked up from his desk and replied with a grin, "Mudir ast!" ("The headmaster is here!"). After we shook hands and exchanged appropriate manly kisses, I introduced the headmaster to the engineer – Maj. Thomas Schmitz. I explained that he would be handling the renovation of the school, and that this was a sign that the project, indeed, would begin.

The headmaster took us on a tour of the facility. The engineer asked some basic questions about the facility, the school year, and what the principal saw as the essential needs of the facility. Included in the discussion was the rebuilding of a perimeter wall, the drilling of a well and the construction of outdoor toilet facilities – separate latrines for boys and girls.

After a couple of hours, we prepared to leave. Before we left, I asked the engineer if we could put a stipulation in the contract. I wanted the contractors to hire as much unskilled and skilled, labor from the local community, as possible. There were so many able-bodied males in my conversational English classes who were over eighteen and unemployed. Rather than use outside labor, I wanted the locals to rebuild their own school. Not only would this provide construction jobs, for a few months, but it would also allow for personal investment by the local population, pride of ownership and a motivation to keep the facility intact. The good major made notes and said he would talk to contracting. We said our good-byes and left the school.

As we rode back with the project engineer to the CJCMOTF, I recounted my first visit to the school and the strange challenge the young female teacher made; "Are you going to be like everyone else; promise us the world and deliver nothing?" The engineer said he would do some digging and see whether another U.S. or NATO unit may have attempted to arrange a renovation of the school prior to our arrival. Thanking him for his time and effort that day, as well as in the weeks to come, we shook hands and departed. On the way back, my new assistant, Piper 13, and I discussed the excitement of this project. I explained more about what the young lady teacher had said...and how she said it, and my hope of one day being able to see her face when the project began. Spring was coming, and our tour soon would end. I just hoped we would be there to see most, if not all, of the work completed.

I wanted to pray in the car, thanking God for this amazing project, but the traffic was bad, so I prayed quietly to myself...with my eyes open!

Chapter 72

Pul-e-Charki School Renovation – Phase One

The renovation project ended up in two phases; the illegal phase and the legal phase. The illegal phase was funded by the Christmas Eve offering and other spontaneous gifts from our soldiers, and churches and donors back in the USA. From this private funding source, we received over $5,000 in two weeks. Never anticipating the blank check from the Task Force 180 Commander, my unit proceeded with the renovation of a large classroom in memory of the four boys killed in the training accident.

Something needed to be done quickly, so we did it.

The headmaster arranged for Afghan subcontractors to complete a series of renovations and improvements to a double-classroom and its immediate environs. The flat roof was repaired, with expansion cracks filled, and a thin layer of tar applied over that segment of the building. Another artisan came in to repair the window frames and install window glass. To protect the glass and add a new level of security, another metal worker designed, welded, and installed steel grating to fit into the outer windowsills' concrete base, sides and upper sections. Another crew came in to lay a new concrete floor. It was amazing how they resurfaced the floor.

The men who repaired the floor cut strips of what appeared to be tempered window glass approximately two inches wide. They proceeded to frame the floor with the glass strips in sections one-meter square. They made a concrete mix with sand and fine pea gravel and poured it into glass frames. They then screed the section flat and smoothed it with a hand trowel. It was an ingenious and economic way to refinish a damaged concrete floor. Several unit members, including team sergeants, who worked in the construction trades back home, came by to see the technique. They, too, were impressed by something they had never seen before. A couple of them took photos for future reference.

Once the concrete floor was laid, the painter – one of the teachers -- started on the walls and ceiling. He patched and painted, applying at least two coats on walls that had been charred and covered by smoke from internal fires built on the classroom floors. One astute soldier observed that these fires had probably contributed to the huge cracks in the concrete – floors and walls alike. As the concrete cured, a carpenter installed a new heavy door frame and lock. With steel bars on the windows, and a heavy locking door, the school building now had two secure areas – the Headmaster's office, and this classroom.

When we started, the school was a mess. It had been closed during the seven-year Taliban reign of terror. The country's schools had closed because eighty percent of teachers were female, and the Taliban prohibited women from working outside the home. While vacant, travelers, gypsies, homeless and refugees had used its thirty-eight classrooms for sleeping, cooking, and latrine purposes. As the Afghan contractors labored, new life seemed to enter the facility. Though officially on school break for the winter, teachers, neighbors and students often visited to see what was going on. News of the classroom renovation spread throughout the village and surrounding area. The American soldiers were starting to rebuild the Pul-e-Charki school in memory of the four boys.

The first portion of the project was not complete. The room was freezing cold in January, and there were no desks or chalk boards for class. Again, I asked the headmaster about classroom furnishings. He said he would contact another local supplier and have a sample desk brought in. We also agreed that two sheet-metal wood stoves and piping would be needed. The main reason for the stoves was to provide heat for special winter conversational English classes. Just before the end of the school year, the older girls asked – literally begged --us to continue teaching while we were still there.

When the sample desk arrived the next week, it was a two-person metal-frame system with wood plank seat and back, and a simple wood writing surface with shelf underneath for book storage. A quick multiplication of the base price by the number required, and I realized that we would not have enough money. Asking how long it would take to build and deliver the estimated twenty-four desks, the builder said about two weeks. In faith, I committed the additional $1,200 to God in a quick prayer, shook hands with the supplier and made the order. The headmaster smiled, patted me on the back, not realizing that our building fund was nearly depleted. On the way back to KMTC, I prayed for God to supply what was needed for the desks.

Back in my chapel office, I checked emails. When I was done, I contacted a church member who had been a real encouragement. I mentioned the need for desks and the approximate cost. Within ten days, a check arrived with the amount needed plus a little bit extra. The next time the Army mobile finance team stopped by, I cashed the check and put the money away for the desks. The finance guys were great, doing everything legally possible to get our donations into useable currency. After a recount of the funds, there was even enough money to buy two wood-burning stoves for the classroom. I didn't know where to find those, but I was sure my interpreter would.

Chapter 73
Back-to-School Shopping

It wasn't like shopping back home in the USA. There were no department stores. There were small shops here and there, but specialty items were concentrated in several main commercial districts in Kabul. There was Butcher Street, Flower Street and Chicken Street, the latter more of a conglomeration of crafts and handmade Afghan goods, as well as gems, semi-precious stones and jewelry. As was the custom, we fueled our vehicle, donned our body armor, my assistant locked and loaded, and we picked up our interpreter for a mid-day shopping trip...destination, the wood stove store.

Out the gate, and right onto East Jalalabad Road, we headed into Kabul. The day was partly cloudy and cool. With me at the wheel, we passed through the first circle, then made a left at the second circle, over a bridge, in the direction of Orphanage. It was a road that was becoming familiar. Tem, our interpreter directed me to a place to park. It was a busy confluence of busses, three-wheeled taxies, bicycles, trucks and pedestrians.

Tem led us to a market area that was shoulder-to-shoulder with people. The street narrowed, obviously only for pedestrians. At ground level were shops selling one item. There was a shop with a conical pile of corn, next to a shop with what appeared to be wheat; clearly, we were in the grain section. We were two U.S. soldiers in body armor, one armed, one smiling and greeting everyone in Dari with a smile and hand across the chest, the Afghan symbol of humility – "I am your servant!" Most men nodded and returned the greeting and gesture, as we walked through the teeming throng. Some stared. I detected a glare or two.

As we moved into the hardware section, I suddenly realized we were in a giant outdoor department store; passing section by section through grocery, hardware, clothing, and even a pet section with kittens and birds in small wire cages. When we didn't see any wood stoves, Tem pointed up ahead and across the main street to a row of stores on the ground floor of a large multi-story building. Braving the heavy traffic, we finally found the wood-stove store. Entering, we found an assortment of hand-made stoves, constructed of light hammered sheet metal soldered and riveted into various shapes and sizes.

After looking at several models and comparing prices, we settled on two identical stoves of medium-large capacity. Estimating the length of stovepipe, we would need to reach the wall vent, we purchased two extra meters, along with the flanges and sheet metal screws to secure the stove pipe to the wall. Through our interpreter, I asked the shop owner about proper venting and mounting procedures. Given my recent experience with carbon monoxide, I wanted to ensure we had all the materials for proper installation and safe operation. Picking up the two awkward stoves and piping, we walked across the street to our vehicle. Surprised it was so close, I realized that Tem had us park close to our destination but had taken us the long way around through the Central Market.

Looking back, I realized it was a dangerous stroll, but an experience I was glad I had. I was reminded of the Portuguese proverb; "Miudo e borracho, Deus tem a mao por baixo," which literally translated means "God catches children and fools when they fall." In other words, God looks out for children and fools. Reflectively, I sensed that I fit that latter category that day. Mission accomplished, we headed back to KMTC and FOB195.

The next day, we delivered the stoves to the school. The floor had hardened enough to walk on, and the painting was nearly complete. When I asked the headmaster about installing the stoves, he said to leave them, and he and the custodian would take care of it. As we surveyed the progress of our special room, I sensed a mounting joy in the eyes of my Afghan colleagues. It was then that the headmaster revealed that he had received a visit from the Afghan contractor who won the Army contract to restore the school. Rock for the perimeter was to be delivered and work begun in a couple days. A foreman from the contractor, who was responsible for constructing the wall, had asked about young men from the village who might be interested in working on the wall. Heartened that my recommendation had been taken, I, too, began to think that this project might be started, if not completed while we were still in country. But time was short, and there was something else, another part of my overall recommendation, that needed to be coordinated and carried out.

Chapter 74

Pul-e-Charki MEDCAP

Back at KMTC, we parked our Toyota Land Cruiser. I dismissed my assistant and interpreter and headed to the "Med Shed" – literally, a slopped roof garage where our battalion aid station and medical clinic was located. I went in to see our senior medical officer, Doc ENZ. Mine was not the only life he had saved during the previous four months. He had treated most everyone on the FOB for one ailment or another, plus he had examined or treated other patients, from the Russian Ambassador to local Afghan children. He had supervised the planning and execution of most of the medical civic action programs (MEDCAP) conducted in country while were there.

The good doctor eagerly listened to my request for a MEDCAP in Pul-e-Charki. We agreed that the school, now in winter recess, would serve as the site of the mobile medical outreach clinic. He gathered his medical team, including available Special Forces team medics, and submitted the contingency operation plan (CONOP) through the operations center to the Task Force-180 Surgeon, along with a request for needed medical supplies. Within a week, approval was received. Now it was a matter of choosing the right date and getting the word out in the Pul-e-Charki area.

Again, the community network established through the Pul-e-Charki school was utilized. The headmaster contacted the local elders and let the faculty (male and female) know of the clinic dates. A medical team conducted a reconnaissance of the school site for security and logistical issues. Local non- governmental organizations (NGO) and Afghan medical providers were invited to participate. Security would be the responsibility of one of our newly graduated Afghan battalions. A map of the facilities and grounds was drawn out with reception, triage, and treatment areas laid out. We even included a room where hygiene and school supplies would be distributed. That would be the ministry team's station.

With planning complete, we gathered supplies and cross-checked details daily. It had the potential to be a significant event – but only if the community turned out. That next Sunday in chapel, we prayed for everything to come together. We had high hopes, but underneath there was some apprehension. Only time would tell.

In the meantime, trucks began to dump loads of rock around the perimeter of the Pul-e-Charki school grounds. Sand and gravel for mortar were piled in a central area, as crews began building the perimeter wall. I came by the next day to observe the project. As I walked, smiling faces of several of my conversational English students called out in English, "Teacher, we build a wall!" and "Come see us work, professor!" Some shouted a traditional Afghan blessing, "Man dana bashi!" ("May you be well!") To each one I replied, "Zan da bashi!" ("May you likewise be well!").

The linear footage of the wall was significant, and the crews worked systematically, choosing and shaping rock with hammers and fitting them into place cemented with mortar. Thick and high, the Pul-e-Charki wall went up. I wondered how its construction might impact our upcoming clinic. Soon we would see.

The day before the MEDCAP, we delivered much of the bulkier supplies, including chairs and tables. Medicine and medical equipment were delivered early on the clinic day for security reasons. Most of it was brought by the ones who would use it. Though the clinic was to begin at 9:00 a.m., we had a team meeting at 7:30 a.m. Afghan Soldiers were given their orders and placed in strategic locations. As the many U.S., Coalition, NGO and Afghan medical providers were assembling; I walked around and greeted them, thanking them for coming. As able, I told the story of the tragic deaths of the four boys and pointed to the building next door that was being renovated in their memory. Some knew the story, others did not. Nodding, with my hand across my chest, I bowed to each one out of gratitude and respect.

It wasn't long before women, most in blue Burkahs, began to gather with their children. They came from every direction – something we had not fully anticipated. The crowd grew so quickly and became so unmanageable, that we had to instruct the ANA soldiers to form them into groups and lines. Soon, one hundred, then two...before long over a thousand bodies milled around the school grounds., and more kept streaming in.

In the meantime, medical and support personnel scrambled to get their clinic stations ready. I worked with my assistant, an interpreter and two Afghan soldiers, to arrange our room – a distribution point for hygiene items...soap, plastic wash basins, dental care items, school supplies and toys. I kept looking outside to see how the crowd was forming. It grew steadily, and the Afghan soldiers started to direct the people, the clear majority women with children, into a long line. Those at the head of the line were anxious to be seen, as they had been waiting the longest. It was then that two strange things occurred.

First, a man that I recognized from my first visit to the Allahuddin Orphanage, starting walking toward the screening point. I recognized his beard and the tweed business suit while still far out. Remembering that he was from the Ministry of Social Services, I figured that he had come to observe our MEDCAP operation. But I was mistaken.

As he approached the building, he stepped over the white cloth tape guides and elbowed his way to the front of the line. I stepped forward to greet him and introduce him to Doc ENZ and the rest of the medical team, but he ignored me, like he didn't recognize me. Instead, he spoke to the screener and told him that he was here to be seen by an American doctor. I was simultaneously embarrassed and angered by his lack of consideration for what was estimated to be approximately one thousand women and children standing in line. Other members of the medical staff saw what he had done and took him aside to talk. Not wanting to make a scene, they decided to attend to his physical complaints. There was too much good to do.

The second "parting of the crowds" occurred shortly after the bureaucrat went through. My interpreter caught my attention and motioned to the far end of the school grounds. A small one-legged woman in a light blue Burkah hobbled quickly through the crowd. As she came, the crowd seemed to part in a very deliberate way, as if she were a recognized celebrity or someone to be avoided. My interpreter asked one of the KMTC officers who she was, and he whispered something in his ear. Calling me aside, my interpreter said, "It's the mother of the youngest boy killed on the range."

Stunned, my heart sank. Only now, six weeks after the tragedy did I see the Burkah-clad mother of one of the four dead boys. I had seen them, their fathers, uncles, and brothers, but not one mother, sister or aunt. I wanted to approach her and offer her my condolences but didn't. She had not come to hear my feeble words of regret intended to help heal her broken heart. She had come to find healing for her ailing body. I respected that and prayed she would find it.

The end of the day, exhausted, we tallied over 1600 Afghans seen by our combined, joint, multi-national medical team. It was a lot effort well spent.

Chapter 75
Pul-e-Charki School Renovation - Phase 2

After the MEDCAP, the school renovation project picked up momentum. Gaps in the perimeter wall began to close, and work on the thirty-eight classrooms began. I was so excited that I came by almost every day to see the progress. Being somewhat of a handyman, I was intrigued by the different construction and repair techniques and tools employed throughout the project. Along with me came other unit members, electricians, carpenters and contractors, all with similar curiosity.

Beyond their unique concrete floor resurfacing technique utilizing strips of glass, we marveled at their carpenters' ability to cut tongue and groove joints in window frames simply with a hand saw right on site. With little more than a sawhorse and a fine-tooth hand saw, local Afghan carpenters systematically built and rebuilt window frames sized and ready for panes of glass and putty. Like a

young boy enthralled with a construction project, I stood mesmerized at the craftsmanship of these tradesmen. Occasionally, I would interrupt with a question through my interpreter. The ensuing conversations were enlightening, to say the least.

In addition to the building renovation, two outdoor toilets – latrines -- were begun off in a corner of the school property. A backhoe was brought in one day to dig the pits for both the boy's and girl's facilities. After some defining of edges and squaring of corners, a foundation made of rock, like the perimeter wall, was set.

As with the wall, the Afghan masons worked quickly, mortaring the stone and brick in to walls and doorways. In a few days, I counted ten pits for the boys and eight pits for the girl's toilets. Though not something many American women would consider acceptable, it was a quantum leap forward for students, faculty and staff, alike, who previously

had to relieve themselves in a ditch less than one-hundred feet from the nearest classroom. These new latrines would be like the public toilets utilized in many state and national parks in the North America, Europe and elsewhere in the world. They were a definite improvement!

We even got the well. Maj. Gen. Eikenberry's promise of a blank check was real. The CCJMOTF engineer contracted a local well-driller to sink a shaft into the water table fed by the Kabul river less

than 1500 meters away. A standard stainless- steel hand pump was installed to cap the well. No sooner than it was installed, the workers and locals began lining up to pump their own water, for the project and personal use.

The building renovation, MEDCAP, wall and water pump were all part of the original school renovation. The latrine facilities were something I never thought of, but the skilled U.S. engineer did. The Pul-e-Charki renovation was turning out to be even more than I had envisioned – oh me of little faith! With the weather warming and days getting longer, the projected time of our departure was getting closer. Though personnel and unit movement were classified information, those we worked with somehow knew our time was winding down. How the subject was broached turned out to be quite interesting.

Chapter 76

Lost and Found – Miracle #2

Word from Chaplain Andy - 3-23-03

I stopped by our local school to check on the classroom renovation project. The assistant principal met me outside with a big smile. I could see the excitement in his eyes and the eyes of the workers, several of whom were students in my English classes and one, a math teacher.

After a few minutes inside to take pictures of the work progress, we boarded our vehicles and headed back to KMTC. As we drove off, I reached for my radio; it wasn't there. After a quick check of the vehicle, I turned around to go back to the school. The convoy turned around and followed.

Back at the school, we did a thorough check and called for the assistant principal. I was angry. The Air Force Special Weather Operator, TSgt. Rob, who was guarding the vehicle, told me that a few students had surrounded the vehicle and opened the doors on both sides, before he could chase them away. Someone had taken my radio and a can of orange juice! The juice I could lose, but the radio I could not.

I told the principal through my interpreter that the radio was a sensitive item…and very expensive. Its loss would cause serious problems for me and my soldiers. He gathered the children and asked them about the radio. No one knew anything, but I had to get it back to our FOB.

After thirty-minutes of pleading with the kids, I called the assistant principal over and asked him if a reward for its return might work. He nodded, and I told the group that I would leave twenty dollars with the principal and he would give the reward to anyone who returned the radio or told where it could be found. We left.

I felt so bad. It wasn't a cheap ordinary radio. It was a high-tech communications device that cost thousands of dollars—and I was responsible for its safe return. It was Saturday night and I went back to my room and not only prayed for its return, but for the first time, I sent out an email prayer alert to several Christian friends and church members back home. I couldn't say what it was, but that it was a sensitive item that I needed to get back. While I slept, many back home prayed.

Sunday morning, I got up and prepared for chapel. I went to call my wife, to see if she got the message to pray. She did and had been praying. While on the phone, a runner came up with the message that a schoolteacher was at the main gate asking for me. I told my wife I had to go and said good-bye. I rarely cut my morale calls short – but this was important.

When I got to the gate, the assistant principal was there. I grabbed the nearest interpreter and asked if he had found the radio. His poker face turned into a big grin as he patted the breast pocket of his coat. He opened his jacket and pulled out a small rectangular-shaped package wrapped in a newspaper and plastic bag. I tore open the wrapping...and there was the radio! I hugged the principal and asked him how he found it.

He told me that he, too, became so upset that he spent the entire evening going from house to house, speaking with the village elders. He told them: "Chaplain Andy has done so much for our school. If he doesn't get the radio back, he'll get in big trouble. Come, help me find his radio."

Around 10:00 p.m., after the word had spread, a young boy came to the village elders and told them he knew who took the radio. They went to the house together and found the radio. They gave the boy a small AM radio he could use in exchange for the military radio. I was back in time for Chapel.

I placed the radio on the camouflaged altar and had the biggest praise to share. The soldiers rejoiced with me, as I stood up in staff meeting to report the radio's safe return. They saw the results of prayer working through a solid relationship with our host nation friends.

A short time later, a newly arrived U.S. Army officer was using one of the local firing ranges. While there, someone stole a backpack containing sensitive military items, more dangerous than my radio. Facing serious consequences, someone told him to contact the KMTC chaplain for help recovering his lost equipment. I shared with him how I got my radio back and sent him off to see the local village elders. His equipment was not recovered by the time of our soon departure.

Part Six: Getting Home
Chapter 77

If you Go, Taliban and Al Qaeda will Return!

One day, when I stopped by to pick up an interpreter, one of the Afghan medical students greeted me with the question: "How long will you stay? When will you go?" Aware that what he was asking was sensitive information, I replied, "Soon." It was our plan all along to come, complete our mission and return to our homes. Suddenly, a look a panic crossed his face, "But if you go, the Taliban and Al Qaeda will return!" He wasn't joking. Recognizing his genuine fear, I replied, "But other Soldiers will take our place to continue our mission." He processed what I said and returned to his seat. It was obvious from the looks of the other interpreters, that this was a shared concern. I understood why.

A week prior, I was taken to the main soccer stadium in Kabul. Curiously, there were what appeared to be Olympic rings painted on the entrance facing the small parking lot. We dismounted our vehicles and walked into the seating area. Our guide/interpreter explained how during the reign of the Taliban, soccer was the only public sport allowed to be played. He also shared that the only thing the crowd could shout after a goal was scored was "Allah Akbar!" – God is the greatest! The other soldiers I was with chuckled at the hypocrisy of the censorship, but outside the U.S., soccer is king.

It was then that I noticed something in the area just off the goals on either end. It looked like the grass had been removed in circles. When I pointed to the round bare spots in the otherwise rare grassy playing field, our interpreter lowered his voice and explained: "Under the rule of Taliban, people were arrested by the morals police for many reasons; women caught walking outside without an adult male family member were often whipped with television cable ripped from homes. Sometimes they were arrested, especially if caught more than once. If a man shaved his beard, against Taliban rules, he could also be whipped or arrested. At half-time period during football matches, there were holes in the ground where these round bare spots are. The Taliban would bring out men and women who had broken their rules and place them into the narrow holes with just their heads and shoulders above the ground. Then a cart of large rocks was brought out and dumped onto the field. People were driven from the stands and made to pick up a rock to stone the offenders till dead. This was Taliban justice. We don't want this in our country anymore." We were all stunned.

Reports of such atrocities by the Taliban made U.S. news, but here we were looking at the very spot where the barbaric practice of stoning took place a little over one year prior. Entering our vehicles, my fellow-soldiers simultaneously locked and loaded their weapons. Witnessing this place of public execution seemed to intensify the reality of the horror and extremism the Afghan people had endured for over seven years. We drove safely back to our FOB with little conversation.

The next day, while walking through the Afghan training area adjacent to our small compound, one of the Afghan colonels, who had participated in Maharamona ceremony waved me over. After we greeted, he asked me in his best English, "When you go home?" It was like all of Kabul was aware of the Special Forces six-month rotation pattern. "Soon." I replied. He looked me in the eyes, nodded, and continued.

A couple days later, I dropped by the school to check on the renovation process. Everywhere I looked, I saw walls being built, windows and doors being installed, floors being systematically resurfaced, walls being painted, and the outdoors latrines being built. Enraptured by the activity, I didn't notice the headmaster come up behind me.

He put his hand on my shoulder, shook my hand and pulled me close for one of those culturally appropriate Afghan male kisses and hugs. Speaking first to my interpreter, he then looked me square in the eyes, waiting for the interpretation; "The Headmaster wants to know when you are leaving." By now I was convinced there was either a concerted effort to get me to reveal departure dates, or a genuine Afghan fear of abandonment – like what occurred when the U.S. stopped supporting the Mujahedeen freedom fighters against the Soviet occupiers in the late seventies. Again, all I could reply was "soon." My Afghan friend looked at me and replied to the interpreter with a nod, "The headmaster wants you to tell him a week or two before you go, so he can have a party for you." Surprised, I said, "There is no need for a party." Not waiting for the interpreter's interface, the school principal replied in English, "We must eat food before you go!" Having already developed a taste for Afghan cooking, I smiled and nodded affirmation to his request. I knew there was someone else who wanted to be there for the party.

Chapter 78
Farewell Meal with Female Students

Throughout the reconciliation and renovation process, I kept Maj. Gen. Eikenberry informed of the other meetings with the Afghan Families, MEDCAP and school reconstruction. When I told him of the request the headmaster made regarding the meal, he was very interested in attending this event. After we agreed on the time and location, I let the general know of the invitation.

In the meantime, the military police (MP) company providing our force protection was preparing to leave and a new MP company was getting ready to take over. This process is called RIP-TOA. It stands for relief in place–transfer of authority. During one of my observation visits to the school, the headmaster told me that the female teachers and students wanted to have a special farewell meal for the female soldiers of our unit – those who taught them English, as well as any other females who would like to come. With the large classroom completed earlier, the luncheon was to be held there.

As was custom, I took the females Army instructors, along with their other female comrades to the Pul-e-Charki School. When we entered the room, I was taken aback! The concrete floors had been covered with woven straw mats, and two large square vinyl tablecloths were placed in the center of the room. Covering these tablecloths was an amazing array of home-cooked Afghan foods. Everything from traditional Kabuli rice, breads, yogurt dishes, salads, sauces and foods I had never tasted or seen before was in a beautiful spread.

The Afghan teachers and students approached their female Army teachers with hugs and kisses. These in turn introduced the female cooks, medic and administration specialists who had chosen to come along. The female Afghan students and teachers likewise welcomed these young ladies warmly. Seeing that I was the only male in the room with the headmaster, I figured it was wise for me to step out and let the females have their party.

Moving to the door, the headmaster motioned for me to stay. Telling him through my interpreter that I knew it was the girls' party, and that I would wait outside, he said, "Come, you stay and eat!" I was directed to sit with him at the head of one "tables," as the U.S. female soldiers were distributed among both sections. I counted approximately eighty students and female teachers. I was amazed.

Here I was, the only American male soldier in a classroom with eighty Afghan females; students ages thirteen to twenty-three, and teachers from early twenties to mid-fifties. My interpreter, Tem, leaned close to me and said, "Not even the U.S. Ambassador has ever been in a party like this." I had to ask him to repeat himself, and when I understood what he said, I nodded. What an amazing experience, indeed.

After a welcome speech made in English by one of the senior Afghan girls, we were invited to eat. I had to pace myself, as I saw so many foods I had never seen or tasted before. I also remembered how sick I got the first time I ate with the contract workers at the FOB. Treating it like a church potluck back home, I started with small sampling of things closest to me. Soon, the Afghan students and teachers seated around me began passing their dishes for me to try. I was in an epicurean paradise surrounded by the future hope of Afghanistan – women who wanted and actively sought an education. Remembering the male soldiers outside providing security, I asked if a plate could be made for each of them. Several girls quickly made plates and delivered them. Looking through the metal bars of the classroom, I saw our soldiers eating with big smiles and flashing a thumbs-up my way.

As I ate and interacted with these ladies, occasionally prodded by the Headmaster on my left, I observed the interaction. Most all the Afghan women made efforts to speak in English. Some spoke more clearly than others. Those who stumbled or became embarrassed were assisted either by their classmates or the American females at their "table." It confirmed our classroom discovery; small group discussions were the preferred way for Afghan girls to learn English. I also noticed that some of the older Afghan female students had a young child with them. It dawned on me at that moment that our meager efforts to teach conversational English were impacting two generations; the student mother and her child. I envisioned in the future some of these mothers helping their children with their schoolwork; and when they struggled with an English word or phrase, their mother would help. When the child would ask, "Mother, how do you know English?" She would reply, "Some female soldiers from America came every week to teach us how to speak English." I was impressed as I supervised the food, fellowship and fun!

After lunch, a lady Afghan teacher - one who talked me into seeing our Doctor with several of her children, nieces and nephews - stood to get everyone's attention. Once the seemingly impossible was accomplished, three female students stood at the head of the classroom to speak. Each speech included words of appreciation for both the
instruction and the friendships that were shared, as well as the Afghan girls' admiration for the courage and sacrifice of their American teachers. The girls

then asked me to come to the front.

One girl, around age fourteen, presented me with a Bic pen that she decorated with a light blue background and the letters "USA" and "9-11" in red and white beads. I could see she was proud and pleased to present it to me – almost as proud and pleased as I was to receive it. Another female student, maybe seventeen or eighteen handed me a small square box wrapped with fine white linen ribbon. I slipped off the ribbon and opened the box. The pen made me smile ear to ear, but the contents of the box made my jaw drop.

On a small wooden base was fashioned with stiff wire and larger beads, what appeared to be a tree. Each branch, thirteen in number, twisted into a trunk on the base and spread out into separate branches that had a large mother-of-pearl type bead encased with smaller gold beads, like fruit at the end. Thirteen branches...I wasn't sure if it represented the "Tree of Life" or the "Thirteen Original Colonies of America." It was a beautiful, handmade expression of appreciation for our simple efforts to provide culturally acceptable conversational English instruction to the high school girls of Pul-e-Charki, Afghanistan. My only sadness was that Maj. Diggs, my teaching cohort, was not present to enjoy the feast, the speeches – in English – and the handmade expressions of gratitude. What gracious students and faculty we had the privilege of getting to know...and love. This event would have been enough, but even more was planned.

Chapter 79

Farewell Meal with Faculty

After the luncheon prepared by the female students and teachers, the headmaster asked me to come back the following week for another special meal. When I mentioned Maj. Gen Eikenberry's interest in coming, he assured me the general was welcome, as well. I sent this message to the general at the embassy, and his reply was that he would do his best to attend.

Having just said goodbye to one MP company and hello to its replacement, I invited the new female MP commander, Capt. Margaret, to attend. Open to all the exposure she could get to local leaders, she readily agreed to accompany me along with another female soldier, and personal security. Arriving around noon, we entered the double classroom which had been prepared for the event.

To my delight, the Afghans had arranged the handmade wooden, multi-colored mini picnic tables that had been made by Sgt. Blackman into one long table. Quietly, these tables had been in the works for several weeks, as the good sergeant, on his own time, scrounged leftover wood to build them, and enough red, blue, orange, green and yellow paint to coat them. This rainbow-colored banquet table was covered with homemade food. Surveying the spread, I expressed my surprise and delight to the headmaster and teachers assembled. Afghan food was tasty and prepared in a healthy manner – even their fried potatoes were made from sweet potatoes!

Looking around the room at the teachers I had come to know over the previous six months, I spied the Afghan English teacher, the one with whom I worked most closely, standing over by the wall. He had a big grin and pointed to a white board that said: "Welcome Chaplain Andy, and other his friends, for a party!" Walking over, I took his hand and gave him a culturally appropriate hug and kiss on both cheeks. We stood smiling at each other for a few long moments.

Beginning with the headmaster, I introduced Capt. Margaret to school faculty and staff present. As I went down the line, I noticed very few female teachers in the room. Those present were arranging the food on the tables, and quietly slipping out. My heart sank. Most teachers were female, and though many of them had attended the luncheon prepared for our female teachers and soldiers, I felt it was wrong to exclude them from this meal, especially with Capt. Margaret as a special guest.

I quietly asked my interpreter if it was inappropriate for the women to eat with the men? His reply suggested that typically men and women ate separately in public – except for weddings – but since this was a group of educated people it would be more acceptable. With a short time left in country, I decided to take another risk. Walking over to the headmaster with my interpreter, I asked why the female teachers were not invited. His hesitant reply about them being busy and having to go home to care for their families was not convincing. Making eye contact with my interpreter and the with the headmaster I said, "If the women do not eat, I will not eat!" The response was predictable.

After double-checking with the interpreter on my reply, the headmaster had a quick conversation with my interpreter. My interpreter, understanding and supporting my desire to include the female teachers, reiterated that they had to attend to duties in their homes. He then pointed to a mature female teacher who had been called into the room. After the headmaster apparently invited her to join us in the meal as a representative of the female teachers, she nodded and replied in Dari. Looking to my interpreter to hear what she said, replied, "She said, 'I will eat for all the ladies.'" Noticing her rather full and mature form, I had to smile at the hidden implication of her statement.

Having delayed the start of the meal for Maj. Gen. Eikenberry, we decided it better to eat before the food got completely cold. Sitting toward the middle of the long table, I gratefully allowed the headmaster to load my plate with Afghan food. Once again, to sample as many dishes possible, I asked for small amounts to try, off for my favorite, Kabuli Rice – a chunk of tender meat covered in flavored rice garnished with slivered carrots, hydrated raisins and roasted sliced almonds. Dessert consisted of an assortment of cakes, yogurt, cookies and fruit.

Well into dessert, Maj. Gen. Eikenberry arrived. Having already eaten lunch, he sampled some tea and cookies. The general could only stay for a short time, so we let him speak. His remarks centered on the progress of the school's renovation and questions on how the families of the boys killed and injured were doing. He was pleased to hear that the injured boy had already returned home and appeared to be recovering well. After this report, he shook hands and left.

Figuring that the event was ending, I started to thank the headmaster for the special lunch, when he beckoned me to sit back down. Dutifully, I responded as an Afghan rug was brought into the room by the Afghan English teacher. He asked me to come up and take the opposite end, as if holding a flag. As I looked alternatingly at him and the rug, he thanked me for coming to Afghanistan with my soldiers. He also thanked me for starting the conversational English class with Maj. Diggs, who I so wished were present at this event. Included in his remarks, occasionally punctuated with clarifying comments by my interpreter, were words of sadness over the death of the boys, but appreciation for my leadership in the reconciliation process, helping start the literacy program for Afghan soldiers and the Pul-e-Charki school renovation. He concluded his remarks by wishing us a safe return home to our families and by letting me know that the rug had been handmade by some of the female teachers for me to take home. With emotion I said, "Tashakor!" (thank you). Even though I offered to help with the cleanup, I was diplomatically escorted to my vehicle where we said good-bye.

Chapter 80
Passing the Torch...with Tears

Word from Chaplain Andy...4-06-03

One of my favorite and most productive duties here as an Army chaplain on the other side of the world has been teaching soldiers of the world's newest army principles of human rights and the law of war. Through this interaction I have learned a lot about these Afghan combat veterans and made many new friends.

During Phase-1, we taught all the classes to the host nation soldiers. In Phase-2 we are developing a new cadre of competent Afghan trainers who will be able to train future cycles of soldiers when we leave.

A while back I was supervising the teaching of a company of new recruits. The officer instructing the class did an effective job. He used some of my illustrations and added some others. He even mentioned "The Golden Rule" as the basis of human rights. He did make one cute mistake when he passionately stated that "America has fifty-one states and they didn't come to make Afghanistan fifty- two—like the Russians tried before!"

At the end of the class I gathered the 250 soldiers around me and told them the story of a WW2 war crime that I personally investigated, fifty-years after the fact. I explained how I went to Italy and spoke with a surviving eyewitness of the shooting of a young Italian girl. I explained both the crime of the attack and the heroic efforts made to save her life.

At the end of the story I told them that the girl who was shot was my own mother, and the eyewitness was my uncle. For the first time, in over four months of teaching the same classes, I found myself choked up before 250 new Afghan trainees and officers. I became emotional, in part over the fact that I was no longer the principal instructor (I love teaching, especially soldiers), and in part due to having the results of war and injury now permanently etched in my memory. A young Afghan soldier kindly handed me his brightly colored handkerchief. When I went to give it back, after wiping away my tears, he beckoned for me to keep it. It was a touching moment where we had connected soldier-to- soldier.

I then asked them what kind of soldier they wanted to be. One who killed and abused innocent, unarmed civilians, or one who fought the enemy and rescued their own people? They all affirmed their desire to be good soldiers in the days ahead. Then I asked "Ayo durastas?" If what we taught them was true...three times, getting louder each time. By the third time, they were on their feet shouting "Durastas!" (It's TRUE!!!) I then said softly, "Tashakor" (Thank you.) and walked off.

They seemed stunned and then were given a break. Over one hundred soldiers mobbed me to shake my hand and individually promise to follow the principles of human rights and law of war in the future.

I got to thinking how what we are doing here in Afghanistan in training new army trainers, is the very thing we are to do in the church. Remember Paul's words to Timothy, "And the things you have heard me say in the presence of many witnesses entrust to reliable men who will also be qualified to teach others. Endure hardship with us like a good soldier of Christ Jesus. No one serving as a soldier gets involved in civilian affairs--he wants to please his commanding officer." (2 Timothy 2:2-4).

How are you spending your precious life? Are you investing it in the lives of others who spread the Good News and serve others in Christ's Name? If not, I challenge you, from the other side of the world, to join me in passing the torch -- if necessary – with tears!

.

Chapter 81

Graduation Day

Word from Chaplain Andy...3-16-03

The winter sun was shining as the Fifth Battalion (Kandak) of the new Afghan National Army assembled on the KMTC parade field. Before the ceremony, I walked up and down the formation proudly taking photos of this battalion of Afghan soldiers. This was the graduation of the first battalion Sgt. 1st Class Dave and I had the privilege of helping train from start to finish. As I moved by, the soldiers called out to me in various ways: "Teacher," "Professor," "Chaplain," "Mawlawee" (Dari for Chaplain) and "Mullah" (Arabic for Preacher).

Foreign dignitaries filled the reviewing stand, along with two tents of VIPs and two new Afghan Army trucks loaded with media representatives. After lengthy speeches by the Minister of Defense and several Afghan generals, the battalion passed in review. Many of the officers and soldiers looked over and smiled at me as they passed my position. I could sense their pride as they goose-stepped by in Soviet-style march.

After the ceremony and a tasty Afghan lunch, the soldiers lined up to turn in their weapons. I took advantage of this one last time to congratulate each one. Part way through the line of over 300 soldiers, one young man asked me if I had copies of the outline of the human rights class, I had taught them eleven weeks earlier? I remembered that I had 500 copies made, so I rushed back to my office to get them. The soldiers swarmed all over me to get their copy of the PowerPoint outline that I had translated into Dari.

Later that afternoon, I was sitting in the courtyard talking with my interpreter, Tem. A group of Junior Afghan officers passing by, stopped, came up and saluted me. I rose to my feet to return their salute. A captain, serving as spokesman for the group said something I didn't understand. My interpreter looked surprised as I nodded for him to tell me what he said. Tem said: "Mr. Chaplain, he said, 'We love you for leaving your family and coming to teach us about human rights and the law of war. We remember the stories you told us about your family, and we will never forget you! Please, chaplain, sir, do not forget us.'" Tears came to my eyes as each young officer came up, saluted me, shook my hand and kissed me on the cheek (in a manly Afghan way).

Somehow, we had connected. God had taken me, a Colorado Army

National Guard Christian chaplain, halfway around the world to teach the Golden Rule to the first battalions of the new Afghan Army. Pray with me that the teaching of the Golden Rule and the example of Christian love I sought to show these soldiers will make a lasting difference in their lives before they reach their final Graduation Day.

Chapter 82
A Day Off

The Apostle Paul and Doctor Luke were a well-known missionary team in the New Testament. They traveled together and ministered to body, mind and soul as they spread the Gospel throughout Asia Minor and Eastern Europe.

In a similar way, God gave me several cohorts in ministry here on the other side of the world.

One of them is Doc Enz, a triple board-certified U.S. Army National Guard physician. He's a rare combination pediatrician, ophthalmologist and public health specialist.

On top of it all, he became my good friend and ministry partner. Though we are almost the same age (he's three and one-half months older), he is a colonel and I am just a lowly major. When we're together, some soldiers jokingly distinguish between us as "Big Sir" and "Little Sir."

When I almost died of carbon monoxide poisoning over New Year's, he saved my life and put me on curfew for two weeks. He directed me to sleep in a bunk next to his in the medical quarters to ensure my full and complete recovery.

Once, when another soldier was seriously ill, he treated him with antibiotics and I with prayer. The result of that combined therapy was, in his words, "miraculous." Under his direction, our battalion medical team has planned and executed more mobile village medical clinics (MEDCAP) than any other medical unit in country. We have been to remote enemy border areas, a mountain clinic, nearby villages, and to the central orphanage of Kabul to treat over 900 resident children ages three to nine.

I have photographed his amazing sight-saving surgery on the eyes of U.S. soldiers and host nation victims of war and watched him correct strabismus in U.S. and Afghan individuals. By straightening the eyes of young Afghan women, they are more likely to become a first wife, and not end up the third or fourth wife of some old Taliban sympathizer.

Once we even took charge of childcare during a service at Community Christian Church of Kabul to allow wives an opportunity to worship with their husbands. Another fun ministry we have jointly developed is supplying local NGO (non- governmental organization) personnel with donated toiletries, books, toys, food, medical supplies and other excess items that are inappropriate for host nation people but excellent for these expatriate relief workers. We started this back in December and it has been a real hoot to drive into the compound of the underground church like an undercover Santa with a pickup load of stuff. We quietly lay out the boxes after the church meeting and stand back and watch with Christmas-like Santa glee as, men, women and children rummage through and find items that they need or want. Then we quietly leave. I remember one young man who found some needed contact lens solution, another mother who found some children's books, an adolescent girl who found an electronic game and one man who picked up a coveted Field & Stream magazine he hadn't read in months. We also delivered some mail and school supplies for their small International Christian School and for a new downtown kindergarten being started by one of their NGOs.

While watching the effects of this heaven-sent mobile Wal-Mart recently with Doc Enz, I was reminded of one of Jesus' rare quotes recorded in the Book of Acts, "It is more blessed to give than to receive." (20:35). During this time of war and chaos, God brought together a pediatric ophthalmologist from Tennessee and a Baptist pastor from Colorado to form the modern-day team of Chaplain Andy and Doc Enz!

Chapter 83

The Curse is Lifted: Miracle #3

As time passed, more Afghan Army battalions graduated and were sent on low-level combat operations. The first battalion went 236 kilometers south-east to Orgun-E on the Pakistan border. The second battalion journeyed to Bamiyan, 240 kilometers north-west of Kabul. Bamiyan is the home of the mammoth, ancient Buddhas carved into the stone. These were destroyed by the iconoclastic Taliban prior to the U.S. entry in support of the Northern Alliance. Ironic as it was, international media was more outraged by the Taliban's demolition of these stone carvings, than by their oppressive actions against women that led to the closing of the Afghan school system.

It had been several weeks since my meeting with Doc Simon (see chapter 68) before his unit deployed under the cover of darkness. Word back had been limited, and I frequently prayed that he would be successful as the chief medical officer of that deployment – especially as it related to the lifting of "the curse" – his seeming inability to secure timely medical evacuation or his team's extraction by air.

Walking through his company's gravel parking area, I heard a shout, "Chaplain!" I turned to see a bearded Special Forces operator running my direction. Bracing for full-body impact, I recognized the eyes and smile of Doc Simon. He grabbed me in a manly bear hug and yelled, "It worked! It worked!" Happy to see him safe and, hopefully sound, I asked, "What worked?" "The curse, it's gone!" He declared with conviction. We slipped and rolled onto the ground, like a couple of third-grade boys. As we got back up, I slapped him on the back and shoulders and invited him to my nearby office to warm up.

He sat down, unzipped his jacket and guzzled a bottle of water. "Tell me what happened." I prompted, leaning forward in anticipation." He proceeded. "On our last mission before returning home, an ear-splitting explosion caused us medics to sprint toward the rising smoke, fearful of what new trauma we would face. A Russian landmine claimed another victim. A young goat-herder had wandered into a minefield in search of a stray, when he stepped on the mine. He lay horribly shattered. It required all our collective skill to save his life, and air evacuation was an absolute necessity. Fear crept back into my mind as I remembered, 'the curse.' For a moment the patient was stable. I dropped to my knees and prayed with all my being for the Lord's help and waited for a response. I watched the patient and scanned the horizon. Finally, a palpable throbbing vibrated the air, heralding

188

the arrival of the MEDEVAC chopper. I held my breath as the patient was loaded and the huge aircraft lumbered into the air. Tears streamed down my face as the helicopter lifted toward the sun." Doc Simon took a deep breath, and with wet eyes concluded, "Chaplain Andy, there was no 'curse' after all, I was simply a lost misguided soul who could not see that the answer to his questions lie in prayer...a soul who is now free."

We hugged and poked at each other like long-lost friends. "I got to go and take care of team business...and do some laundry." He said. "Any word on the Afghan boy we saved on the mountain?" I quickly explained what had transpired, since the original Maharamona meeting. Another event was being planned for the teams who were involved in the incident. "Would you like to see the young man whose life you saved?" I asked. "Sure, is that possible?" I told him what was in the works and assured him I would keep him in the loop as to time and place. One last hug, and Doc Simon said, "I'll see you in chapel on Sunday!"

Grateful for Doc Simon's positive report and the obvious spiritual breakthrough in his life, I thanked God for hearing his and my prayer. Now that Doc Simon's team was back, we could have a final meeting that I hoped would bring closure to both the families of the dead boys, and the soldiers involved in the incident.

Chapter 84
A Surprising Offer

Over the previous six months, we conducted six humanitarian missions to the Allahuddin orphanage in Kabul. These efforts included food, clothing, school supplies, hygiene and medical support, much of which came from private U.S. donations. The largest donation consisted of 850 sweaters collected and mailed to my Afghanistan APO address by Saint Catherine Siena School of Storrs, Connecticut. (Remember my visit with the Army Postmaster?) The student body worked together to provide warm clothing for the 900 children of this orphanage. Once we got into a rhythm of promoting and receiving donations, we completed one to two missions per month. After our initial twenty-two soldiers returned from "Operation Christmas Blessing," we had no lack of volunteers for succeeding missions.

The orphanage staff and residents seemed to enjoy the visits as much as we did. Each time our vehicles reached the facility, the caretaker would open the gate and wave us in. Soon, children would pour into the courtyard, mob the soldiers, who came laden with candy and soccer and kick balls. Within minutes groups of boys and girls would form with soldiers organizing various games, including that American favorite: "Duck, Duck, Goose!" Though in the minority, female soldiers who came were swarmed by young girls who asked them to take off their hats, so they could see their hair! The girl and boys' choirs would come out and sing for us and the staff would often bring us tea. The largely female staff would stand in the windows of the surrounding buildings, watching the visit. Many had to stay indoors to care for the babies and toddlers and those who were sick.

After the sixth visit, the director invited me and my interpreter into his office for a visit. Once the tea was brought in, he closed the door and we sat down. After exchanging pleasantries and accepting the hot tea, the director looked me in the eyes and through my interpreter said. "You and your soldiers have been very kind and helpful to our orphanage. The staff and I appreciate the material support during these desperate times. There was an initial outpouring of international aid after the Taliban was deposed, but that was short-lived. Since you came last fall, you have made several visits with food, clothing, school and medical supplies; and have asked for nothing in return."

My reply was simple. "When we became aware of the needs of the children, our hearts were broken. The food and medical supplies were part of our Army's humanitarian aid budget, but the clothing, toys and school supplies came from our families, schools, churches and social organizations. You are wrong in one way. We received much joy with each visit by being allowed to play with your children. Bringing needed supplies was our excuse to see the children."

He smiled and continued, "Do you know what I did prior to this assignment?" I responded, "No, tell me." "I was the intelligence officer under Najibullah." * (My Afghan history was weak, but I recalled that he served as president prior to the Soviet invasion and occupation.) "That must have been an interesting time in your nation's history," was my reply. "It certainly was." He grunted. I felt like he was driving to a point.

"I have something in which I think you might be interested." He said. "What might that be?" I queried. His response surprised me. "How about a list of high-level Taliban and Al Qaeda leaders living in hiding in Kabul and the surrounding area?"

I considered how I should handle this. As a chaplain, I believed that this was outside of my lane, but I didn't want to pass up actionable intelligence, so I replied, "Though I can't do anything with such information, I know someone who can. Would it be okay if I brought one of our intelligence officers to speak with you?" The director thought briefly and agreed to deliver the list at a future meeting. We scheduled a tentative time, thanked him for his hospitality and willingness to help. I left wondering where this would lead. Later that evening I spoke with our intelligence officer. He agreed that we should pursue the offer and recommended going back with our chief counter-intelligence officer. I briefed the chief, and we coordinated our meeting with the director.

A few days later, we entered the director's office. I introduced the chief and we sat down. The director had on his desk what looked like legal-size sheets of paper clipped together. Written in Arabic script, the information was organized into several columns. Though I couldn't read it, it appeared to include name, affiliation, and address.

The director reiterated what it was. "These are the names and information of high-level Taliban and Al Qaeda leaders living in hiding in Kabul. How accurate I cannot say;
maybe ninety percent, maybe fifty-percent." He then picked up the sheets. As the chief leaned forward to accept them, the director intentionally handed the document to me. Understanding the gesture, I received the document with a nod and then passed it to the chief. Following culturally appropriate manly hugs and handshakes, our small team departed. That was my last visit to the orphanage.

What came of the list, I'll likely never know. What I do know is that none of us, including our intelligence officer, could have predicted the second-order effects of extending humanitarian efforts and simple human kindness from the battalion and our generous donors from home. *

https://en.wikipedia.org/wiki/National_Reconciliation

Najibullah Ahmadzai February 1947 – 27 September 1996), commonly known as **Najibullah** or **Dr. Najib**, was the President of Afghanistan from 1987 until 1992, when the mujahideen took over Kabul. He had previously held different careers under the People's Democratic Party of Afghanistan (PDPA) and was a graduate of Kabul University. Following the Saur Revolution and the establishment of the Democratic Republic of Afghanistan, Najibullah was a low profile bureaucrat: he was sent into exile as Ambassador to Iran during Hafizullah Amin's rise to power. He returned to Afghanistan following the Soviet intervention which toppled Amin's rule and placed Babrak Karmal as head of state, party and government. During Karmal's rule, Najibullah became head of the KHAD, the Afghan equivalent of the Soviet KGB.

Chapter 85

Final Meeting: "We Are Not Going to Apologize."

As our deployment was ending, I was amazed that all the recommended projects at Pul-e-Charki were nearing completion. The Maharamona meal was eaten with salt, and the sheep were accepted, along with burial assistance, and the death gratuity was processed expeditiously by the JAGs of CJCMOTF. School renovation was progressing steadily with newly built outdoor latrines. The well was drilled, the aluminum pump was installed and functioning. The MEDCAP treated over 1600 patients. In all, six official meetings were held with the fathers of the boys killed. Still I felt there was one thing missing.

Having served during the Vietnam Era, I was aware of the emotional struggles of some returning Veterans, especially those involved in close combat and incidents of collateral damage, with innocent non-combatants. Though I couldn't see into the hearts and minds of my Soldiers, I could look into their eyes and hear their words in private conversations. The death of the four boys was probably the most devastating incident of the deployment. It's one thing to fire on and kill enemy combatants – those who are trying to kill you. It's another to accidentally kill innocent young boys hunting for scrap metal or semi-precious stones. I pondered and prayed for a way to help those most closely involved with the incident process their personal pain and feelings of guilt.

Talking with one of our doctors who worked in the emergency room on an Indian Reservation in New Mexico, he mentioned the benefits of debriefing – processing the incident by reviewing what happened and how it made those involved feel. Though we had done that with those involved immediately after the incident – within twenty-four hours, I thought we needed to do more. As we dialogued, the idea of a face-to-face meeting with the fathers, over tea, was brought up. Having our soldiers who were leading the live fire exercise meet with the bereaved fathers to simply sip tea and express sorrow over the loss of their sons lives, seemed like a bridge too far. Still, I felt like I had to attempt something for the sake of the fathers and our soldiers who were directly involved.

Later, I went to see Master Sgt. Moses, one of the team sergeants. He was a respected leader in the battalion. His reaction frankly was not surprising: "I'm not going to sit with those fathers and apologize for what happened! We didn't do anything wrong. We chased them off twice! It was their fault for coming around back into the firing range. No one knew they were there. We've got nothing to apologize for!" He declared. I agreed. We didn't know they were there. We did chase them off. Still, they were accidentally killed during an exercise we ran. "I'm not asking you to apologize. I'm simply asking you to sit, man-to-man, father-to-father, and tell them that you regret their loss – that's all." Then I said. "In the long run, I think it will do well for both you and your men, and these fathers. Just think how you would feel in their place." I knew I had said enough. Moses agreed to think about it and talk with his men, so I left. I had another team sergeant to visit.

Sgt. 1st Class Dave was the other team sergeant running the range with his men. A unique blend of discipline and sensitivity, he was initially more open to the idea, but still wanted to know the expected end state of the meeting. When I explained it was intended to help bring closure to both the fathers and the soldiers most directly involved with the incident – more conciliation than reconciliation, he agreed to speak with his team. Though I understood from my soldiers' perspective, it was a totally unintended accident, resulting from the boys own natural curiosity, I believed that having tea with these fathers, would go a long way to bringing closure.

Why did I think so? Upon reflection, it probably came from the time my youngest brother, Luke was hit by a car driven by a local farmer who had come into town to do business. Only four or five years old, Luke broke from our mother's grasp and ran into the street in front of a parked car. I know because
I was watching from our front yard across the street, when I heard the thud and our mother's scream. The driver slammed on the breaks as soon as he saw Luke. After he stopped, he picked up my youngest brother, put him in his car along with our mother and rushed them to the local hospital emergency room. A day later, the farmer stopped by to see how little Luke was doing. Though it was Luke's fault, the farmer felt bad and cared enough to respond, try to save his life, and even later check up on him. As a result, there was never any animosity or ill feelings between our families. Though linguistically and culturally different people, I had found them no different to us in our basic humanity. The meeting would be as much for our benefit as theirs.

After a couple days, I checked with both team sergeants for their decisions. I knew I couldn't force them, but I prayed they would participate. Sgt. 1st Class Dave said his men were all in. They would have tea and express condolence over the death of the four boys and explain their efforts to save them afterwards. Master Sgt. Moses was less sure of the purpose and benefit of the event. "We'll go." He said. "But I am *not* apologizing for something that was not my fault!" I assured him that he was free to express his sentiment in any way he chose. I went back to the village elders, some of whom were members of the KMTC military staff, and they set up an afternoon meeting in one of their homes.

When the day came, we set up our departure time and location on our compound. Several Toyota pickups and my Land Cruiser loaded with members of two Special Forces teams, a public affairs officer, and senior interpreter convoyed to Pul-e-Charki. Arriving at the designated home, we left a couple guards with our vehicles and proceeded to enter the home, led by a KMTC officer in civilian Afghan dress, followed by me and the team members. I took off my shoes at the door, as was custom. Inside, the fathers were waiting, as we shook hands, we placed our hands across our chests and greeted them in Dari and Pashtu. As we sat, I removed my body armor, as did my soldiers, most placing their weapons on the floor and then covering their rifles with their body armor.

As was the custom, a teenage boy came in with warm water, a basin and a towel. It reminded me of Jesus and the Last Supper; how Jesus washed his disciples' feet, but when he came to Peter, he refused to allow Jesus to wash him. Some of the men initially refused my proposal but were now committed. How it would turn out, I would soon see. I prayed it would be positive for both parties.

The boy poured warm water over our fingers and offered the towel, as he went around the room. Cookies, nuts and Jalalabad oranges were already laid out on the floor before us. When all hands were washed, he brought out hot tea. For a few minutes we snacked, drank tea, grunted and nodded approval of the delicacies and hospitality provided. After a nod from our trusted public affairs officer, I explained the purpose of our visit.

"One day soon, we will be leaving to return to our homes. Before we go, we wanted to come, one last time to sit with you and mourn the loss and injury of your sons. As their chaplain, I am concerned about the burden my soldiers will carry with them because of this terrible accident." Our interpreter conveyed my opening remarks. All the fathers present nodded, acknowledging the hopeful intent of my words. I continued, "Many of us are fathers too, and if our sons were taken from us in this tragic way, we would be broken beyond belief." I prayed for just the right words of transition. "We'll never know what they might have grown up to be, a teacher, an engineer, a medical doctor, a general, a president, but we have come for a few moments to share your pain." Looking over to Team Sergeant Moses, I saw a tear trickle down his cheek. His opening words broke the invisible dam of emotions in the hearts of everyone in the room. "Please forgive us, we didn't know they were up there. We couldn't see them and didn't know until it was too late!" Blurting out the very words he insisted he'd never say, caused the eyes of everyman present, Afghan and American, to well up with tears.

Following his lead, soldier after solder, every Green Beret team member present spoke similar words of sorrow, regret, and even apology for the incident that unintentionally claimed the lives of four of their sons and wounded a fifth. The men of both teams who had primary responsibility for that live-fire training exercise, as well as the emergency medical responders exposed their hearts. All spoke in gentle, humble words, conveyed through an interpreter, himself an Afghan medical doctor, specially chosen for this event because of our confidence in his linguistic skill, intelligence, and maturity. During much of the time, he, too, had tears in his eyes.

Up to this point, the Afghan fathers had said little, beyond the theologically correct Islamic assertion that "Allah had willed them to die as martyrs." When the last U.S. soldier had shared his words, the fathers spoke. They thanked the men for coming and having tea with them. One confirmed that retaliation was never an option in their minds, as such an attempt would have been suicide on their part. They did express concern that no American official came to their homes during the mourning period, if it was, indeed, an accident. My fruitless conversation with the battalion commander came to mind.

Near the end of the hour-long conversation, the Afghan father-spokesman who had lost both his son, and his nephew, motioned with his hand that he wanted to speak a concluding word. All eyes turned to him. "We know that you did not intend to kill our sons – that it was an accident. Allah willed that they should die as martyrs. You have done your jobs well. Now go home with no heaviness of heart. We forgive you." I let his words sink in.

Unsure of what would be the outcome of this risky encounter, I believed I had just heard the best words and sensed the best emotional responses possible. Though unimaginable at the outset, I witnessed humility, genuine sorrow, sympathy, brokenness, and forgiveness – all the essential elements of not only conciliation, but reconciliation. In my pastor's heart I was satisfied that this was a healing moment for both our soldiers and the bereaved Afghan fathers.

I thanked them for their time and hospitably, this and the many times prior – this was meeting number seven for me – and I asked if we could take a group picture outside to commemorate this special gathering. We filed out, put on our boots and leaving body armor aside, we took a group photo through the cracked lens of my digital camera and the good lens of the public affairs officer. After many strong, lingering, culturally appropriate, manly Afghan hugs, and even kisses on the cheeks of these American warriors - including my own -- we boarded our vehicles and returned to base.

As part of our daily routine, I reported my significant actions in the Commanders Update Brief. No questions were asked, and few comments were made, but I knew that one of the most important missions of our deployment had just been accomplished.

Chapter 86

Lunch at the Golden Lotus Restaurant

The Pul-e-Charki school renovation continued as our time of transition began. Classified plans were made to pack up and return home in stages, as our replacement unit came in. Interestingly, the unit we originally replaced, came back to relieve us. Rumor had it they were none too pleased. I wasn't sure why, as we had improved the base considerably – new dining facility, buried water pipes, Cat5 wire, new chapel carpet, and all.

During my last few remaining days, I received word through our interpreters, that a local businessman wanted to have lunch with me in "downtown" Kabul. When I enquired who this man was and why he wanted to meet, the reply was that he was a businessman interested in meeting the chaplain who had organized the Pul-e-Charki Maharamona and school renovation. I spoke with my Command Sergeant Major, and he thought it would be okay, if I had a security detail stationed inside and out. My assistant coordinated an outside team to watch while we went inside.

Three of us, my assistant, my interpreter, Tem, and I, entered the Golden Lotus Chinese restaurant where we were introduced to two clean-shaven Afghan gentlemen dressed in western business suits. We exchanged greetings and introductions and were seated. I took my mother's advice and sat with my back to the wall and face toward the entrance. My armed assistant sat to my left and my interpreter to my right. The Afghan businessmen sat across from us at a round table. Tea was brought, and our order taken. Then it was time for conversation and lunch.

Since I was invited, I let my hosts speak first. Their English was as limited as was my Dari, so we fell into a conversation through my interpreter. "We heard about your teaching English at Pul-e-Charki School, the food, clothes and medicine you brought to Allahuddin Orphanage, and the way you helped the families of the dead boys. We wanted to meet you, and we wanted to know why you did all these things?" Both men stared at me as the interpretation was made. I was taken aback. At first, I didn't know what to say. I looked first at Piper 13, then at Tem. Taking a deep breath, I asked God for a simple, succinct reply to a complex question.

I told them how our unit came to remove Al Qaeda from Afghanistan, after the Talban allowed them to train and launch an attack against our country that killed many people in New York, Washington and

Pennsylvania. Part of that included deposing the radical Taliban regime, and helping install a government elected by the Afghan people. One of our main purposes was to train the first battalions of the New Afghan Army. I also explained that humanitarian projects, like teaching English in the school, providing food, clothing, toys and medical support were part of our way of showing our genuine concern and support for the oppressed and poor Afghan people.

The men listened intently but pressed further. "But why did you do this when others who also came from other countries did not?" At first, I was confused by the question, but I decided to take a stab at what they were asking. "I did what I did because as a Christian Chaplain, a follower of Isa (Jesus), I believe that He wanted us to sow seeds of peace and not war, love and not hate. The Ingil (Gospel) teaches that we show our love for God by loving people. We came to stop and prevent evil men from continuing to do harm against our country and yours." The two men looked at each other and nodded. They seemed satisfied with my answer.

I then went on to explain how the different projects were resourced: school reconstruction and medical projects through the U.S. Army Civil Affairs budget. And how school supplies, toys and clothes came from donations of individuals, organizations, schools, and churches back in the U.S. and Europe sent through the Army Postal system – how these donors even paid to have their gifts sent to Afghanistan. They seemed genuinely impressed by the spontaneous, private generosity of Americans to Afghan people.

Before we got up to leave, one asked, "What do you seek in return?" I replied, "Security for us, and peace for you!" They paid for lunch, thanked me for the opportunity to meet, and for my leadership in our humanitarian projects.

As we departed, I noticed that my outside guard had also eaten. The two Afghan men also ordered meals that were taken out to them to eat in their vehicles. Driving off, I wondered who these two men were. I never did find out.

Chapter 87

Packing Up and Heading Back to KIA

Though we couldn't divulge the exact time of our departure, it became increasingly obvious by our activities that it was imminent. Pallets and small containers laid out on our parade field were systematically filled, as our organizational and personal gear was inspected by our newly arrived MP Company. I did my best to utilize old wooden Soviet weapons' crates to carry my gear, and accumulated mementos – Afghan wood sculptures of animals, a few hand-woven rugs and as many Soviet bayonets and as I could scrounge – the latter packed inside an empty old Soviet artillery shell casing that had been used as a cigarette butt receptacle on our compound.

As we packed, a problem arose. While we were rotating out of Afghanistan, a much larger military invasion force was massing around Iraq. Aircraft that had transported us into Afghanistan were now moving personnel and equipment into Kuwait and other allied Gulf States. Every day we listened intently to the logistics briefing for news on our departure, but the U.S. Air Force had a new priority.

After a while, our innovative support center commander, Lt. Ted, came up with the idea of contracting civilian cargo aircraft to bring us home. He floated the idea of leasing a Boeing 747 cargo plane. After doing some online research, he led a team to Kabul International Airport to see if they had the necessary equipment to load our pallets and containers. It was ultimately decided to wait on our U.S. Air Force C17s to come and bring us home in stages. As usual, someone quipped that it was the chaplain's job to ensure that the planes arrived on time. Next came the task of deciding who would return in what order, and on which plane. Administrative and logistics personnel were divided strategically in the first and last "chalks," as the aircraft were typically designated. The movement team decided that the chaplain and a medical provider would be on the first chalk, and other medical personnel would be divided up between the remaining two chalks. With that decision made, I continued preparations to transition from my ministry at FOB195 back to Ft Carson, our demobilization station.

In the meantime, I did pray, and led our soldiers in prayer for airflow to allow adequate aircraft to take us home. Without specifics, I employed prayer warriors, family, friends and church members back home in praying for a "ride home." With Operation Iraqi Freedom kicking off, we needed all the prayer support we could muster. And pray they did.

As winter melted into spring, our hopes of returning home grew with the increasing daytime sun. In late March, the logistics officer announced that C17s indeed would be arriving the next week. With half-hearted hope, we completed our packing and started living out of our rucksacks. I turned in the keys of my Toyota Land Cruiser to our motor sergeant. Our equipment was packed onto pallets and readied for transport by Afghan "Jingle" trucks. Next stop, KIA. I wondered how we would say our final good-byes to our Afghan partners, interpreters and ANA officers we had come to know and love.

Shortly we would see.

Chapter 88

Farewell to Arms and our Afghan Partners

When the word came for "Chalk 1" to be ready to leave in two days, I knew I had to bid a difficult farewell. My interpreter, Tem, who became known as "the chaplain's son," had become my trusted, personal interpreter. He turned nineteen during the time we were in Kabul. I met his family and ate with them several times. They were very hospitable, inviting me and other soldiers, male and female, over for meals in their home. Though they were poor, by American standards, they were possessions: their food and their fellowship.

Tem's father, a health professional, became my Afghan brother, his mother, my sister. His almost blind grandmother, "mother Kalan," adopted me as her American son. They took risks having us in their home several times, but the warmth of their hospitality was the finest pleasure we experienced in their country. Their simple means notwithstanding, their generosity toward family and neighbors was obvious. Tem's mother did laundry by hand for her large extended family, and this after a long day at work.

As our days ended, the sight of his mother's hand-washed laundry impressed me. I asked Tem if they sold washing machines in Kabul. He nodded affirmatively, so I quickly sent home for one-hundred- fifty dollars to buy one.

A few days prior to our departure, I asked Tem to guide me to a local store that sold electric washing machines. It was the "Appliance Factory Outlet of Kabul." It had a small variety of electric washing machines to choose from, but I had to find a model that would work in their home. We settled on a green plastic electric washing machine, that resembled the old ringer-washer my mother had in the U.S. back in the fifties. It had an ungrounded 220v plug and a plastic hose receptacle for the tub drain. The cycle was semi-manual. First, you filled the tub with water and laundry soap. Then you closed the top lid and plugged in the unit for the wash cycle. Then, you unplugged the unit, and opened a plastic spigot to drain the tank of dirty soapy water. Next, with a hose or bucket, you filled the tank with clean water and ran the electric-powered rinse cycle. After draining the rinse water, the clothes are wrung out (by hand or through a ringer) and hung out to dry.

Tem's mother was home the day we dropped it off. She looked at me with a fake cross look, "I would be angry with you, but it would not help." She sighed. All we had done up to that point was deliver leftover toiletries, small electronics (CD player and a digital camera), toys, food, toilet paper, personal office supplies, clothes, school supplies, and other excess donations. Rather than throw useful things in the trash or burn-barrel, we periodically dropped them off at their home – usually at night.

Most Westerners would cringe at the wash-rinse-dry cycle described, but Tem's mother was ecstatic. She was able to do four loads in the time it used to take her to do one. Soon, she was doing the laundry for other family and neighbors.

Many of my comrades were sharing their excess supplies with interpreters, day laborers, and members of the Afghan military staff of KMTC. Rather than waste it, we felt compelled to share with those with whom we had worked and learned to love and appreciate.

Finally, the day came. "Chalk One," was directed to be ready with two carry-on bags at 9:00 a.m. the next day. A small shuttle bus (unarmored, of course), drove onto the parade field. We dropped our bags in a line prior to boarding. These items would be loaded onto a five-ton "Jingle Truck" along with our prepackaged pallets. Taking advantage of the loading time, I hustled over to the interpreters' building. Tem was inside looking out onto the commotion on the parade field.

My emotions were strong and near the surface. I called to him, using every word of social greeting in Dari that he had taught me; "Hello! How are you? Is your body good? What's your name? How old are you? Are you good?" The other interpreters smiled and some giggled at my staccato delivery. Tem looked at me with lachrymose eyes. He struggled to remain composed, almost as much as me. I hugged him, thanked him, told him that I loved him, and that I would pray that we would see each other again. My greatest fear was that I would not. Stifling a sob, I turned and almost ran out of the room.

The bus was boarding. Lined up shoulder-to-shoulder, was the staff of KMCT: Brig. Gen. Assifi, Col. Kharoudim, all the senior officers who had worked with us in the training of seven new Kandaks of the New Afghan Army. Among them were the faces of three or four senior officers who had set with my soldiers and me during the reconciliation meetings with the fathers of the four Afghan boys accidentally killed three and one-half months earlier.

As we shook hands along the line, every one of them pulled me close, kissed me – in a manly Afghan way of course - and either offered or replied to a simple Afghan blessing I had learned: "Man dana, bashi!" The reply, "Zan da, bashi!" Teary eyes lubricated the smiles they wore. We had ostensibly come to kill terrorists who had used their country as a training and staging area for attacks against our homeland, but we were leaving as their comrades and collaborators in the training of the first two brigades of the New Afghan Army...and so much more.

General Assifi was the last to say farewell. He hugged me tight, kissed me three times, and said, "Well done, chaplain. I will remember you. Please remember me in your prayers." With tears streaming, I replied, "I will, my friend...'cha daw fez'" (Good-bye!) and boarded the bus.

As we pulled away, the interpreters off in the shade, and the staff of KMTC standing in the sun, waved us out the main gate. As I looked back, I wondered what would become of our work, our friends and their country.

Next stop, KIA – the place where we began our adventure, eight months before.

Chapter 89
Freedom Bird

After spending a day and a night on the tarmac of KIA, our C17 cargo plane finally arrived. We loaded our pallets, our rucksacks and ourselves into the Globemaster characteristically dubbed, "Freedom Bird." Seventeen hours later, sleeping much of it on the floor of the main cargo bay, we touched down in Charleston, SC for refueling, potty stop, calls home, snacks and a fresh crew. With short time and long lines, I first called my mother – to let her know that I was back on U.S. soil. It was in the middle of the night, so all she said was, "Good." She went back to sleep. I hung up and was unable to make any more calls go through with my telephone calling card.

Warned not to divulge our arrival time to anyone, I purchased a snack and re-boarded when called. All I could think about was a real bed and hot shower, but that was still many hours away.

Once airborne, I found my spot in the cargo bay. The vibrations soon lulled me back to sleep. My next memory was a tap on my shoulder, telling me to get back into my seat for landing. I belted in for an early-morning landing into Colorado Springs. Cheers erupted as we touched down. High fives flew everywhere, as we gathered up our rucksacks and duffle bags. As the tailgate lowered, we marched out single file onto the tarmac of Peterson Air Force Base. Squinting in the early morning light, I dropped my bags and went into the front leaning rest position. I slowly lowered my face to the concrete and kissed Colorado ground. I was grateful to be home.

EPILOGUE – A: Trip to GTMO

It was Spring of 2007. My office phone rang. "This is S.A. Smith. Are you the chaplain who served with the 5/19th Special Forces in Afghanistan in 2002?" Missing the caller's first name, I said. "I didn't catch your first name." "The name is Smith, Special Agent Smith, CID, from Baltimore." The call took me by surprise. I was now working fulltime at Colorado's Joint Forces Headquarters in the office of the Chief of Staff as Quality Manager, and part-time as chaplain for the 89th Troop Command.

"Yes, I'm the chaplain that deployed with that unit." I replied. Then he asked, "Were you present for the interrogation of Mohammed Jawad at KMTC?" "Yes, I was the human rights observer. What is this about?" Special Agent Smith asked if I could get to a secure line to continue the conversation. I told him I would check and took his number to call back.

After checking into secure telecommunications options, I called Agent Smith. When I explained the limitations of access, he decided to speak over the commercial line. He asked about my role as human rights observer in the interrogation. Near the end of the conversation, he asked if other unit members involved in the incident were still around, and if I had their contact information. I thought a moment and started writing down names of those I could remember – four or five immediately came to mind. Before hanging up, he asked about a good time to come out and conduct interviews. I checked the yearly training calendar and gave him some dates. He said he would check with his supervisors and confirm his visit.

Two weeks later, Agent Smith was in my office. After interviewing me and other unit members involved, he left with little comment. Within days, I received another call. This time, it was from a JAG officer from the Office of Military Commissions (OMC) – out of the Pentagon...and Naval Station Guantanamo Bay, Cuba. He introduced himself as the lead prosecutor of a team of military attorneys assigned to the case of Mohamed Jawad. He asked similar questions regarding my role as human rights observer in the interrogation. After I outlined my involvement in the incident and informed him of the physical evidence in my possession, he asked if I would serve as a witness in Jawad's pre-trial hearing at GITMO. Assuring him of my personal willingness, I thought it best to secure authorization from my military supervisors.

Shortly after hanging up, I walked down the hall to see my boss, Col. Joe Reiter, Chief-of-Staff. Already aware of the visit by the special agent, Col. Reiter affirmed the importance of my testimony and authorized me to proceed. He simply asked me to keep him in the loop as things developed. The lead prosecutor was pleased with both my willingness, and our command support. He told me to block out specific dates and wait for travel orders. That, it turned out, was easier said than done. A week prior to my scheduled departure, I was called with travel instructions. I was to fly to Baltimore, catch a rotator flight to Guantanamo Bay, Cuba, and ride a ferry to the OMC facility. That, it turned out, was the easy part. With thirty years in the military, I knew the importance of having printed (and funded) orders in hand prior to departing on any military duty – especially one taking me outside the U.S. – as GITMO technically was. After a rushed, last-minute process, completed through the support of Col. Ken Sanchez, G3, I had the necessary authorization, orders, and travel arrangements in hand. It was time, once more, to fly into the unknown.

At the Military Airlift Command (MAC) terminal in Baltimore, I checked in and waited. While there, I received a special visit from stepdaughter, Diane and her baby daughter, Caroline. They drove over to bring me some BBQ ribs from a local restaurant. It was fun to see them and savor the snack on the ensuing flight.

After take-off, the group of approximately thirty passengers began mingling and visiting. My first contact was with my former battalion counterintelligence officer. He gladly shared my ribs, as we caught up. Before long, the U.S. Marine Corps interrogator from the Kabul embassy was smacking his lips and licking his fingers over a meaty rib.

Upon return from washing up after a hearty shared, lunch, an unfamiliar gentleman invited me to sit with him. He introduced himself as an Air Force Reserve attorney – a JAG. He said that he was teaching at a third-tier law school in California but hoped to do a good job in Guantanamo as a lead defense attorney, make a name for himself, and secure a teaching position at a tier-one law school, like Harvard or Yale. He then asked me what I was heading to do in Guantanamo. I told him my purpose. He asked a few questions and picked up a book to read, as did I.

Landing in Guantanamo, we passed through customs and security. Boarding a nearby ferry, we took a twenty-minute trip to our destination. After signing in, we were issued security badges and keys to our lodging and vehicle – a 15 passenger van.

At the security check-in and base security briefing, the four of us who were the prosecution's key witnesses linked up. Three of us were involved directly or indirectly, Marine interrogator from the Kabul Embassy, our counterintelligence team chief, and me, the chaplain, appointed as human rights observer. The fourth member was a former criminal investigation division (CID) warrant-officer who did the follow-up investigation of the attack among the Afghan witnesses at the scene, in addition to the general investigation background.

Since we were there for the same purpose, we hung out together to meet our timelines and purpose. The second day, we found our way to the military court facility. It was in an old headquarters building adjacent to an abandoned landing strip. Included in the complex were old airplane hangars and a village of temporary structures, all built to support the detainee judicial process.

Passing through the court facility security, we were directed upstairs to the prosecution's offices. There we met the team of military prosecutors. The lead attorney was a male Air Force Reserve Lieutenant Colonel, assisted by a male Navy Lieutenant Commander, and a female Navy Lieutenant – all Staff Judge Advocates (SJA/JAG). After introductions, they showed us the offices, explained the pre-trial process and proposed timetable. Then I showed the physical evidence I had maintained in my possession for over five years: the stomach bandage used for a blindfold, and the sand-colored sandbag used to cover his head, in addition to printed photos and notes of the events surrounding the attack, interrogation and initial medical treatment. I also showed them a printed PowerPoint presentation of the entire incident, including a log with photos of the wounded Soldiers, and a storyboard of them in the ISAF intensive care unit and final movement to the MEDEVAC helicopter.

They were impressed with what I had and planned to introduce it in the hearing. Security concerns over the physical identification of our Special Forces member were addressed. It was decided that he would wear a balaclava that would only leave his eyes uncovered. This later caused consternation with the outer court security personnel. With a proposed agenda in hand, and an outline of the prosecution's strategy, we left for lunch and a tour of the unique, historic naval base.

Piling into our fifteen-passenger van, we headed out for a self-guided area tour. We wanted to see the sights, check out base amenities, and meet the residents; human and otherwise. Following a coastal road, we were immediately struck by the lack of trees on this wind-swept Caribbean island. The few palm trees we saw were in housing areas and around naval facility buildings. They were obviously planted. Otherwise, the island was covered with low bushy vegetation, less than ten to fifteen-feet high.

As we passed though housing areas, we came to a school complex that was replacing its football field with synthetic turf. Across the road was a Navy Exchange with food court. We stopped in to see what souvenirs were available, as well as the unlikely sale of Cuban cigars. There was an ample supply of stuffed iguanas, tee-shirts, hats and postcards, but, no Cuban cigars

– though other Caribbean cigars were in ample supply. I purchased some tee-shirts and hats for folks back home, especially those who helped get me here.

Following a quick shop, we headed to a local fast-food place. As we pulled into the parking lot, we spied a huge iguana – seven to eight feet in length. As we got out, he froze and just stared at us. Warned in our briefing not to disturb the wildlife – especially the iguanas, I was none-the-less wanting to get a close-up photo and visual examination. He bore a striking resemblance to a monster dragon I once saw in a Godzilla movie. As I approached, the lizard raised a front leg and then bolted for a hole in the grassy area next to the parking lot. I jumped back and quickly followed my colleagues into the food court. It became quickly apparent that the massive iguanas were in charge – and knew it.

Over lunch, we each shared our role in the incident that brought us to the Caribbean island. The new member of the team was the retired CID agent. With time to kill, we decided to take a tour of our historic garden spot and see what else lay along its wind-blown shores. Back in the van, we headed out of the housing area. Before long, we passed an overgrown area with high fences and wooden corner guard towers. One team member suggested that these were refugee holding areas from the 1995 Haitian boat exodus that claimed the lives of many seeking asylum in the U.S. Later local queries confirmed that assumption.

A few miles down the asphalt road, we came to the various facilities of the Guantanamo (GITMO) facility. We drove by areas for detention and military operations, to include what appeared to be temporary lodging for military personnel. Our first impression was that the detainees lived in the better facilities than the troops. One facility, Camp America, was located on a bluff overlooking the sea with a beautiful view of the setting sun. After we passed through the detention area, we turned around and began to make our way back. Up ahead, we saw a soldier limping along the side of the road in a walking cast. We pulled alongside and asked if he'd like a lift. He looked us over and said, "Sure."

We introduced ourselves as guests of the OMC. Our hitchhiker told us he was on a six-month security rotation with the Puerto Rico Army National Guard. When I inquired about his foot, whether he had injured it on a run or other athletic event, he looked at me with a serious look: "Hell no! I got my instep stomped by a detainee when I was trying to give him his meal." He went on to explain that many of the MPs and other detention facility personnel had been injured during duty, to include kicks, punches and bites. When I asked him if they had to get rabies shots to work there, he replied, "And then some!"

A half-mile down the road, we dropped off our serendipitous GITMO guide. In that brief courtesy ride, we learned enough to convince us of the inherent danger of these prisoners and the wisdom of keeping these irregular enemy combatants offshore and away from the U.S. civilian population. With the sun going down, we turned into our lodging for our first night in the Pearl of the Antilles, Cuba's nickname.

Reporting the next day as directed, we met our prosecution team on the second floor. We discussed our proposed schedule and were briefed on the pre-trial process. Timing was critical, as other proceedings were in process. As we concluded, the lead paralegal showed us a break room where we could watch on closed-circuit television, the ongoing proceedings in the courtroom below. That would help us know when to go down to present our testimony. As we stood in the break room, a bearded man was on the witness stand. He looked vaguely familiar, but it wasn't until the paralegal announced, "Sheik Khalid Mohammad, the alleged mastermind of the September 11th attack is being examined right now." As he said it, the hair on my neck stood up. Later, I shared that with other members of the prosecution team. Most of them admitted to the same reaction. We all agreed that we were in the presence of pure evil. Briefing completed, we left to get ready for the first day of the proceedings.

I was number three of four key witnesses in the pre-trial hearing. Prepped by the prosecution team on general courtroom procedure, I was sworn in by the pre-trial judge, an Army Staff Judge Advocate Colonel in a black robe. He looked like "Judge Judy," but without the white lace collar.

The prosecution began by asking me basic questions to establish my standing and credibility as a witness; "Were you deployed with the Special Forces battalion in December of 2002 when two soldiers were attacked in downtown Kabul?" I replied, "Yes, I was." "Explain how you came to be involved in the handling and interrogation of the suspect." I flashed back to the visit in my office by our operations officer, Maj. Ken, shortly after I had returned from the ISAF field hospital where our two soldiers were undergoing emergency surgery and treatment. "At approximately 2200 hours on 16 December 2002. our operations officer, an experienced Denver Police Lieutenant, came to inform me that the suspect who threw an explosive device into the jeep carrying two Special Forces soldiers and Afghan interpreter, was in custody and on the way to our facility for interrogation. He asked me to be the 'human rights observer' for the interrogation. He told me that he thought that I was the best person for the position, given my role as chaplain and primary trainer in human rights and law of land warfare for the several Afghan battalions we had trained up to that point. He said that if at any time I felt the suspect's human rights were being violated, I was to intervene. He closed with, 'This is as much for our protection as for his.'"

The prosecutor then led me through the reception, processing, interrogation and transfer of the person under custody (PUC). I noticed the stoic judge paying close attention and the defense attorneys taking copious notes. The prosecuting attorney then asked me the most difficult question: "Can you identify the accused in this courtroom?" It had been five years since I saw that young man, and I was fearful that I would not recognize him. But as I looked over to the defense area, there was the face of the man who was brought into my chapel, blindfolded and bagged. "That's him over there." I pointed to the now twenty-four-year-old man, some thirty-five pounds heavier and with a semi-bearded face, like Abraham Lincoln. "How can you be sure?" The prosecutor asked. "Well, I admit that he is significantly heavier and has more facial hair, but I recognize his eyes and facial structure...plus, if you have doubts, you can verify his identity with the items that I kept." The judge broke in, "What do you have, chaplain?"

"Your honor, I kept the blindfold and sandbag that was over his eyes and head when he was brought into our facility. The guards took them off and left them on the floor of the chapel area that led into the conference room where he was interrogated. I simply picked them up to keep the entry area clear and put them in my chapel office. Later I placed them in plastic bags to be placed in the unit's historical display case back home. When I was contacted about this hearing, I told the investigator and legal team what I had, and they recommended that I bring it as evidence." The magistrate was very interested in my "exhibits." "So, you have had these in your possession from the night of the interrogation until today?" The magistrate confirmed my statement. "Yes, sir. Seems to me that the stomach bandage used as a blindfold should contain DNA that would match that of the accused. Also, the lack of blood stains will corroborate the condition of his face and head when he came into our custody." The magistrate tried not to smile. "Bring those here, please. These will be entered into the prosecution's case as evidence." The prosecutor took my two bags and gave them to the judge. "That wasn't so bad." I thought to myself. But the show wasn't over.
Next it was the defense team's turn.

"So, chaplain, you say that you were there the whole time?" The Air Force Reserve defense attorney looked at me and then to his client. I replied, "From the time he entered my facility, through the walk to the medical clinic for examination, and back, through most of the interrogation, and when he was transferred out..." The JAG spun around and snapped, "Most of the time? When were you gone?" I knew this was coming. "I had visual or auditory contact the entire time he was in our custody." He took a step closer, "How is that possible?" He was looking for inconsistency in my testimony. "I was in the conference room where the interrogation took place starting at approximately 2330 hours, until approximately 0130 the next morning. After that, I moved into my office on the other side of a three-sixteenth-inch plywood wall where I could hear everything going on." The defense attorney continued his probe. "So, what did you hear?" "I heard questions asked through an interpreter; some questions asked by our interrogator from the U.S. Embassy, as well as by one of our intelligence officers." He continued; "So how can you be sure he was treated humanely?"

I focused on the facts, as the prosecution had directed. "I listened to how he was questioned, the tone and volume of speech. I was impressed with the self-control of our interrogators. In fact, the Afghan interpreter got more animated than our interrogators." "What do you mean?" The defense attorney asked. "Sometimes our interrogator would speak in a normal tone, but the interpreter raised his voice, something I was trained not to do, as a former U.S. Army interpreter." I replied. "You were an interpreter? Explain." The defense queried. "Yes, I was a U.S. Army linguist in the Army Security Agency trained at the Defense Language Institute from 1972-1976. In fact, I was a technical language instructor in the Portuguese department of the Defense Language Institute." He homed in, "So you don't speak Dari or Pashtu." I was getting tired of the line of questioning, "I learned combat commands in Dari and Pashtu as part of my pre-mobilization training. After arriving in Afghanistan, I picked up some basic social dialogue."

As he prodded, I sensed he was trying to discredit my testimony, "Could you understand any of the interrogation?" I had to be careful, "I heard what was asked in English that was interpreted,
followed by the reverse interpretation. I knew when he said, 'Yes, No, or 'I don't know.' I also heard when he didn't reply." Next, he tried to lead me, "What kinds of things did they ask? I explained some of what I recalled. "So, did the accused ever admit to the alleged crime?" That was easy. "In fact, he did early on, with a tone of defiance." The defense then asked, "Did he ever change his story?" I thought and said, "Not his story, but his attitude. He came in defiant and proud but ended up less so as the questioning went on." Curious, the defense counsel asked, "What changed his attitude?" I met his stare. "It was the questioning about whether the Koran taught that it was right to kill innocent bystanders, who did you no harm." He stepped closer. "How did he respond?" I looked him in the eye, "He bowed his head and said 'No.'." He turned away, "No more questions, but I reserve the right to recall the witness."

The questioning continued over the next two days. At the end of each day, we had a huddle with the prosecution team. After the second day of testimony, we were prepared for closing arguments and an anticipated motion by the defense to dismiss charges and let the suspect go.

This time I was called last in the sequence of witnesses. Most of the questioning was made by the defense. After the magistrate reminded me that I was still under oath, the defense lawyer came right at me. "One time you said that you heard no shouting, but another time you said that you did. Which is it?" He was fishing for a contradiction. "I said that our interrogators kept themselves under control, but at times the Afghan interpreter significantly exceeded the vocal intensity and volume of the U.S. interrogators." He picked up a copy of my journal of the event that was also previously admitted establishing the timeline of events. "That's not what you wrote here." I sensed he was seeking to discredit me by showing contradiction in my testimony. "When I wrote that I didn't hear any shouting or screaming, I was referring to our U.S. personnel." He rolled his eyes, concluded his remarks and sat down.

The magistrate called for a brief recess before closing arguments. Our prosecution team informed us that we were to sit together for the closing arguments. I had no idea how things would turn out, because I had not heard all the other testimony, in part because some of the U.S. Embassy interrogator's testimony was given in private due to security reasons.

Rather than dominate the prosecution's case, the lead USAF attorney, allowed his U.S. Navy JAG Lieutenant Commander counterpart to present the closing argument. This man was tall, well-mannered and professional. His statement was eloquent and succinct. "Your honor. This was a picture-perfect interrogation." He went on to describe the interrogation as well-planned, and carefully executed according the rules of the U.S. Military interrogation manual, principles of human rights and law of land warfare. He indicated that the suspect was transported carefully, given an initial physical exam, treated humanely, and offered food and water, even allowed to sleep after questioning. He highlighted the fact that the unit assigned a chaplain to serve as a human rights observer, something he had never seen or heard before. He underscored that the suspect admitted to the attack. He concluded: "Your honor, we believe this man is guilty of the charge of attempted murder of two U.S. soldiers and their Afghan interpreter; three men who still carry the scars and injuries of this unprovoked attacked. We move that this case proceed to trial, as this was a picture-perfect interrogation."

The defense attorney was next. Unlike his counterpart, he did not share the stage with his two military attorneys. He went on for at least ten-minutes picking apart each one of our testimonies; the criminal investigator's report was late and incomplete, interrogation techniques were coercive and intimidating, etc. Then he turned and looked at me, "What was masked as an attempt to ensure the safety and humane treatment of this young boy, was a cover-up by a right-wing Christian religious bigot, bent on vengeance over the injury suffered by his comrades." Inside I fumed. This third-tier law professor, who had admitted to me on the plane ride over his self-serving intent to use this case to propel himself into a first-tier law school, was impugning my character and testimony – simply because he could. He didn't care about the truth, he just wanted to get his client free, so his name would make the headlines. I tried not to show my true emotion. The unscrupulous attorney concluded, "Your honor, I move that all charges be dismissed, and that this young man be allowed to return to his mother who lives in a refugee camp in Pakistan." He sat down near the defendant.

All eyes were on the magistrate. He made some notes, shuffled some papers, and looked up. After the character assassination I endured as a key witness, I fully anticipated the announcement of a full dismissal of charges. The magistrate looked up and said, "Defense motion is denied. There is ample evidence of the alleged crime. Detainee is remanded for trial."

I thought twice about what I heard. Looking over to the prosecution team, I saw restrained looks of satisfaction and nods to one another. We all stood as the magistrate left the room. As we filed out of the courtroom, I passed one of the many signs posted throughout the make-shift courthouse. It had two sentences,

> **"The eyes of the world are on Guantanamo Bay. Justice must be done there, and must be seen to be done there, fairly and impartially."**

It was a statement made by Judge James Robertson of the District Court for the District of Columbia in another detainee trial (Hamdan v. Gates, Civil Action No. 04-1519 (2008)).

In the prosecution team's office, we processed what had just transpired. The legal team explained what this meant and the additional work that needed to be done to prepare for the future trial. The CID agent suggested ways to secure the missing testimony of Afghan eyewitnesses of the attack – difficult as that might be, and the prosecution team made a list of critical pieces of information and evidence that would be needed to answer some of the defense counsel's main objections.

214

All four of us, the CID agent, the Marine interrogator, the Green Beret intelligence officer, and I, the human rights observer chaplain, would be needed for the trial. The prosecution agreed to contact us as details were forthcoming. Thanking our legal team, we left for a visit to the Base Exchange to shop for local souvenirs, eat a quick supper, and an early turn-in so we could make the ferry ride and plane trip back to Baltimore.

My alarm went off at 3:30 a.m. After a quick shower, I packed by bags and jumped into the van. We drove to the airfield and dropped off our vehicle. It was pitch black as we waited near the dock for our ferry. I felt like I had successfully completed my pretrial mission. I was looking forward to a quiet trip home.

The intel chief asked if we could go for a walk while we waited. As we started down the cracked old navy runway, he told me a story I would never forget. Following our shared tour in Afghanistan in 2002, he redeployed to Iraq. It was during the height of counterinsurgency operations, when kidnapping, torture and videotaped beheadings were rampant. He was assigned to a special joint hostage recovery team. He told about a mission when his team successfully rescued Italian journalists just minutes before their planned videotaped execution. Through an amazing combination of battlefield intelligence and interagency cooperation, his team was able to locate and fight their way into an insurgent safe house and rescue several Italian civilian journalists.

He said, "Chaplain, when we broke into the room where they were staged, bound and gagged, they looked up into our faces as if we were angels. They cried for joy as we removed their shackles and carried them to safety. It was a scene I will always remember, and a feeling of satisfaction I will never forget." I asked him if he wanted to tell me about any other operations. He became still.

"Actually, I do." The chief stopped for a few moments, as if to regain composure in the predawn light. Turning away from the ferry dock, he stopped and sat on a concrete barrier. "There was another time. We got intel on the possible location of a captured U.S. Army officer. We worked our sources and got a local informant to take us to the place where he was being kept. Our team stormed the building..." The chief halted. I waited. He started to sob, "We were too late." I put my arm around his shoulders as he wept tears of regret. After a time, he asked me one of those questions I could not answer. "Why, chaplain? Why did God allow us to save those civilians from another country, and not our own American brother? Why?"

After he shared his heart-wrenching story, I asked him if he remembered the time he was lying sick in the battalion aid-station in

Afghanistan...when I came in to pray for him. He said he didn't, so I reminded him of what had occurred from my perspective; how I asked if I could pray for him, his affirmative reply, the prayer, and subsequent "miraculous" recovery – with photos taken with Doc ENZ to document it. I explained to him how God didn't always answer my prayers the way I intended—like on that day with him in Afghanistan, but that I was commanded and committed to pray whenever the situation dictated – and leave the results to God. He nodded pensively.

As dawn broke over the eastern Caribbean horizon, two soldiers cried together on the old GITMO airfield. When the horn signaled the ferry's arrival, I prayed an audible prayer of thanksgiving for the heroism and daring of this soldier and those like him, for the loved ones of the lost, and for a successful pre-trial effort. We hugged, in a manly appropriate Special Forces way, and wiped our eyes, as we walked to the dock. Back in Baltimore, we again went our separate ways.

On 31 July 2009, I received an email from Major Ken, with a link to a news article reporting that Mohammad Jawad was released from GITMO and sent home to his family in Kabul, Afghanistan.

---

1   http://www.dailymail.co.uk/news/article-1208978/One-Guantanamos-youngest-detainees-claims-tortured-camp.html

EPILOGUE – B: Meeting Tem, Again

It was an exciting trip to the airport. My wife and I had done it may times, welcoming visiting family, military members returning from deployment, and WW2 and Korean War veterans returning home from Honor Flights to our nation's Capital. But this time it was different.

After leaving Afghanistan in 2003, I maintained contact with my main interpreter – the one the others called, "the chaplain's son." In 2006, the U.S. Government, under President George W. Bush, established a program offering a quota of special immigrant visas (SIV) to Afghan and Iraqi personnel who worked closely with the U.S. Armed Forces, especially those whose involvement may have compromised their personal security in their home countries. Having applied and finally received a visa for his service as an interpreter, my Afghan son and wife needed a U.S. sponsor as a final step. One mealtime discussion, and my wife was on-board, concerned, but willing to assist this young Afghan couple enter the United States to begin a new life. We reviewed the State Department documents on the program, prepared a guest bedroom and awaited their springtime arrival.

The last email before they arrived came just a week prior. We copied the flight info and checked the airline website to make sure we were tracking. We could only imagine the potential fear and apprehension they were facing, so we wanted to help them enter and adjust to a new and very different way of life, with the least amount of stress possible.

We arrived early at Denver International Airport and checked the flight arrival board. Their plane was on time. As we stood in the meeting area at the top of the escalators, we continued our discussion of what they would need in their first twenty-four hours; food, sleep, shower, assurance, calls home, etc. We both agreed that we would lay out options and let them choose where feasible.

Though it had been six years since I had seen Tem, we had seen photos of his recent wedding. Positioning ourselves so we would have the best vantage point behind the barriers, I recalled the day, six years earlier when we said good-bye. That sadness would soon turn to joy in what, to me, was another incredible and amazing turn of events.

After a thirty-minute wait, I spied Tem's head and shoulders – only bulkier and stronger. Obviously, he had been working out. Next to him was his dark-haired beautiful bride of less than a year, Permilla. As we greeted them with hugs and handshakes, I rattled off all the Afghan greetings I had ever learned. Looking them over and pausing for some photos, we led them to the baggage claim area and then to our car. On the way home, we tried to ascertain their most pressing needs, such as sleep, food, and hydration. Assured they were not yet ready to eat or sleep, we took them for a quick tour of the Denver skyline.

After an hour, we arrived at our home. Introducing them to our two parrots, we then showed them to their upstairs bedroom. We placed them in a room with a double bed down the hall from a full bathroom. Fairly certain that they had limited experience with Western conveniences, I tried not to take things for granted. I explained to my wife how they had no indoor plumbing and only short periods of low wattage electricity from a gas-powered 300-watt Chinese Tiger generator.

We showed them the bathroom with full tub and shower, opened the cabinet drawers and doors so they could see the hair dryer, curling iron and other hygiene items we had prepared for them. It was late, and we could see that they were getting tired. We said good night and went to bed.

The next morning, we fed them an American breakfast of eggs and toast. Permilla was gracious, but a bet hesitant to eat very much. Tem, on the other hand, was used to American food, so he ate heartily. After clearing the table, Permilla went to the sink and started washing the dishes. As she cleaned the plates, she asked her husband in Dari where to put the scrapings. My wife told them she could put them down the "garbage disposal." So, she did. We explained that we didn't expect her to do the dishes because we had a dishwasher, but they insisted that they help with home chores...just like they did back home. We thanked them for their willingness to pitch in.

Uncertain how long they would be with us, we sat down and tried to get an idea of what they needed and wanted to do during their time with us. Their wishes included sightseeing, completing their visa application, opening a bank account, and visiting former battalion members with whom Tem had served. The days went quickly, especially as my wife and I were both working fulltime jobs outside the home.

After a long weekend together, my wife and I left early Monday for our jobs. We showed them where the food was, and encouraged them to relax, watch TV to help improve their English language skills and get outside to see the neighborhood.

That evening, my wife and I arrived home at almost the same time. I closed the garage door and entered to the delightful smells of something cooking. Stepping into the kitchen, we noticed the sink full of water. Looking in we saw no stopper. When we asked if they had any problems with the sink, Tem replied that the water backed up after they used the garbage disposal. A look into the drain revealed something white. After a little fishing, we retrieved a series of items that would have normally gone into the pantry trash can. Tem and Permilla were relieved when the water began to drain normally.

After a couple questions, we found out what happened. When we showed them the sink disposal, we failed to specify what kinds of garbage the unit would take. We all had a good laugh, as Tem explained to Permilla, what had occurred. The meal she prepared was hot and delicious, including Afghan-style bread and fried potatoes. Over the next couple weeks, we would eat some simple, delicious and healthy Afghan meals.

That kitchen experience helped us realize how important it was to explain all our home systems, in the kitchen, bathroom, living room, etc. Our role turned out to be a basic one of familiarization and orientation to life in suburban United States. We helped them register with local immigration, open a bank account, and purchase a cell phone with international access.

We also helped them consider options for schooling. Tem came to secure a college education in a field that would help him support his family. That, it turned out, would be in another state. After three weeks, we took them to the bus station with their bags. Next stop would be Seattle where they would reconnect with another friendship made in Afghanistan.

Three and one-half years later, we received a graduation announcement. Tem had successfully completed his degree program and had several job interviews. Within a few months he had a job, moved his family and was actively pursuing the American Dream.

In May of 2013, we received news that Tem's job had been eliminated. We emailed them some local employment contacts, with the assurance of our prayers for a new job. The following week, we got an email informing us of their interview for U.S. Naturalization. Unfortunately, the time was too short for us to adjust our schedules and secure flights to their location.

On the day following their formal Naturalization Ceremony, we received a sweet email with photos of their biggest day in America. With the photos came news that Tem had been hired by a major
U.S. corporation on the East Coast. We replied with rejoicing and invited them to stop by and stay with us on their east-bound cross-country trek. Tem told us that Permilla wanted to drive across America so she could get a better perspective of their newly adopted homeland.

Three weeks later, on Memorial Day Weekend, 2013, we again embraced our adopted Afghan son and daughter and their two American-born children. We clapped our hands in delight as their car drove up.
Anxiously, we allowed them to unbuckle their children – the two Afghan-American grandchildren my wife had the privilege to name. Through tears of joy, we hugged and kissed our Afghan children and grandchildren. Once

again, I used every Afghan phrase of greeting and congratulation I could remember – causing their four-year-old daughter to stare at her mother with a strange look. Cautious not to overwhelm the children, we invited them out of the warm sun into our air-conditioned home, where they had begun their U.S. orientation five years prior.

We spent the next several hours eating, catching up and listening to the wonderful employment opportunity that awaited Tem. The American Dream appeared to be alive and well, along the established path of legal immigration. In our conversation, they both expressed their burning desire to one day meet former President George W. Bush, to thank him personally for the Special Immigrant Visa program he had authorized.

The evening passed too quickly. After tucking everyone into bed, my wife and I discussed how far they had come in such a short time. After three weeks with us, we put them on a bus to Seattle where they reunited with another family, whose husband Tem had worked with in the development of the Afghan National Police. As an adjunct professor at a Washington State University, he arranged a Presidential Scholarship with work study option. Within three and one-half years, Tem completed a bachelor's Degree in computer science with a minor in mathematics. Upon graduation, he was hired by a Silicon Valley computer company, where he gained valuable work experience in his field of expertise. When that job ended due to layoff, he reapplied to Boeing, and was readily accepted for a position in his chosen field of endeavor. Now, they were driving across America, "from sea to shining sea," to continue their pursuit of happiness.

As was their practice when they first entered our home five years earlier, they were up, packed, the guest beds made, and bathroom spotless – this time with two young children. We ate breakfast and helped them pack their car. Tem had plotted their trip and they had miles to go on day three of their great American Journey. On our front lawn we reaffirmed our pride for their diligence and focused effort – the kind that originally built America. We joined our arms in a circle and I prayed another prayer of blessing, on their travel and new life ahead. Again, tears filled our eyes, as their young children looked on with curiosity.

Someday, mom and dad would tell them the story of how their dad met an Army National Guard chaplain, who came to Afghanistan with a Green Beret unit to help free their Afghan family from the oppressive Taliban regime, and the Al Qaeda terrorists who used their country to attack the USA on September 11, 2001, their land of birth. How their dad worked with this chaplain in humanitarian projects, restoring a school, rescuing starving, sick, destitute Afghan orphans, and helping Afghan widows earn a living. How their dad helped the chaplain teach conversational English classes to Afghan school children, and classes in human rights and the law of land warfare to the first 2500 soldiers of the New Afghan Army. How they worked together to heal the deep wounds accidentally caused by a training accident that took the lives of four young Afghan boys, and how, in the process, they had developed a deep, lasting bond – that of a second family – their new American family!

Looking back, I stand amazed at the impact our battalion made in history, at the personal and geopolitical levels.

Glossary/Acronyms:

ANA	Afghan National Army
AOB	Advance Operating Base
CJSOTF	Combined Joint Special Operations Task Force
CSM	Command Sergeant Major
CUB	Commander's Update Brief
DFAC	Dining Facility – "Mess Hall"
FID	Foreign Internal Defense
FOB	Forward Operating Base
JAG / SJA	Judge Advocate General / Staff Judge Advocate (Military Attorney)
KIA	Killed-In-Action / Kabul International Airport
KMTC	Kabul Military Training Center
MRE	Meals-Ready-to-Eat
MEDCAP	Medical Civic Assistance Program
OMC	Office of Military Commissions
UH60	Utility Helicopter Model 60 officially named "Blackhawk"

Made in the USA
Coppell, TX
23 May 2020

26350976R00136